THERE'S A PLACE FOR US:
THE MUSICAL THEATRE WORKS OF
LEONARD BERNSTEIN

For Jason

There's a Place For Us:
The Musical Theatre Works of
Leonard Bernstein

HELEN SMITH

ASHGATE

Published by
Ashgate Publishing Limited
Wey Court East
Union Road
Farnham
Surrey, GU9 7PT
England

Ashgate Publishing Company
Suite 420
101 Cherry Street
Burlington
VT 05401-4405
USA

www.ashgate.com

British Library Cataloguing in Publication Data
Smith, Helen.
There's a place for us: the musical theatre works of Leonard Bernstein.
1. Bernstein, Leonard, 1918–1990 – Criticism and interpretation. 2. Bernstein, Leonard, 1918–1990. Musicals. 3. Musicals – United States – History and criticism.
I. Title
782.1'4'092-dc22

Library of Congress Cataloging-in-Publication Data
Smith, Helen, 1975–
There's a place for us : the musical theatre works of Leonard Bernstein / Helen Smith.
   p. cm.
Includes bibliographical references and index.
ISBN 978-1-4094-1169-7 (hardcover : alk. paper) 1. Bernstein, Leonard, 1918–1990.
Musicals. 2. Bernstein, Leonard, 1918–1990. Operas. I. Title.
ML410.B566S65 2011
782.1'4092–dc22
                                                                                    2011002918

Reprinted 2013

ISBN 9781409411697 (hbk)

Bach musicological font developed by © Yo Tomita

Printed in the United Kingdom by Henry Ling Limited, at the Dorset Press, Dorchester, DT1 1HD

Contents

List of Tables

List of Music Examples

Acknowledgements

A number of people have been invaluable in the assistance they have given me during my research, and my thanks must be extended to them: at the Library of Congress in Washington, Mark Eden Horowitz, who has helped me with the Bernstein Collection, both while in the Library and with countless e-mails; at The Leonard Bernstein Office in New York, Marie Carter and Eleonor Sandresky; Boosey & Hawkes in London, for the lending of unpublished Bernstein scores; Bernstein's personal assistants Jack Gottlieb, Charlie Harmon and Craig Urquhart, who have helped me clarify details; John and Roberta Graziano, for advice, information and accommodation in New York; and others who have given help and advice: Geoffrey Block, Adolph Green, John Jansson, Mark Lavine and Stephen Sondheim. I must also offer my thanks to Andy Chan at Boosey & Hawkes, Charlotte Mortimer at Faber, Angus Fulton and Pete Beck at Warner/ Chappell and Ruth Searle at Music Sales for assisting me with copyright details and permissions; and to my friend Sarah Beedle, for checking my manuscript. My deepest gratitude to Heidi Bishop and Barbara Pretty at Ashgate, and to Sara Peacock, my highly astute proofreader.

I offer special thanks and gratitude to Professor Stephen Banfield, for his supervision, guidance and friendship over the past years.

I must also thank my husband, Jason, who has lived in a Bernstein-filled world for many years, for his help and encouragement, and my parents for their support, especially of my musical activities over the years.

Grateful acknowledgement is made to the following for permission to reprint materials:

Extracts from letter from Marc Blitzstein to Mina Curtiss reproduced by kind permission of the Blitzstein Music Company.

Extracts from libretto of *Peter Grimes* by Benjamin Britten and Montagu Slater. © Copyright 1945 by Boosey & Hawkes Music Publishers Ltd. Reproduced by permission of Boosey & Hawkes Music Publishers Ltd.

The words of Aaron Copland are reproduced by permission of The Aaron Copland Fund for Music, Inc., copyright owner.

Musical examples by Jack Gottlieb (4.3 and 6.12a) reproduced by kind permission.

On the Town

Trouble in Tahiti

Wonderful Town

and Polygram International Music Publishing Ltd. (PRS) All rights administered by Warner/Chappell North America Ltd.

Music and lyrics from 'Christopher Street', 'Conquering New York', 'What a Waste', 'A Little Bit in Love', 'Conversation Piece', 'A Quiet Girl', 'Conga', 'Swing', 'It's Love', 'Ballet at the Village Vortex' and 'Wrong Note Rag': words by Betty Comden and Adolph Green; music by Leonard Bernstein © (Renewed) 1953 Chappell & Co Inc and Polygram International Music Publishing. Warner/Chappell North America Ltd, London, W6 8BS. Reproduced by permission of Faber Music Ltd. All Rights Reserved.

Candide

Lillian Hellman libretto quotations reproduced by special arrangement with Creative Artists Agency.

Music and lyrics © 1956, 1994 Amberson Holdings LLC. Leonard Bernstein Music Publishing Company LLC, Publisher. Reproduced by permission of Boosey & Hawkes Music Publishers Ltd.

West Side Story

Lyrics from cut songs reproduced by kind permission of Stephen Sondheim.

Music and lyrics © 1956, 1957, 1958, 1959 by Amberson Holdings LLC and Stephen Sondheim. Leonard Bernstein Music Publishing Company LLC, Publisher. Reproduced by permission of Boosey & Hawkes Music Publishers Ltd.

Mass

Music and lyrics © 1971 by Amberson Holdings LLC and Stephen Schwartz. Leonard Bernstein Music Publishing Company LLC, Publisher. Reproduced by permission of Boosey & Hawkes Music Publishers Ltd.

1600 Pennsylvania Avenue

Excerpt from the libretto of *1600 Pennsylvania Avenue* by kind permission of the successors to Alan Jay Lerner and Leonard Bernstein.

Music and lyrics © 1976 by Alan Jay Lerner and Amberson Holdings LLC. Leonard Bernstein Music Publishing Company LLC, Publisher. Reproduced by permission of Boosey & Hawkes Music Publishers Ltd.

A Quiet Place

> Music and lyrics © 1983, 1988 by Amberson Holdings LLC and Stephen Wadsworth Zinsser. Leonard Bernstein Music Publishing Company LLC, Publisher. Reproduced by permission of Boosey & Hawkes Music Publishers Ltd.

Chichester Psalms

> © 1965 by Amberson Holdings, LLC. Leonard Bernstein Music Publishing Company LLC, Publisher. Reproduced by permission of Boosey & Hawkes Music Publishers Ltd.

Fancy Free

> © 1950 by Harms, Inc. Copyright renewed. Leonard Bernstein Music Publishing Company LLC, Publisher. Reproduced by permission of Boosey & Hawkes Music Publishers Ltd.

Hashkiveinu

> © Copyright 1946 by M. Witmark & Sons, NY. Copyright reassigned to Amberson Holdings LLC, Copyright renewed. Leonard Bernstein Music Publishing Company LLC, Publisher. Reproduced by permission of Boosey & Hawkes Music Publishers Ltd.

Kaddish

> © 1963, 1965, 1977, 1980. Copyright assigned 1999 to Amberson Holdings LLC. Leonard Bernstein Music Publishing Company LLC, Publisher. Reproduced by permission of Boosey & Hawkes Music Publishers Ltd.

Yigdal

> © 1950 by Amberson Holdings LLC. Leonard Bernstein Music Publishing Company LLC, Publisher. Reproduced by permission of Boosey & Hawkes Music Publishers Ltd.

Introduction

Background and Context

Leonard Bernstein was a man filled with a love for life and all that it could offer him. His passion for music inspired him to reach out to audiences through his conducting, performing, teaching, writing, television programmes and, of course, through his compositions. He was an innately theatrical and dramatic person, extrovert and exuberant, who enjoyed the spotlight, and appeared to feed on the attention of the public. This theatrical personality was reflected in many of his own compositions, whether written specifically for the theatre, or as a piece of orchestral or chamber music. Bernstein himself noted that 'I have a suspicion that every work I write, for whatever medium, is really theatre music in some way' (prefatory note to *The Age of Anxiety*, 1949).

In the twenty years since his death, Bernstein's popularity has not waned: his musicals continue to be performed, not least on Broadway and in the West End, and his orchestral pieces still appear on the programmes of orchestras around the world. As a measure of one aspect of his legacy, in the last few years two new recordings of his *Mass* have been released, the first conducted by Kristjan Järvi and the second by Marin Alsop. A former conducting student of Bernstein, Alsop also directed performances of *Mass* in July 2010, as the culmination of a season-long 'Bernstein Project' at the South Bank Centre in London. Other recent celebrations have included 'Bernstein: The Best of All Possible Worlds', a series of concerts and lectures presented by the New York Philharmonic at Carnegie Hall in 2008, and an international festival and conference titled 'Leonard Bernstein: Boston to Broadway' hosted by Harvard University in 2006. On the academic front, scholarly attention remains focussed on Bernstein's compositions for the stage: in December 2009 Nigel Simeone's in-depth study of *West Side Story* was published, and Carol J. Oja's survey of the theatre works will appear soon as part of the Broadway Masters series for Yale.[1]

There is a duality in Bernstein's music, a tension between the highbrow and the lowbrow, paralleled by the dichotomy between the two most prominent sides of his musical persona: the conductor and the composer. The conflict dogged Bernstein throughout his life, as he was constantly moving between the two professions, and when engrossed in one would feel that he should be giving more time to the other. As Bernstein's biographers tell,[2] his life was certainly lived to the full, and

---

[1]   Gottlieb's insightful and fascinating memoir *Working with Bernstein* was also published in 2010.

[2]   Burton 1994; Myers 1998; Peyser 1987; Secrest 1994; Seldes 2009.

often ran into excess. It seems that he loved life so much that he wanted to cram as many experiences as possible into his time, and this led to problems in his professional life, as he tried his hand at many different aspects of musical creation, presentation and education, which was a cause for concern for him, even in 1946: 'It is impossible for me to make an exclusive choice among the various activities of conducting, symphonic composition, writing for the theatre, and playing the piano. What seems right for me at any given moment is what I must do' (1982, p. 103). Yet this struggle in styles and ideals is integral to the sound of Bernstein's music, which endeavours to embrace both sides of his personality.

My book aims to survey the musical theatre works of Bernstein as a whole, and, through consideration of the musicals, operas and theatre piece, to observe how both his compositional technique and his approach to composing developed and evolved. I have chosen these works as I believe that the musical theatre works in particular provided the ideal outlet for Bernstein's aspirations and passions, allowing him to contribute to the development of American opera, a genre that he considered important. This survey will concentrate on eight works: the musicals *On the Town* (1944), *Wonderful Town* (1953), *Candide* (1956), *West Side Story* (1957) and *1600 Pennsylvania Avenue* (1976); the operas *Trouble in Tahiti* (1951/2) and *A Quiet Place* (1983); and the theatre piece *Mass* (1971); see Table I.1. These compositions span nearly 40 years, almost the whole of Bernstein's composing career, and so encompass the majority of his musical life, and the changes and growth that occurred within.

Such a study of musical theatre works, as opposed to orchestral or chamber music, or other genres of composition, is complicated by the fact that the composer is only one part of a team behind the finished product. Lyricists, librettists, choreographers, directors and producers all have a stake in the work, and so share in the creative process. With this in mind, it is difficult to isolate the contribution that the composer has made, and even then it is a certainty that he will have been, at least, influenced by others; at worst he may have been forced to change his work to fit in with a larger scheme. Despite this, I still consider Bernstein to be totally and individually responsible for the music for each show; no matter what may have happened in the period between original idea and opening night, it is Bernstein who is given sole credit, even when other composers have been involved in the processes (Sondheim and Schwartz are both composers in their own right, yet only contributed lyrics to *West Side Story* and *Mass*). Songs, scenes and whole concepts may come and go between run-throughs, tryouts and the actual opening performance of a work, and even then it may still evolve. Issues may be confused further if there are changes in the personnel, as happened with *Candide* and *1600 Pennsylvania Avenue*, forcing more alterations in the libretto, lyrics and music. However, it would be reasonably safe to assume that all people involved in a show would wish it to be successful and so work together to create the best outcome; whether or not this is achieved is another matter, as shall be seen later. As far as is possible, I have based my analyses on the productions as they were first seen in

Table I.1   Bernstein's musical theatre productions

Show	Source	Book	Lyrics	Tryouts/preview	Première	Director/ Musical Director
On the Town	Jerome Robbins	Betty Comden Adolph Green	Comden and Green	13 December 1944 Boston	28 December 1944 Adelphi Theatre NY	George Abbott/ Max Goberman
Trouble in Tahiti			Leonard Bernstein (LB)		12 June 1952 Brandeis University	Elliot Silverstein/ LB
Wonderful Town	Ruth McKenney	Joseph Fields and Jerome Chodorov	Comden and Green	19 January 1953 New Haven	26 February 1953 Winter Garden NY	George Abbott/ Lehman Engel
Candide	Voltaire	Lillian Hellman	Richard Wilbur, John LaTouche, Dorothy Parker, Hellman and LB	29 October 1956 Boston	1 December 1956 Martin Beck Theatre NY	Tyrone Guthrie/ Samuel Krachmalnick
West Side Story	Shakespeare and Robbins	Arthur Laurents	Stephen Sondheim and LB	19 August 1957 Washington	26 September 1957 Winter Garden NY	Jerome Robbins/ Max Goberman
Mass	Roman Catholic liturgy		RC liturgy, Stephen Schwartz and LB		8 September 1971 John F. Kennedy Centre, Washington	Gordon Davidson/ Maurice Peress
1600 Pennsylvania Avenue		Alan Jay Lerner	Lerner	24 February 1976 Philadelphia	4 May 1976 Mark Hellinger Theatre NY	George Faison and Gilbert Moses/ Roland Gagnon
A Quiet Place			Stephen Wadsworth and LB		17 June 1983 Houston Grand Opera	Peter Mark Schifter/ John DeMain

their premières, and looked at original published librettos; any departures from this approach will be detailed when discussing the associated musical theatre work.

The following chapters attempt to explore connections and relationships both within and between the different works, looking at the changing techniques Bernstein employed and the various influences on each of them. Rather than a blow-by-blow examination of each work, I will consider pertinent issues and details within individual shows. Each chapter begins with a consideration of the background and context[3] before going on to look at specific details from each work. There are certain recurring ideas, principally the concepts of motifs, structures and forms, and pastiche, the importance of which will be discussed in the relevant chapters.

Bernstein's Life and Compositions up to *Fancy Free* (1944)

Bernstein's parents were Jewish immigrants: his father Sam and mother Jennie had both travelled to America from Russia when they were children, and had married in the US in 1917. Leonard, originally named Louis but always called Leonard by his family, was born on 25 August 1918 in Lawrence, Massachusetts. His sister and brother, Shirley and Burton, were born in 1923 and 1932 respectively, completing the Bernstein family. Despite a tense home environment, Bernstein began to flourish when his father's younger sister Clara gave the family a piano in 1928: the love affair with music had begun, and for Bernstein it would never end. In 1929 he began attending Boston Latin School and in 1932 he gave his first public performance as a pianist, playing in a concert arranged by his piano teacher, Susan Williams. Although Sam had initially been reluctant to encourage his son's musical abilities, he now began taking Bernstein to classical concerts, and allowed him to change piano teachers to help develop his playing; Helen Coates, his new tutor, would remain part of Bernstein's life, first as teacher and later as his secretary, until her death in 1989. The piano played a pivotal part in Bernstein's life, and the majority of his early compositions were for the instrument, or included a piano part: in 1937 he produced a Piano Trio and *Music for Two Pianos*, and in 1938 he completed *Music for The Dance Nos. 1 and 2*, and a Piano Sonata (music from these juvenile compositions would reappear later in several of his mature works).

Bernstein's musical studies took him to Harvard in 1935,[4] and, although the education provided there was more theoretical than practical, Bernstein created his own opportunities for creativity; in 1939 he wrote and conducted the music for a production of *The Birds* by Aristophanes. His conducting debut was witnessed by Aaron Copland, whom he had met in 1937, and who had become Bernstein's

---

[3]   The subtitle for the first section in each chapter is taken from the first words heard in each show at its première.

[4]   1935 is also the year of Bernstein's first significant composition, a setting of Psalm 148 for voice and piano.

Chapter 1

On the Town

In the 1920s and 1930s, American culture began to develop an identity of its own, distancing itself from the influence of its European forebears. America was now capable of producing great works of literature, art, theatre, film and opera, each with a clear and distinct native voice. On the musical stage, new works by American composers including Jerome Kern, Oscar Hammerstein II, Irving Berlin, Richard Rodgers and Lorenz Hart succeeded the Austro-German-influenced romantic operettas of émigré composers such as Sigmund Romberg and Rudolf Friml, and in their quest for a sense of national individuality, detached from the sway of the Old World, musicians looked to their own dance and popular music heritage for inspiration and ideas. In time, musicians working in 'serious' genres, including Paul Whiteman and George Gershwin, absorbed the jazz music that had become the new vernacular musical language and created a bridge between the highbrow and the lowbrow. The influence of this new style spread into other fields, and in 1922 John Alden Carpenter wrote the music for a 'jazz pantomime' based on George Herriman's *Krazy Kat*, a cartoon character originally created for the American press; Carpenter later followed this with the ballet *Skyscrapers* (1923–24), a lively depiction of New York using the new rhythms. It was in this environment, as American artists aimed to create American works for the American public, that new organizations were established to help fulfil these aims. One such group was the Ballet Caravan, set up in 1936 by Lincoln Kirstein with the intention of generating American ballets, distinct in style from European dance, which had previously dominated the genre. In Kirstein's own words, 'The Caravan will continue to collaborate with younger American designers and musicians to find a direction for the classic dance ... rooted in our contemporary and national preferences' (quoted in Cohen 1998, vol. 2, p. 279).

One of the most successful productions by the Ballet Caravan came in 1938, with the ballet *Filling Station*, choreographed by and starring Lew Christensen to music by Virgil Thomson. *Filling Station*, set in a gas station attended by the unassuming character of Mac, was described by George Balanchine as 'not only one of the first modern ballets on a familiar American subject, but one of the first ballets to employ American music, scenery, and costumes by an American, and American dancers' (Balanchine and Mason 1978, p. 235). Thomson's music included waltzes, a tango, and music based on popular dances of the time,

particularly the syncopation of the jazz/ragtime-derived rhythms: ♩ ♫‿♩ ♩, and
♪♩ ♪♪♩ ♪.[1] The drive for an identifiable national style of ballet, instigated by groups
such as the Ballet Caravan, also led to the commission of Copland's *Billy the Kid*
later in 1938, and to the setting up of other professional companies and schools
focussed on the development of an American style. The young dancer Jerome
Robbins was a member of one such company, the Ballet Theatre group in New
York, and he also had aspirations to become a choreographer. He had an outline for
a ballet on an American theme, and in the search for a suitable composer Robbins
was directed to Leonard Bernstein's door by Oliver Smith, a designer who
went on to work closely with the pair for many years (Robbins, interviewed by
Burton 1996).

By 1944, a year had passed since Bernstein had composed any major orchestral
music; his *Jeremiah* symphony had been completed in December 1942, and the
composition of the smaller-scale song cycle *I Hate Music* had occupied him during
the first half of 1943. The remainder of the year had been dedicated to conducting,
following Bernstein's appointment as Assistant Conductor of the New York
Philharmonic Orchestra in August, and his well-documented, and well-received,
substitution for the indisposed Bruno Walter on 14 November 1943. Bernstein's
willingness to write ballet music is unsurprising given the success enjoyed in the
field by prominent composers including Stravinsky, and more particularly by
his friend Copland, whose aforementioned *Billy the Kid* and *Rodeo* (1942) had
both proved very popular with the American public. However, for Bernstein and
Robbins, neither of whom had had any previous experience of choreographing or
composing for Broadway, the creation of a ballet was quite a gamble. Luckily, the
collaboration paid off and the audience attendance for *Fancy Free*, which opened
on 18 April 1944 at the Metropolitan Opera, broke box offices records (Burton
1994, p. 128). The overall effect of the production certainly appeared to please the
critics: 'The music by Leonard Bernstein utilizes jazz in about the same proportion
that Robbins's choreography does … It is a fine score, humorous, inventive
and musically interesting. Indeed, the whole ballet, performance included, is
just exactly ten degrees north of terrific' (Martin 1944, p. 27). The rest of the
programme at the Metropolitan Opera included excerpts of more traditional ballet
from Tchaikovsky's *Swan Lake* and *The Nutcracker* (Martin 1944, p. 27), the
classical sounds of which could only have served to emphasize the contemporary
nature of Bernstein's work.

Fancy Free featured three sailors, familiar characters at a time when America
was playing its part in the conflict of the Second World War. The ballet followed
their shore leave in New York, each hunting for a female companion to enliven the
24 hours before they are recalled to the ship: 'they meet first one, then a second
girl, and … they fight over them, lose them, and in the end take off after still a
third' (Bernstein 1946). The contest to impress the girls takes the form of a dance

---

[1]   The first of these can be found in the movements 'Mac's Dance', 'Big Apple' and
'Finale', and the second also appears in 'Mac's Dance' and in the 'Introduction'.

competition between the three men, who individually display their prowess in a galop, a waltz and a danzón; the music for all three being derived from the previously encountered themes, from the opening 'Enter Three Sailors'.[2] The music throughout the ballet is characterized by its energy, and a jukebox playing a blues-style pop-song (of Bernstein's composing) called 'Big Stuff' establishes the atmosphere before the curtain rises.

Bernstein's usage of jazz elements in *Fancy Free* reflects the sounds of the city, 'urban jazz, which is the essence of American popular music' (Bernstein 1969, p. 177), and contrasts with the cowboy music that influenced Copland's ballets. *Fancy Free* was not alone in using jazz – Bernstein's Clarinet Sonata of 1942 showed some level of the same influence, and was described by the *Boston Globe* as containing some 'jazzy, rocking rhythms' (quoted in Secrest 1994, p. 103, no author given). Neither did the *Jeremiah* Symphony escape the touch of jazz, although its presence is not overt, as the composer himself explained: 'The scherzo of my *Jeremiah* Symphony, for example, is certainly not jazz; and yet I am convinced I could never have written it if I had not had a real and solid background in jazz' (Bernstein 1982, p. 119).

This background was derived, in part, from three of Bernstein's main musical influences – Hindemith, Copland and Stravinsky. These men had already incorporated the sounds of jazz into their music, especially during the 1920s, when the genre was seen as a raw expression embodying the feelings of the time. Although it was absent from his early ballet scores, Copland utilized jazz to depict urban cityscapes in two of his works in the 1920s: *Music for the Theatre* (1925) and the Piano Concerto (1926). In both of these orchestral pieces, Copland created symphonic jazz to reflect the excitement of the city, and contrasted this with the slower and more seductive sound of the blues: 'Copland uses such styles metaphorically, in order, if not actually to portray New York, at least to impart a sense of life in a great American metropolis' (Pollack 1999, p. 134).[3] Bernstein was very familiar with Copland's work, and he had used sections of the Piano Concerto to illustrate points about jazz rhythms in his 1939 BA thesis at Harvard (Bernstein 1982, pp. 74–81). The older composer had advised the younger on his thesis; Bernstein wrote to Copland in November 1938:

> I will try to show that there is something American in the newer music, which relies not on folk material but on a native spirit, (like your music, and maybe Harris' and Sessions' – I don't know), or which relies on a new American form, like Blitzstein's. Whether this is tenable or not, it is my thesis, and I'm sticking to it.

---

[2]   These dances are variations not only in the musical sense, but also in ballet terms, where the word indicates a solo dance (Chujoy and Manchester 1967, p. 940).

[3]   The lively music of these pieces contrast with the music Copland wrote to portray New York in *Quiet City* (1930), which is more subdued and restless than excited.

Now how to go about it? It means going through recent American things, finding those that sound, for some reason, American, and translate that American sound into musical terms. I feel convinced that there is such a thing, or else why is it that the Variations [Copland's *Piano Variations*] sound fresh and vital and not stale and European and dry? (Quoted in Burton 1994, p. 50)

To which Copland replied:

You sound as if you were very much on the right track anyhow both as to ideas and composers' names. Don't make the mistake of thinking that *just* because a Gilbert used Negro material, there was therefore nothing American about it. There's always the chance that it might have an 'American' quality despite its material. Also, don't try to prove *too* much. Composing in this country is still pretty young no matter how you look at it. (Quoted in Burton 1994, p. 51)

To Bernstein, the rhythms in Copland's Piano Concerto embodied what he called a 'great development of Negro rhythms by an American into an independent idiom' (Bernstein 1982, p. 74), and the influence of Copland's music is certainly in evidence in *Fancy Free*.

Like Copland, Bernstein used symphonic jazz to reflect the atmosphere of the city. His ballet has an immediate rhythmic exuberance, with cross-rhythms, syncopations and changes in time signature that add an edginess and restlessness to the music, reflecting the enthusiasm and vigour of the sailors and of the metropolis itself. There are seven sections to the work: 'Enter Three Sailors', 'Scene at the Bar', 'Enter Two Girls', 'Pas de Deux', 'Competition Scene', 'Three Dance Variations' and 'Finale'. The rhythmic vitality is seen at the outset, in the syncopation of the opening bars of the first section, 'Enter Three Sailors'. This melody recurs at various points and in different guises throughout the ballet, and already by its second appearance in b. 6, the tune has changed rhythmically from the first presentation at b. 2 (see Example 1.1).

In his analysis of *Fancy Free*, Laird describes Bernstein as making 'obvious Latin and jazz references here, with a swinging melody that includes syncopation in the second measure approaching the *tresillo* rhythm (3+3+2) of the *rumba*, and the third measure [b. 4] with dotted eighths and sixteenths meant to swing like Count Basie's orchestra' (Laird 2002, p. 33). There is also an interesting rhythmic twist in the second dance variation, with its changing time signatures that are most uncharacteristic of the waltz that lies at its basis: $\frac{3}{8}$ $\frac{4}{4}$ $\frac{3}{4}$; the shifting accents and syncopations of both sections of Bernstein's music are reminiscent of Copland's Piano Concerto.

The influence of jazz on Bernstein's music is apparent not only in the use of rhythm, but also in the harmonic and melodic language employed. Use of the blues scale can be found at various points in the score, including the opening of the third section, 'Enter Two Girls'. Here a semitone clash between C♯ and C♮ played simultaneously (the major and minor third of the chord together) creates the effect

Example 1.1 *Fancy Free*, 'Enter Three Sailors', bb. 1–8

of a blue note. Bernstein described the use of the scale in his thesis, and mentions specifically the use of both flattened and natural notes on the third and seventh degrees of the blues scale, where

> the actual note of the scale is somewhere between the natural tone and the flatted [*sic*] tone ... It is for this reason that when swing is played on the piano – which, being a mechanically exact instrument, cannot produce quarter-tones and the like – the pianist must resort to such impressionistic approximations as [playing both notes together (shown by Bernstein in musical examples)]. (Bernstein 1982, pp. 53–4)

The effect can also be found in the 'Pas de Deux', where the tune from the opening song, 'Big Stuff', returns as the main musical material. In the first phrase, we find the flattened and natural fifths in close proximity to each other (F♯ and G), a flattened third (E♭), and a flattened seventh (B♭) in the accompaniment that is raised again in the following bar. Bernstein was selective in his employment of jazz elements in *Fancy Free*, utilizing the scale and the rhythms of the vernacular music, but combining these with forms and techniques of development that stemmed from his classical training:

> From its very opening, the symphonic treatment of jazz is clearly taken beyond Gershwin and Copland. The changing metres and cross accents look Stravinskian on paper, but, without using jazz structures or improvisation, the aural impression is one of the sounds of the big band era and the nervous energy of jazz. (Schiff 2001, p. 445)

Bernstein began integrating jazz into his own music at a time when the genre was changing in function as people danced less and listened more; it was metamorphosing from a commercialized art to an intellectual art. But Bernstein had grown up with the sounds of jazz, and had worked for a time at Harms-Witmark, notating music from recorded improvisations of famous jazz musicians (Burton 1994, p. 103). He had also turned his own hand to performing, and had certainly impressed Copland, who wrote: '[Bernstein] is also a whizz at the piano – including jazz style' (Burton 1994, p. 102). So in his inclusion of such elements, Bernstein was not only following the lead of those composers important to him, but also embracing a significant part of his own musical experience.

It was the stage designer Oliver Smith who suggested that the success of *Fancy Free* could be built upon by expanding the ballet into a musical (Burton 1994, p. 129). Work on *On the Town* began in June 1944, only two months after the première of the ballet. Jerome Robbins again choreographed, and Bernstein suggested that Betty Comden and Adolph Green be brought in to work on the book and lyrics. He had known the nightclub performers for about five years,[4] and on occasion had played piano for their satirical group, The Revuers, at the Village Vanguard in New York (Burton 1994, p. 102.). There is a sense of innocence and simplicity about the show, almost certainly a result of the show being the first foray onto Broadway for the collaborators. *On the Town* feels like the result of a group of friends writing the show they wanted, rather than aspiring to create a commercial success. Jerome Robbins later remembered,

> We just went ahead and did what we felt we wanted to do. We weren't asking ourselves, 'What would be far out here?' We were just pouring it out the way we wanted to see it, that's all … And you have to remember that we were all very naïve and had no Broadway experience. (Quoted in Guernsey 1985, pp. 5 and 6)

Despite all the enthusiasm, excitement and drive, the show still needed a steadying hand, and this was provided by the experienced Broadway director George Abbott. It was Abbott that took the raw material created by the team and shaped it into a viable show, making some quite drastic cuts and changes along the way (as will be discussed later). The friends set a 'credo' for themselves when they began work, which Betty Comden wrote down on a yellow legal pad, stating how the show was to be 'integrated': the book, lyrics, music and dancing should all 'tell the story … The show was the important thing, not any individual element' (Comden, interviewed by Burton 1996). Rodgers and Hammerstein's *Oklahoma!*, which had enjoyed great success the previous year, was considered an integrated musical, and itself built on an approach to dance on the stage which had begun eight years earlier. Rodgers and Hart's *On Your Toes* (1936) not only introduced ballet into the Broadway musical comedy, but also made this dance integral to the plot, as it carried the drama forward to its climax in the final scene.

---

⁴   Bernstein had actually first met Green in 1937 at summer camp at Pittsfield in northwest Massachusetts, where they had worked together on a production of *The Pirates of Penzance* (Burton 1994, p. 38).

Oklahoma! subsequently included important dance scenes that explored the psyche of the show's heroine as she slept, the concept of the dream ballet giving the opportunity to 'do in dance what the script and score could not do in words and music' (Mordden 1999, p. 77). Rodgers and Hammerstein's show had important repercussions on Broadway, raising the function of dance from visual spectacle to a narrative device: 'there were some wonderful side effects as well, not least in a new sophistication in the composition of dance music. Indeed, *Oklahoma!* made dancing so integral to the … well, the integrated musical that high-maestro choreography became the fourth Essential' (Mordden 1999, p. 79).

However, the dance music that was created for *On the Town* was different from any that had been heard before. Bernstein outlined this in his programme notes for the *Three Dance Episodes* that he extracted from the musical for concert performance two years later:

> It seems only natural that dance should play a leading role in the show *On the Town*, since the idea of writing it arose from the success of the ballet *Fancy Free*. I believe this is the first Broadway show to have as many as seven or eight dance episodes in the space of two acts; and, as a result, the essence of the whole production is contained in these dances … That these are, in their way, symphonic pieces rarely occurs to the audience actually attending the show, so well integrated are all the elements by the master-direction of George Abbott, the choreographic inventiveness of Jerome Robbins, and the adroitness of the Comden-Green book. (Bernstein 1945)

Such use of symphonic music in a musical comedy was not to be repeated by Bernstein: 'Lenny didn't do that again really, not quite in that way, because *West Side Story* [which also employs symphonic methods] is a serious story, and this was mostly lighthearted' (Comden, interviewed by Burton 1996). The combination of elements obviously appealed to a great many people, as following its première on 13 December 1944, the show was a success, enjoying 463 performances in its initial Broadway run (Suskin 1992, p. 350). One review talked of the music being 'excellent. [Bernstein] has written ballet music and songs, background music and raucously tinny versions of the blues. The music has humour and is unpedantic; Mr Bernstein quite understands the spirit of *On the Town*' (Nichols 1944, p. 11).

The only aspect of *Fancy Free* that remained in the new musical was the trio of sailors, again beginning 24 hours' shore leave. In *On the Town* they are intent on seeing the sights, but are waylaid by amorous females: Chip, the innocent country boy, is seduced by Hildy, a rather insistent taxi-driver, and the clown of the group, Ozzie, falls for the anthropologist Claire. Gabey, the dreamer among the boys, decides he has to find Ivy Smith, who has been featured as 'Miss Turnstiles for June' on posters in the subway. He finds her in Carnegie Hall,[5] loses her again, and

---

[5] Carnegie Hall is where Jerome Robbins found Bernstein when looking for a composer for *Fancy Free* (Burton 1994, p. 126).

with the help of his friends and their newfound sweethearts is reunited with her just as the men have to go back on board their ship (see Table 1.1 for the structure of the show, pp. 16–17).

Originally, the whole story was to have been shown as a recollection of the events of the past 24 hours, but Abbott was not so enthusiastic about the idea, as Betty Comden remembered:

> We'd written an almost final version as a flashback. The show opened in a night court where all the characters were gathered, and the judge rapped his gavel and said, 'Now tell your stories one at a time', and then you told the story and did *On the Town*, and then you came back to night court where everybody was sitting around and the judge was making his final decisions. We thought it was great. It gave the show form, shape and importance. Then one day Mr. Abbott told us he loved the score, the book, everything – we were so excited. Then he said, 'there's just one thing. Cut that prologue, that flashback. You don't need that'. (Quoted in Guernsey 1985, p. 8)

And so the prologue was cut,[6] and the court appearance at the end was avoided by the intervention of Claire's jilted fiancé, Judge Pitkin W. Bridgework, who it appears has had a dalliance of his own during the evening (as he has caught the distinctive sneeze of Hildy's flatmate, Lucy Schmeeler). In the cases of the other relationships formed that day the script implies, if it does not make it overtly clear, that Ozzie and Chip both consummate their brief relationships.[7] It was was not shocking for a musical comedy to portray casual relationships, as there had been other shows that contained sexual content or implication, such as *Pal Joey* and some Cole Porter productions, but in *On the Town* the protagonists are clean-cut individuals, innocent provincial boys serving their country in a time of conflict. It is important to remember that *On the Town* was written and performed during the war, and such behaviour was widespread as 'young men, still in their teens, were facing death. They wanted to taste a little of life before dying. And many young women thought they deserved to and were happy to oblige' (Haagenson 1994/5, p. 32).

Although the six young people are important to the story, there is a further plot component which is perhaps even more significant: the city of New York itself. The nature and energy of the tale reflect completely the location in which it occurs, and the affection that the city inspired in its creative team is obvious, as Oliver Smith noted: '[*On the Town*] wasn't about three sailors, it was about the

---

[6]   It is conceivable that the night court and flashback concept was borrowed from Marc Blitzstein's *The Cradle Will Rock*, which Bernstein certainly knew (he had mounted a production of the show at Harvard in 1939, through which he had got to know Blitzstein himself (Burton 1994, p. 53)).

[7]   Both sailors are alone with their new partners in their respective girls' apartments, although there are strategic blackouts at the end of each scene.

enormous love each of us felt for New York City. It was a valentine to New York. We each adored New York in our own way, and that became a unifying theme' (quoted in Guernsey 1985, p. 11). The six main players in the story behave the way they do, to some degree, because they are in the city, specifically *this* city. The different locations around New York, and the diversity of the characters found there, create opportunities for enormous variety and fast-moving action, moving from Brooklyn Navy Yard, via the subway to the Museum of Natural History (found at Central Park West and 79th Street), Carnegie Hall (57th Street and 7th Avenue), Times Square, several nightclubs, to Coney Island, and back to the Navy Yard; this is a significant distance to travel around Manhattan and Brooklyn in a 24-hour period. Bernstein's urban jazz music encapsulates the vigour of the city in sounds that were being heard in the streets, clubs and concert halls of New York itself, but for each location there is a different musical feel. The streets of the city are a lonely place for Gabey, but exciting for Chip in Hildy's taxicab. Carnegie Hall is characterized in the 'Pavane', with its singing exercise patterns, and Times Square is musically vibrant and active. The nightclubs echo with parodies of songs heard in such establishments, and while Coney Island is sophisticated in Gabey's dreams, it is somewhat tacky and vulgar in real life. 'Like a time capsule, *On the Town* has captured all the giddy, gaudy, bawdy, frantic days of New York during the war' (Kreuger 1972, p. 78). The musical told a contemporary story using contemporary music, created by a young and energetic production team. It was the beginning of a relationship between Bernstein and the musical theatre that was to last for 40 years, and the first of Bernstein's tributes to the city that had become his home.

Intervallic Composition

Bernstein's approach to composition is similar to Stravinsky's as he employs comparative techniques. Stravinsky talked of 'composing by intervals' utilizing the repetition of sound patterns and 'cells' of notes. He briefly outlined this method in one of his lectures as Norton Chair of Poetics at Harvard, given the year after Bernstein had graduated from the same institution:

> So our chief concern is not so much what is known as tonality as what one might term the polar attraction of sound, of an interval, or even of a complex of tones ... Composing, for me, is putting into an order a certain number of these sounds *according to certain interval relationships*. (Stravinsky 1942, pp. 36–7 [italics added])

Although Stravinsky is talking about *intervals* rather than *motifs*, there is an obvious connection between the two, as the latter contains the former. Bernstein offered a concise definition in the last of his lectures whilst he held the Norton

Table 1.1   Structure of *On the Town* (not including encores or scene changes)

	Setting	Main events	Musical numbers	Performers
Act I Scene1	The Brooklyn Navy Yard	Sailors begin their shore leave	'I Feel Like I'm Not Out of Bed Yet' 'New York, New York'	Workmen Gabey, Chip and Ozzie
Scene 2	A Subway Train In Motion	Gabey spots Ivy's picture	'Chase Music'	Orchestra
Scene 3*	A New York City Street	Chip and Ozzie advise Gabey on romantic issues	'Gabey's Comin'	Gabey, Chip, Ozzie and Chorus
Scene 4	Presentation of Miss Turnstiles	Ivy is 'crowned' Miss Turnstiles for June	'Presentation of Miss Turnstiles'	Announcer
Scene 5	A Taxicab	Hildy accosts Chip	'Come Up to My Place'	Hildy and Chip
Scene 6	The Museum of Natural History	Claire and Ozzie meet	'Carried Away'	Claire and Ozzie
Scene 7	A Busy New York City Street	Gabey searches for love	'Lonely Town' 'High School Girls' 'Lonely Town Pas de Deux' 'Lonely Town Choral'	Gabey Orchestra Orchestra Gabey and Chorus
Scene 8	A Studio in Carnegie Hall	Gabey meets Ivy, and arranges to meet her later Ivy has her ballet lesson	'Carnegie Hall Pavane'	Ivy, Madame Dilly and Chorus
Scene 9	Claire's Apartment	Claire introduces Ozzie to her fiancé	'I Understand' (one verse)	Pitkin
Scene 10	Hildy's Apartment	Hildy demonstrates her many talents	'I Can Cook Too'	Hildy

* Scene 3 was cut prior to opening on Broadway in 1944; it was later reinstated.

	Setting	Main events	Musical numbers	Performers
Scene 11	Times Square	Ivy doesn't show up, and Gabey begins the search for her	'Lucky to Be Me' / 'Times Square Ballet: Finale Act 1'	Gabey and Chorus / Orchestra
Act II Scene 1a	Diamond Eddie's Nightclub	The friends try to cheer up Gabey	'So Long, Baby' / 'I Wish I Was Dead' / 'I Understand' (one verse)	Chorus / Diana Dream / Pitkin
Scene 1b	The Congacabana	More attempts at cheering up Gabey	'I Wish I Was Dead' / 'Ya Got Me' / 'I Understand' (one verse)	Dolores Dolores / Hildy, Claire, Chip, Ozzie / Pitkin
Scene 1c	The Slam Bang Club	Gabey discovers where he can find Ivy	'I Understand'	Pitkin
Scene 2	The Subway Train to Coney Island	Gabey falls asleep while on the way to find Ivy, and dreams	'Subway Ride and Coney Island'	Orchestra
Scene 3	Dream Coney Island	Gabey dreams	'The Great Lover Displays Himself' / 'Pas de Deux'	Orchestra / Orchestra
Scene 4	Another Subway Train to Coney Island	The friends follow Gabey, and think about what they will miss out on	'Some Other Time'	Claire, Hildy, Chip and Ozzie
Scene 5	Real Coney Island	Gabey finally finds Ivy again	'The Real Coney Island'	Rajah Bimmy and Orchestra
Scene 6	The Brooklyn Navy Yard	The sailors return to the ship, leaving the girls on shore, and more sailors begin their 24-hour leave	'Finale, Act 2'	Entire Company

Chair himself 30 years later, during 1972–73, a definition that underlined the relationship between the components in Stravinsky's technique:

> Stravinsky's asymmetrical structures are mainly based on the juggling of motives [*sic*], rather than what you ordinarily think of as melody. By 'motives' I mean simply brief melodic fragments, concise formations of two, three, or four notes which are then subjected to a kind of Cubist treatment … All these cells are conjoined, embedded, permuted, expanded, and relentlessly repeated, always in different patterns. (Bernstein 1976, p. 349)

Bernstein had played Stravinsky's *Concerto for Two Solo Pianos* whilst still at the Curtis Institute in December 1941,[8] and during his early days at Harvard he had encountered *Le Sacre du printemps*, having played a four-hand arrangement of the piece at a music club that Bernstein himself had organized at Harvard (Wright 1999, p. 8). Bernstein had also met and conversed with Stravinsky following a concert in early 1943.[9] A further influence of the Russian's compositions can be seen clearly in Bernstein's first symphony, the *Jeremiah*, specifically in rhythmic figures that appear in the second movement.

Several figures recur throughout Stravinsky's music, particularly two motifs that each contain two notes, the first outlining the interval of a fourth, and the second describing a semitone; additionally, there is a third pattern created by the combination of the two (see Example 1.2a).

Example 1.2(a)   Stravinsky's motif

Example 1.2(b)   Bernstein's *Urmotiv*

This resulting three-note motif can be found in several significant works, including *Dumbarton Oaks Concerto*, Concerto for Strings, *Symphony of Psalms* and the

---

[8]   According to a concert programme in the Library of Congress, Bernstein also conducted Stravinsky's Suite from *L'Oiseau de feu* (28 and 30 January 1944) prior to working on *On the Town* (box 335, LBC).

[9]   A letter from Copland to Bernstein, dated 6 May 1943, asked what impression Bernstein had of Stravinsky following the meeting (box 16, LBC).

Symphony in C (Routh 1975, p. 137). In fact, in his Symphony in C, Stravinsky uses the motif as the cell for the entire piece:

> he not only adopts the thematic exposition and the technique of development inherent in this form, but he adopts them in a most consequential and rigorous manner, i.e. he accepts the cyclic form based on a single motif or thematic idea which permeates the whole work – in this case the basic motif is an extremely simple figure consisting of the three notes B, C, G. (Vlad 1967, p. 136)

Similarly, Bernstein bases his compositions on small cells of notes: 'it can be said that he actually composes with intervals as his main source materials. The interval is used not only in its natural state as a musical building block, but is treated as an entity unto itself. It has meaning *sui generis*' (Gottlieb 1964, p. 19). This technique was seen to be typical of those 'influenced by the *note choisie* philosophy of Nadia Boulanger' (Gottlieb 1964, p. 21), and it is not insignificant that Boulanger was a tutor to Bernstein's teachers Walter Piston and Arthur Tillman Merritt, and to his friends Aaron Copland and Marc Blitzstein; she was also a friend and colleague of Stravinsky (Kendall 1976).

One example of the process of composing by intervals can be seen in the first movement of Bernstein's *Jeremiah* Symphony, where 'most of the subsequent melodic ideas are in some way either related to the opening horn melody or the derivative woodwind motives [*sic*] that set in at its conclusion' (Gottlieb 1964, p. 72). The figures are employed throughout this movement, both in their original forms and in variations; there are also links to the following two movements derived from these motifs. Intervallic composing on a smaller scale can be observed in the second of Bernstein's *Seven Anniversaries* for piano ('For my sister, Shirley'), where both the accompaniment and the melody are dominated by the interval of the perfect fourth; his Clarinet Sonata demonstrates a further development of the technique.

It is interesting that Bernstein's most frequently recurring pattern, described by Gottlieb as the *Urmotiv* (1964, p. 34),[10] can be seen to be closely related to Stravinsky's aforementioned motif: a descending minor second followed by a descending major third (see Example 1.2b). This motif is evocative of the folk idiom, owing to the omission of the second degree of the scale, which lends a pentatonic feel to the phrase. It can be found in the music of various composers, including Copland, and of those wishing to portray a folk sound, for example Grieg and Bax; the motif also occurs in some African American spirituals.

In Bernstein's music the figure is primarily used at cadence points, descending to the tonic, and so can be labelled $\hat{4}$ $\hat{3}$ $\hat{1}$, taking the figures from the degrees of the scale. The *Urmotiv* always forms a principal part of the melodic line when it

---

[10]   Gottlieb describes the term as being derived from the theories of Heinrich Schenker, in the manner of his terms *Urlinie* and *Ursatz* (letter to the present author, 16 February 1999).

appears, and Bernstein utilizes it in this way in *On the Town*, most significantly in 'Lonely Town'.

'Lonely Town' is the first solo by a principal character in *On the Town*, and is sung by Gabey, who is lamenting his own situation as he remains alone whilst both Chip and Ozzie have found girls to spend the day with; there is irony in Gabey feeling a sense of loneliness in a city of thousands. The chorus of 'Lonely Town' consists of two ideas, which are repeated to form an AABAB structure. The *Urmotiv* appears as the last three notes of the B section, therefore being heard as the last three vocal notes of this piece, and the significance of the phrase is underlined by being coupled to the words of the title (see Example 1.3).

Example 1.3 'Lonely Town', bb. 83–86

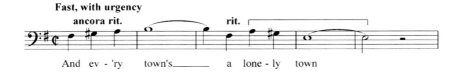

The *Urmotiv* is also seen in *On the Town* in the opening song, 'I Feel Like I'm Not Out Of Bed Yet', sung by a workman at the Navy Yard in Brooklyn, as he bemoans the early hour in a bluesy hymn to the comforts of home. This is an exposed solo reflecting the same theatrical manner of the opening moments of several of Bernstein's works; Gottlieb describes this device as a 'manifestation … of [Bernstein's] theatrical impulse' (1964, p. 10).[11] The use of a solo curtain raiser, rather than beginning the action with a large-scale chorus number, can also be found in Rodgers and Hammerstein's opening to *Oklahoma!*, in the solo 'Oh, What a Beautiful Mornin''. However, it is possible that the stronger influence here is that of Blitzstein, as his *The Cradle Will Rock* also commences with a solo item in 'Moll's Song'.

In addition to the *Urmotiv*, another motif that plays an important part in this work is contained within what is probably the best-known theme of the show: the figure that accompanies the title words of the song 'New York, New York', $\hat{1}$ $\hat{2}$ $\hat{5}$. The motif is first heard in the basses of the orchestra, where it forms the first bar of an ostinato (see Example 1.4a). This follows the 'hooter' introduction that announces 6 o'clock, when the sailors' 24-hour shore leave begins. At b. 45 the canonic vocal entries, which add the anacrusis $\hat{5}$ before the motif (E–A–B–E), loudly proclaim the city in which the action is about to unfold, and so the figure

---

[11]   Gottlieb details how many of Bernstein's orchestral works begin with solos, or duets: '*Jeremiah* – [2] solo French horns; *Facsimile* – oboe; *Age of Anxiety* – clarinet duet; *Serenade* – violin; *Fancy Free* – snare drum; *Trouble in Tahiti* – clarinet; *On the Waterfront* – French horn; *Kaddish* symphony – speaker' (1964, p. 10). Of works completed after Gottlieb's dissertation, only *Mass* has a similar opening (soprano and percussion).

becomes a motif that symbolizes the city at various points within the show, a fanfare for the metropolis (see Example 1.4b).[12]

Example 1.4 'New York, New York'

(a) bb. 9–12; (b) bb. 45–47

The same four-note figuration can be found within the first bars of an earlier panegyric depicting a city: Vaughan Williams's *London Symphony* (1913). However, it is unlikely that the English composer influenced Bernstein's writing, and the comparable contexts of the use of the motif appear coincidental. The appearance of the four notes at the opening of a different symphony, Sibelius's Symphony No. 5 (1915), is more significant.[13] Burton relates how, when Bernstein met Adolph Green for the first time, Green introduced Bernstein to one of his favourite symphonic works, the Sibelius symphony (1994, pp. 38–9). This meeting took place in 1937, seven years before the two friends began work on

---

[12]   Jaensch also labels this the 'New York, New York fanfare' in his 2003 book (p. 49).

[13]   Gottlieb pointed out the relationship between the two phrases (1964, p. 40), as the motif reappeared in *The Age of Anxiety*. He also demonstrated the resemblance between these two phrases, a section from the *andante* of Brahms's *Double Concerto*, and a nineteenth-century German synagogue tune (2004, p. 54).

On the Town, and it is conceivable that some memory of the piece lingered and re-emerged, unconsciously, as their collaboration began in June 1944.

Another interesting point in 'New York, New York' concerns the instrumental figure that begins at b. 15, over the $\hat{1}$ $\hat{2}$ $\hat{5}$ ostinato. This pattern can be seen to be an inversion of the $\hat{1}$ $\hat{2}$ $\hat{5}$ motif: where the latter ascends from tonic to dominant via a tone step, the figure at b. 15 *descends* from tonic to dominant via a tone step, $\hat{1}$ $\hat{7}$ $\hat{5}$. This could also be seen as a variant of the *Urmotiv*, the descending minor 2nd – major 3rd pattern becoming major 2nd – minor 3rd.

The New York fanfare motif appears next in the ballet 'Presentation of Miss Turnstiles', where we first meet Ivy Smith, the object of Gabey's desire. The figure appears in its original guise in the introduction to the dance; the 'Miss Turnstiles' concept is based on a real New York practice of naming a 'Miss Subways' (Mordden 1999, p. 123n), and so is integrally linked to the city. There are also other subtle connections, as the music labelled 'Allegretto di "Ballet Class"' has two main phrases, each of them beginning with the figure $\hat{1}$ $\hat{2}$ $\hat{5}$. This refers back to the fanfare, although in this appearance it is somewhat disguised by its ♪ ♩ ♪ rhythm and more leisurely nature.

In 'Times Square Ballet', the figure can be heard when the music of 'New York, New York' is reused in a depiction of the city at night, rhythmically altered at one point into $\frac{6}{8}$, and appearing in an elaborated form at another. The next two appearances of the fanfare are also in ballet sections, first in Gabey's dream at the end of 'The Great Lover Displays Himself', as the Master of Ceremonies announces an imaginary clash between Gabey and Ivy. The second is a brief reference to the figure in 'The Real Coney Island', reminding us that the action is still taking place in one of the boroughs of the city. At the end of the show, the song 'New York, New York' is reprised as the sailors return to the ship, and the next group leave for their day in the city. Despite the intervening action and individual stories, New York remains unchanged by its inhabitants and visitors, and life goes on the same.

Other musical ideas that recur through the show are found in the song 'Gabey's Comin'', the 'pick-up song' where Chip and Ozzie are attempting to teach Gabey the finer points of approaching women. There are three phrases from this number that reappear, the first of which is found in the introduction, a phrase based on a simple auxiliary note pattern and its subsequent development (see Example 1.5a). This motif can be seen in later ballet sections, where it forms an important part of the musical material. In 'Lonely Town Pas de Deux' the pattern is used and expanded in the central section of the piece (see Example 1.5b). This expansion also occurs in 'Subway Ride and Imaginary Coney Island', where the auxiliary note figure is a significant part of the accompaniment at the start of the piece. The full motif is the basis for a later section, where it is developed by octave displacement (this dance will be discussed in more detail later in the chapter). In the section that follows, 'The Great Lover', the introduction figure is used, with some rhythmic alteration and at a faster tempo (see Example 1.5c). The motif appears to be associated with Gabey's yearnings for romance, as it appears in situations where is he dreaming of or wishing for love.

Example 1.5   Appearances of the 'Gabey's Comin'' motif

(a) 'Gabey's Comin'', bb. 1–2
(b) 'Lonely Town Pas de Deux', bb. 12–15
(c) 'The Great Lover Displays Himself', bb. 33–36

This is not the only idea from the song that is repeated, as the first phrase from the chorus, characterized by dotted rhythms that contrast with the earlier triplets, is reused in the verse for Gabey's 'Lonely Town'; the encouragement from his friends has had little success as he still dreams of finding his perfect woman, and the jaunty dotted notes are replaced by equal-length quavers.

The final element of 'Gabey's Comin'' that is employed elsewhere is the first half of the melody from the verse, which is utilized in 'High School Girls'. This tune was composed some time before *On the Town*, as it appears in Bernstein's Piano Trio from 1937, one of his earliest compositions.[14] In the 'Tempo di Marcia' movement of the Trio, the music is presented in a simple canon between the violin, piano and cello. The simplicity of the melody is retained in 'Gabey's Comin'', and in its reuse in 'High School Girls', which will be discussed in more detail later.

All the numbers which contain components from 'Gabey's Comin'' are, perhaps obviously, connected with the romantic hero himself: the song acts as positive reinforcement from his friends as they venture into the big city; 'Subway Ride' and 'The Great Lover' form part of his dream in the second act when he is hunting for Ivy; 'Lonely Town' is his solo song lamenting his situation. 'High School Girls' and 'Lonely Town Pas de Deux' are ballets showing Gabey watching as other sailors are more successful with women, while he remains alone. However, in the original show, the song 'Gabey's Comin'' was cut, as director George Abbott felt

---

[14]   On the cover of the manuscript book containing the music for the Trio, Bernstein has added the note, 'op.2' (music in LBC).

that it slowed the action down (Mordden 1999, p. 128n). Two of the collaborators described the change in an interview:

> Jerome Robbins: ...there was a number called 'Gabey's Coming' [*sic*] early in the show. Two sailors were trying to teach Gabey how to pick up a date and how to make out with girls. A lot of the show's music was based on that song. That song was cut, and I saw Lenny holding his head and saying 'Everything is based on that'. In putting on a show, that can happen time and time again: some thematic material upon which a lot of the score is built doesn't work, and it's cut, and the composer wonders, 'My God, where do I put my foot down?'

> Bernstein: There are two places remaining in the score that are seriously based on that number, including the climax of the second-act ballet. (Quoted in Guernsey 1985, pp. 9–10)

Although some connections between the motifs may still have been obvious to the audience, with the initial presentation of the material no longer being heard, not all the references will have been apparent.[15]

There is one final motif that appears in various numbers in the show, and that is a descending chromatic phrase that is first seen in 'Subway Ride' (see Example 1.6).

Example 1.6 'Subway Ride and Imaginary Coney Island', bb. 8–9

Once again, this is music that existed before the show was composed, as it was written for Bernstein's *Music for Two Pianos* (1937). A fragment of the motif is used in the 'Pas de Deux' later in the same ballet sequence (the first five notes only). A variant of the descending figure appears at the opening of the verse for the song 'Some Other Time', and the triplet rhythm goes on to form the basis for the music of the chorus (see Example 1.7), where the pattern is inverted and developed.

The final appearance of this motif is in 'The Real Coney Island', where it is elaborated and 'jazzed-up' (see Example 1.8). This is actually a further extract

---

[15]   The song has since been reinstated into the show; it appears in the 1997 Boosey and Hawkes vocal score, and the scene in which it features is included in the published libretto (Comden and Green 1997).

Example 1.7 'Some Other Time', bb. 3–6, bb. 11–14

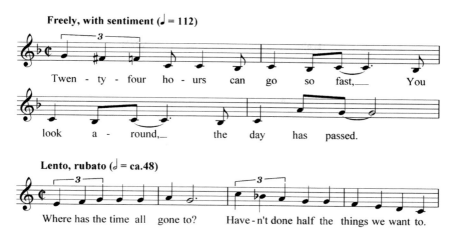

Example 1.8 'The Real Coney Island', bb. 1–3

from the *Music for Two Pianos*, where Bernstein included this variation on his own tune later in the music. The four numbers that include this figure are connected by virtue of the fact that 'Subway Ride and Imaginary Coney Island' and 'The Real Coney Island' depict two visions of the same place, Gabey's dream idealization and the reality, while 'Pas de Deux' and 'Some Other Time' both appear between the two ballet sections. It seems that Bernstein wanted to maintain a sense of continuity between the two scenes of Coney Island, and this also included the song that interrupts them.

As can be seen from the above discussion, the four motifs mentioned appear predominantly in the ballet sections of the show, and also in the songs 'I Feel Like I'm Not Out of Bed Yet', 'New York, New York', 'Gabey's Comin'', 'Lonely Town' and 'Some Other Time'. These may be seen as the most significant songs in the show, as it seems to me that they contain the essence of the story: the two sides of the city in the sense of excitement, contrasted with the isolation of the individual, and the desire for love and romance that drive the whole plot forward. The remaining songs, which do not contain references to the motifs, function primarily as character songs, and as such are not essential to the narrative of the story. The linking of the ballets and important songs by the use of motifs introduces an almost symphonic level of thematic connection and integration throughout the show, echoing the integration of elements they were trying to achieve within the musical itself, and initiating a new concept for the Broadway stage.

Melodic Techniques

'Subway Ride and Imaginary Coney Island' forms part of the ballet sequence during which Gabey travels to find Ivy, and, having fallen asleep on the train, he dreams of his upcoming romantic encounter. This piece is a good example of both Bernstein's composing by intervals and his integration of motifs. It is an especially clever instance, as a large amount of the material in this ballet came from his earlier composition, the *Music for Two Pianos* from 1937; despite the seven-year gap between the two works, Bernstein combines the piano piece with ideas from the show and still manages to create a piece with contextual links to the rest of the musical.

The ballet begins with a simple clarinet figure derived from the 'Gabey's Comin'' introduction motif, and this music continues when an accompanying chord progression enters at figure A (see Example 1.9). As can be seen, this chord progression originated from a rising tone, with a leap of a fourth in the upper part in the fifth bar, a pattern which echoes the figuration in the 'yearning' motif; this chord pattern is from the piano piece, as is the descending chromatic phrase which enters at figure B (see Example 1.6). This can be seen as a elaboration of the motif, the intervals of the fourth and the second being present in inversion, with some chromatic movement. At figure D there is a key change, and the 'Gabey's Comin'' introduction motif is employed again as the basis for the next section, with some octave displacement, over a variation of the chord pattern that continues beneath for the first four bars. The developments of the figure demonstrate clear associations with the original motif, showing a strong emphasis on the rising fourth and the second. The melody changes direction in the last two bars of this section, and the descending arpeggio figure appears as a retrograde variant of the preceding B♭–E♭–A♭ phrase. In fact, this whole six-bar section was heard in the first act as part of the 'Lonely Town Pas de Deux', without the octave displacement in the motif at the start, and appears to have been transplanted into the second act to link the two

Example 1.9 'Subway Ride and Imaginary Coney Island', bb. 1–5

ballets and their contexts; this will be discussed more later. The music of the next section, beginning at figure E, appears less motivically connected to the preceding sections, but the upper auxiliary-note figure of the introduction is inverted to a lower auxiliary-note which occurs three times in these five bars (see Example 1.10); this 'upside-down' version is then taken up by the clarinet, reminiscent of the opening, and provides a link into a repeat of the three sections: a very subtle touch. In the repeat, each section is shorter than in the original presentation, and the ballet ends with a coda based on the 'yearning' motif, leading directly into the next section of the dance.

Bernstein's ability to easily combine his old and new ideas underlines the fact that, during this period, most of his music was composed with intervals as the basis. By selecting motifs that were similar in nature, two pieces could be amalgamated successfully.

Motivic and intervallic composition can also be observed in Bernstein's earlier work, the Clarinet Sonata (1942). The slow introduction to the second movement, although lasting only 26 bars, uses five musical ideas that can all be derived from the first motif, a rising linear third. It is subsequently heard in several different versions, varied through development, inversion and reversal. Furthermore, the accompaniment is again constructed of the same figures as the melody, and, in common with 'Subway Ride', is dominated by a rising tone figure. The sonorities within the accompaniment also reflect a basis on the initial cell, as there is a predominance of notes that lie within a third (although in the piano part they are spread over octaves).

The technique employed by Bernstein in 'Subway Ride and Imaginary Coney Island' and the Clarinet Sonata would appear to owe something not to Stravinsky's composing by intervals, but rather to a method used by Copland in his Piano

Example 1.10 'Subway Ride and Imaginary Coney Island', bb. 27–31

Variations (1930), based on a serial treatment of material. In the Variations – as in his preceding work, the Symphonic Ode (1928–29) – Copland creates music from a minimal amount of material, and in the piano work 'everything that happens in the Variations is strictly derived from the theme which is also a "row"' (Mellers 1964, p. 85). Bernstein knew the Variations intimately – indeed, he played it for Copland at the composer's birthday party on the day that the two met (Bernstein 1982, p. 285) – and he had analysed the piece during his time at Harvard, when he 'fell in love with the music. It seemed so fierce and prophetic, and utterly new' (Bernstein 1976, p. 5). This method of composing may seem a very involved and technical process to be utilizing in a musical theatre show, but it underlines both Bernstein's training and background prior to arriving on Broadway, and his willingness to combine vernacular and traditional ideas and methods.

Song Forms

In the thesis he wrote for his bachelor's degree, Bernstein was somewhat scathing about the structure of the popular song: 'The popular song in the twentieth century is more or less a stale and stereotyped melody set over a 4/4 accompaniment, plunged usually into a ternary form (strain and repetition, release, and strain). It has never yet dared to advance harmonically further than Schubert' (Bernstein 1982, pp. 50–1). This AABA form had emerged as a favourite amongst popular-song composers, and, although the pattern may seem limiting, musicians exploited the form creatively, as described by Hamm: 'the skill and genius of Tin Pan Alley composers (and lyricists) was revealed by what could be done within a tightly restricted formal structure, rather than flights of fancy soaring to new and complex designs' (1979, p. 361).

In his 1943 art-song cycle, *I Hate Music*, Bernstein utilized classical structures: ternary ABA form (nos. 3 and 4), rondo form (2 and 5) and through-composed music (1). However, in 'Big Stuff', the blues song that opens the ballet *Fancy Free*, Bernstein turned to popular music for his structure, and created an AA¹BA² song. Despite his criticism of the form five years earlier, Bernstein appears to have decided that within the context of the ballet, which employs vernacular music sounds, such a structure is appropriate. Similar reasoning can be applied to *On the Town*: Bernstein seems to have changed his mind, and decided when writing a Broadway show it was reasonable to use the song forms employed by other Broadway composers.

Bernstein employed the AABA form, labelled 'Popular Song Form' by Citron (1991, p. 55), in four numbers in the show, most notably in the second of Gabey's two solo songs, 'Lucky to Be Me'. The form is found in the chorus, which follows a recitative-like verse, sung over semibreve and minim chords. The A section contains a lyrical melody, with a simple rhythm and melodic shape dominated by arpeggios. This music contrasts with the B section, where there is almost a full chromatic scale in the vocal line, ascending from C to C with only the A natural missing. This section's key is unclear, especially after the unambiguous F major of the preceding music, but this is ambiguity is a trait that can be found in other songs in this form:

> many songs of the era have a B section which is tonally unstable, moving through a sequence of chromatic chords back to the tonic for the return of A; the character of such a section is more often that of a bridge between the second and last statements of A than of a contrasting section. (Hamm 1979, p. 363)

Following the solo presentation, the whole song is reprised by the chorus in four-part harmony: Gabey's indefatigable optimism spreads to those around him, and they echo his positive sentiments. In this song, the rhythms and the accompaniments are relatively simple, demonstrating the typical Tin Pan Alley bass-line pattern of a low bass note followed by a mid-range chord. 'Lucky To Be Me' is in the style of a Broadway ballad,[16] which emphasizes the fact that it is being sung by the romantic hero of the tale, and it contrasts with some of the high-energy numbers sung by the other characters.

Another example of a ballad in AABA form can be found near the end of the show, in the song 'Some Other Time', when Claire, Hildy, Chip and Ozzie are lamenting the shortness of the time they have left together; they have not really had time to get to know each other and to do the normal things couples do: 'There's so much more embracing, / Still to be done, but time is racing', 'Didn't get half my wishes, / Never have seen you dry the dishes', 'Can't satisfy my craving, / Never have watched you while you're shaving' (Comden and Green 1997, p. 80). The verse of this song has already been mentioned, as the opening melody is used in 'Subway Ride', and features the descending chromatic figure (see Example 1.7). The feeling of longing in this song is increased by lengthening the crotchets in the triplet figure at the opening of the chorus (see Example 1.7), and because of the three beats pulling against two. The 16-bar verse is sung three times, once each by the two women, with all four characters joining in the last four-bar phrase of Hildy's verse, and then once by the quartet, including canonic imitation and four-part harmony.

A further song that is in the Popular Song Form is 'So Long, Baby', sung by Diamond Eddie's Girls at the first nightclub of the evening heard at the opening of the second act; there is also an extension in this song, resulting in an AABABA structure, although the final two sections are predominantly instrumental to allow for a short dance. The rather loud and vulgar character of the song is a contrast to the romantic nature of the other songs in the same form, but the song is labelled 'Fast and corny', suggesting that it is a perhaps a parody of a popular song.[17]

The structure of 'I Can Cook Too', Hildy's solo seduction song, appears a little strange on first consideration (Table 1.2). However, closer examination reveals that it contains a simple AABA form refrain, repeated twice in the main song, with the verse appearing after the first chorus, rather than at the beginning; this structure is confirmed by the encore that immediately follows. The repeated A sections allow the lyricist various references within a list song dedicated to cooking and food; the first five notes of the A section return to the same concept over and over again, emphasizing the title of the song and developing the idea:

---

[16]   Jaensch states that 'despite the unusual B-section "Lucky to Be Me" is "sugary-sweet", the melody moving with parallel thirds typical of the Broadway ballad' (2003, p. 53, translation by present author).

[17]   'So Long, Baby' reminds me of the tacky nightclub songs created by Rodgers and Hart for *Pal Joey*.

Table 1.2   Structure of 'I Can Cook Too'

intro	4 bars	Key of G
A+A+B	4+4+8	G > F♯ min
A¹	6	G
instrumental	4	G > F
C	8+8	F > G
A+A+B	4+4+8	G > F♯ min
A¹	6 + 2	G
dance (AAB)	8+8	D > C♯ min
A¹	8	G
encore		
intro	4	G
C	8+8	F > G
A+A+B	4+4+8	G > F♯ min
A¹	8	G

Chorus 1:
'Oh, I can cook, too', 'And I can cook, too', 'Oh, I'm a gumdrop'

Chorus 2:
''Cause I can bake, too', 'Yes, I can roast, too', 'Oh, I'm an hors d'œuvre'

Encore:
''Cause I can fry, too' 'Yes, I can broil, too', 'Oh, I'm a paté'

In *On the Town* Bernstein also utilizes simple strophic structure in three numbers: 'I Feel Like I'm Not Out of Bed Yet', 'I Wish I Was Dead', and 'I Understand'.[18] It is interesting that all three of these songs are performed by minor characters: the First Workman, with his four work-mates providing echoes at the end of each of his three verses; Diana Dream and Dolores Dolores the nightclub singers (two verses from the first and one from the second); and Pitkin, who sings one verse and two fragments of his music at points throughout the show before his final four-verse version.

The standard Broadway structure that Bernstein employs in *On the Town* is that of the verse and chorus. This can be observed in several numbers: 'New York, New York', 'Ya Got Me', 'Gabey's Comin'', 'Come Up to My Place' and 'Carried Away'. In the last three, the sense is less of 'verse' and 'chorus', and more of alternating

---

[18]   The common feature of the first person pronoun appears to be purely coincidental.

contrasting material. This contrast is usually strong, as in 'Gabey's Comin'', the two sections of which have already been discussed. Similarly, in 'Come Up to My Place', the two sections are distinct; the fast moving quavers of the first part give way to the seductive blues sound of the second, where Hildy gives excuses for not visiting the various landmarks that Chip wishes to see, trying to persuade him to return to her apartment with her.

Gabey's first solo song, 'Lonely Town', is another which contains two contrasting sections in the chorus, an AABAB[1] structure. However, this is not an extended 'Popular Song Form' number, as the climax of the chorus clearly occurs at the end of the first B section, not in the following repetition of A – unusually an instrumental presentation of the music. The A section is interesting as it wavers between E major and E minor, as the sentiment moves between Gabey's loneliness and his desire for love. The B section starts in the dominant, a reasonable modulation to a closely related key, but does not remain there for long: another demonstration of the chromaticism already seen in the corresponding section of 'Lucky to Be Me'. A further notable feature of this song is the function of the verse, a portion that by the 1940s had become discretionary. It was considered that the most important and memorable material would usually be found in the chorus:

> As single verse became standard in the 1920s, and even this was often omitted in performance away from the stage, perhaps because the dramatic setting was unimportant when it was heard over the radio or from a phonograph. And in less than a decade, composers themselves began treating the verse as an optional part of a song. (Hamm 1979, p. 359)

Hamm's description underlines an important point regarding the purpose of the verse, the relating of some aspect of the drama or narrative (similar to the function of an operatic recitative), whilst the chorus could frequently be removed from its context and still be understood, due to the more general emotional or dramatic message (as is often the case with an aria). This happened with Bernstein's 'Lonely Town' – when the song was released as sheet music, a different verse had to be created. The version in the show included Gabey's name and references to the Navy, and also used music that was derived from 'Gabey's Comin'', allusions that would not be relevant in an independent song. The replacement lyrics were more general, referring to the city rather than people and situations, and the music included fragments of the melodic theme from 'New York, New York', which would be more familiar to the listeners and purchasers of the music.

There is one further song that contains interesting structural details: 'Carnegie Hall Pavane'. This song shows Ivy at her singing lesson at the Hall in a simple musical *scena*, based on a vocal exercise that she is practising. There are a number of significant points regarding the number. First, the song is not a pavane; there is nothing regal and stately about the number. The misnomer appears to have been applied to underline Ivy's artistic pretensions; it is an ironic as the number has little to do with a baroque dance form.

Although the majority of dance items in the show are presented as stylized pantomime or ballet, there are several numbers that include more traditional dance 'breaks', where music is repeated instrumentally to provide the opportunity for the performers to dance, but without advancing the story. 'Carnegie Hall Pavane' employs this device, and the form of the number fits within a standard mould, although there is an unexpected excursion to D♭. The opening of the song is based on simple figures, following the pitches indicated by the tonic solfa words in the lyric: 'Do-do-re-do / Do-re-mi-do' (c^2–c^2–d^2–c^2/c^1–d^1–e^1–c^1) and 'Do-ti-la-do' (c^2–b^1–a^1–c^2) (Comden and Green 1997, p. 43); the figures gradually increase in their range until the final phrase contains a full descending C major scale. The scalic patterns and stepwise movement reflect the diegetic function of the song,[19] emulating the patterns used in vocal warm-ups. The bass line is also quite simple, moving stepwise in six out of the eight bars in this section. As with many of these songs, the second melody (B) presents ideas that originate from the opening figure. However, here they seem to be a jazz-derived break from the monotonous scales of the exercises; a brief diversion from the academic studies into music a little more interesting and contemporary. The first note is slightly altered, and instead of the tonic we hear a flattened third in b. 15. There is no resolution back down to the tonic (although this resolution does occur two bars later). The original motif becomes the answering phrase to this new idea. In this contrasting area, or release, the style of the accompaniment changes; a dotted quaver-semiquaver 'swing' rhythm is seen in the bass part, and there is also syncopation and an altered harmonic language, including flattened and chromatic notes.

In 'Carnegie Hall Pavane', a further significant structural element is a degree of golden section proportion,[20] as shown in Table 1.3. The structure of the song follows golden-section proportions, allowing for an error of up to 1.9 per cent (at a ratio of 1.6296 as compared to 1.618), remembering that the phrases all consist of four, six or eight bars. If one more bar existed in the second section, the structure would reflect golden section proportions to within 0.02 per cent (in the ratios 55/34 and 89/55). This proportion can be seen specifically in Hindemith's Sonata No. 2 for Piano, a piece that Bernstein performed in his first full-length piano recital in 1938 (Burton 1994, p. 48).[21] As he read fine arts and classical European literature, including Socrates and Plato, at Harvard (Burton 1994, p. 33), it is highly probable

---

[19] The term diegetic is used here to distinguish between music that the characters know that they are singing, and other numbers that appear as sublimated song that in real life would be heard as speech.

[20] The golden section is the mathematical ratio used by mathematicians and artists since the Renaissance to produce what they consider to be aesthetically pleasing works, although it can also be traced back to the Greeks and Romans. It can be found in nature, and is also governs the numbers of the Fibonnaci sequence. Numerically, the ratio equates to 1.6180339887...

[21] It is very probable that Bernstein later met Hindemith at Tanglewood in 1940, when the former was a student at the summer school, and the latter was presiding over a composition class (Burton 1994, p. 75).

Table 1.3   Structure of 'Carnegie Hall Pavane', demonstrating golden section division

Intro	2 bars	Key of C	
A	12	C	
B	4	C	34
A¹	8	C	bars
B¹	8	C	
A²	18	D♭	
Dance break	24	C	54
A¹	4	F	bars
Coda	8	F	

that Bernstein would have discerned the classic division entwined with the traditional sonata-form within Hindemith's work. Golden-section division was, for Hindemith, part of ancient theory relating to 'the basic concepts of time and space, the very dimensions of the audible as of the visual world ... constructed in the very same proportions as the overtone series, so that measure, music and the cosmos inseparably merged' (Hindemith 1937, pp. 12–13).

No doubt the appeal the golden section division held for Hindemith, together with its facility to be combined with traditional forms, also attracted Bernstein. He utilized the proportion in several of his early works, revealed by analysis, including four out of the five songs of the *I Hate Music* cycle (nos. 1, 2, 3 and 5), and the second movement of his Clarinet Sonata (although the original manuscript contains extra bars that remove this proportion, bars that were deleted early in the composition process, possibly to accommodate the ratio). It is perhaps an unusual element to find in a musical-comedy song, but is another instance of Bernstein combining the highbrow with the lowbrow, a subtle underlining of Ivy's striving towards a classical and educated existence.

The Dances

As has already been discussed, the ballet sections of *On the Town* played an important part in the narrative of the story, and this is a significant contrast to the dance breaks mentioned in the last section. The two previously mentioned dance types have distinct functions, as, when the dances occur as part of songs, the flow of the plot is halted for the spectacle of the action on stage. In the ballets, the story is moved on and continued, being advanced through the dancing that takes place. In *On the Town* there are eight ballet numbers, some of which are linked in continuous sections, and all of them develop the scenario in some way.

The first ballet can be found near the beginning of the first act, in 'Presentation of Miss Turnstiles'. In this number, we are introduced to the character of Ivy

Smith, and her various attributes, as described on the 'Miss Turnstiles' poster that the sailors find in the subway. Some of Ivy's character traits appear contradictory, and apparently the result of some shrewd public relations: 'She's a home-loving girl, / But she loves high society's whirl. / She adores the Army, the Navy as well, / At poetry and polo she's swell' (Comden and Green 1997, p. 18). Following the fanfare figure based on the $\hat{1}\ \hat{2}\ \hat{5}$ phrase, and semiquaver underscoring over which the Announcer describes the reasons behind the Miss Turnstiles title and the manner in which the new holder is chosen,[22] there is the section labelled 'Allegretto di "Ballet Class"'. The 13 bars are divided into two phrases of seven and six bars, mostly written in $\frac{3}{4}$, and each of the two phrases begins with the figure $\hat{1}\ \hat{2}\ \hat{5}$. This section is followed (after a short four-bar bridge) by the only vocal passage in the number, sung by the Announcer using the words quoted above; these 13 bars further demonstrate Bernstein's awareness of the highbrow musical styles used Copland and Hindemith, as the melody contains 11 out of the 12 tones available, eight of them in the first three bars. The notes within the first few bars do not fall within a single diatonic framework, and the first two bars are also syncopated within the $\frac{3}{4}$ time signature. The chromatic nature of this melody is similar to the tune for 'Big Stuff', the song used to open *Fancy Free*, where again eleven tones are heard within the opening bars of the song. In 'Miss Turnstiles' there are then six variations, each forming the basis for a pas de deux for Ivy and one of the men, followed by a final section for all seven dancers. The first five variations demonstrate development of some or all of the material of the vocal theme, changing the style of the melody to match the character being described in dance on stage: military, seductive, and so on. The sixth, however, does not use this theme; instead, it is a variation on the second half of the 'Ballet Class' section. In the 'Pas de Sept', where all the men are dancing with Ivy, a further fanfare figure appears, once more developed from the vocal theme, creating a seventh variation. The number ends with a repetition of the semiquaver underscoring, as it is explained that a new Miss Turnstiles is chosen after a month, and as 'Ivy balks at returning' (score note, Bernstein 1997, p. 45), the 'Ballet Class' theme, which now appears to be a leitmotif for Ivy[23] is heard over the vamp in a rhythmically altered version.

'Presentation of Miss Turnstiles' demonstrates an expansion of the technique already seen in *Fancy Free* where three contrasting dances were created for the three sailors to display their dancing expertise. Seven variations are written, one for each of Ivy's supposed character facets, but, as in the ballet, in addition to the

---

[22] This semiquaver section is also based on an early Bernstein composition, the *Music for the Dance* (1938), although Gottlieb (1964, p. 262) lists the sections as *allegretto, vivicissimo, moderato* and *allegro non troppo*, while the manuscript containing the semiquaver phrases is marked *non troppo presto*.

[23] The phrase forms the basis for the second act 'Pas de Deux', as Gabey dreams of dancing with Ivy, his presence indicated by the 'blues' rhythm and harmony of the accompaniment, similar to that heard in 'Gabey's Comin''.

reuse of musical ideas there is a connecting idea: the competition for the girls in *Fancy Free*, and the character of Ivy in *On the Town*.

In *On the Town*, Bernstein deviates from the traditional variation form used in the dance routines of earlier and contemporary shows. In other musicals, repeated refrains of a previously heard song were presented with slight deviations in melody, harmony and instrumentation, but generally within the same phrase lengths and structures. This can be seen in the first-act ballet in *Babes in Arms* (Rodgers and Hart 1937), which is based on repetitions of the preceding song, 'Johnny One Note'. In contrast to this, the 'Slaughter on Tenth Avenue' ballet in Rodgers and Hart's *On Your Toes* (1936)[24] is an example of a dance based on a melody not derived from a previously heard song. The central contrasting section of the number is based on 'Three Blind Mice', which, following its initial presentation, is varied three times. The choice of theme and the number of imitations is symbolic, as three policemen enter the bar in which the ballet is set, and see nothing of the wrongdoing that is occurring. However, the whole section of the music is repeated, accompanied by different action on the stage, suggesting that the musical form is not integral to the drama, but merely reflects the usual development of material. In 'Miss Turnstiles', Bernstein creates two original themes, one of which is highly chromatic, and the other of which is linked thematically to other numbers in the show, and from these generates a set of variations that follow a narrative in describing Ivy's differing aspects. A similar technique was also used in the film musical *An American In Paris* (1951), where a girl's varying features are demonstrated in dance as her boyfriend describes her, to variations on the Gershwins's 'Embraceable You'.[25]

The next two ballet numbers form a pair, and appear later in the first act. The first of these is a relatively short number, 'High School Girls', which lasts only 25 bars. This bridges Gabey's solo, 'Lonely Town', and the 'Lonely Town Pas de Deux', and is based on material from the verse of 'Gabey's Comin'', as explained earlier. 'High School Girls' is divided into three short sections, the first containing the music of the song verse (see Example 1.11). In the following repetitions, the music is varied, mainly in the manner and texture of the accompaniment, whilst the theme retains its basic shape and rhythm in all three sections. However, at b.12, in the second version of the tune, a fragment of the theme is heard in E major, in crotchets, on the piccolo and glockenspiel over the chromatically altered second half of the 'verse', while the first eight notes of the theme are being played in minims, in C sharp major, in the basses of the orchestra; this is complex counterpoint for such a short musical number. This music accompanies a dance

---

[24]   Bernstein certainly had a respect for Richard Rodgers's work, and particularly for this ballet: 'there was a great amount of wonderful dancing in shows which preceded *On the Town* ... And "Slaughter on Tenth Avenue" is not to be sneezed at' (quoted in Guernsey 1985, p. 10).

[25]   It is perhaps not a coincidence that *An American in Paris* was partly created by Gene Kelly, who had starred in the 1949 MGM film of *On the Town*, although in the film version the Miss Turnstiles dance was performed to different music, still written by Bernstein.

Example 1.11 'High School Girls', bb. 1–4

that shows high-school girls being approached by a group of sailors. Most of the girls leave, with the men close behind, but one remains, and the music moves into the 'Lonely Town Pas de Deux' as Gabey misses a romantic opportunity: he moves towards the girl, but she approaches the last sailor and dances with him before they exit together.

In his programme notes for the dance episodes that he extracted from *On the Town*, Bernstein elaborated on the situation during the 'Lonely Town Pas de Deux': 'Gabey watches a scene, both tender and sinister, in which a sensitive high-school girl in Central Park is lured and then cast off by a worldly sailor' (Bernstein 1946). Again, the music for the ballet is in three sections, arranged in an ABA structure, a form that is governed by the material quoted in the music. The A section, which begins with a very un-Broadway like clarinet figure, includes a reference to Gabey's preceding song, with the music of the chorus of 'Lonely Town' played on a trumpet, punctuated and accompanied by the triplet patterns introduced by the clarinets (see Example 1.12).

Schiff points out that this section 'sounds like an echo of the slow movement of Gershwin's Piano Concerto' (2001, p. 445), and there are definite parallels between the orchestration (dominated by homophonic clarinets and a muted trumpet solo), and the general mood of the two pieces. The Gershwin work was another that Bernstein had studied before writing his thesis, and it is mentioned in passing in his writing (1982, p. 55). Bernstein's blues-style opening then leads into the central B section, which is based on the music of the introduction of 'Gabey's Comin'', and it builds to a fortissimo climax before falling away again. The contrast between the two sections is emphasized in the modulations in the music: the A section is in D major, 'lifting' to E major for the B section, which moves through B and F♯ majors before returning to D major for the shortened repeat of the A section. The connection between the materials used is obvious, as both the 'Lonely Town' music and the 'Gabey's Comin'' motif are linked with the character of the sailor searching for romance. Mordden describes the latter theme as being 'dramatic, specific: the American Musical's Unshakeable Belief in Romance' (1999, p. 128), but, of course, this subtle reference to Gabey's earlier song would not have been recognized by the original audience, who were denied

Example 1.12 'Lonely Town Pas de Deux', bb. 1–4

the opportunity to hear 'Gabey's Comin''. However, they would still have been able to discern that this music recurs several times throughout the show.

The first act ends with another ballet section, this time on a larger scale, in 'Times Square Ballet: Finale Act 1', when the nightlife of New York is portrayed as the principals go off to enjoy themselves. Not surprisingly, as it is a number that celebrates the city, there is much use of the music from the opening song 'New York, New York'; several musical ideas are utilized from this earlier number, usually undergoing some degree of development and variation. The ballet opens with the music of the verse of 'New York, New York', with no alterations, and this is followed by the chord pattern heard in the introduction to the song. Later in the song, at figure C, the verse of the song appears in the orchestral bass instruments, while syncopated chords are played over the top. The chorus of the earlier song also provides the basis for an interesting section from figure F, when the music moves into $\frac{6}{8}$, and the 'New York, New York' melody is transformed into a sexy blues tune. A fragment of 'Come Up to My Place' appears at figure R; Hildy's 'seductive' section is repeated, before the ballet moves back into music derived from 'New York, New York'. The allusions within the ballet are clear, the music from the song that praised the city being used to underline the location, and the segment from 'Come Up to My Place' suggesting the objective of perhaps the majority of the people who are in Times Square that night. The rousing panoramic vision of the city brings the first act to an exciting close.

In the second act, there are two major segments of ballet, the first of which incorporates three different sections of music in the framework of a dream ballet. Gabey is travelling to Coney Island to look for Ivy, a place that Madame Dilly has led him to believe is very high-class and exclusive. As he sits on the subway train, he falls asleep and dreams of this fantastic place and of finding Ivy. In his fantasy, however, to overcome his shyness and inexperience, his place is taken by a dream counterpart, the 'Great Lover', who dances for the rich women in Coney Island before facing Ivy in a boxing ring. In the end, Gabey, in the shape of his dream-self, is overcome by Ivy, and the real Gabey moves quickly out of the scene. As with the earlier ballets, there is reference to earlier themes and songs, creating musical and dramatic associations. The music of the first ballet section, 'Subway Ride and Imaginary Coney Island', has already been discussed in some detail earlier in this chapter, and, as previously noted, it also employed the 'Gabey's Comin'' yearning motif and reused a section from the 'Lonely Town Pas de Deux'. In both of these situations, Gabey is dreaming about romance: either day-dreaming, as he watches the other sailors in the first act, or really dreaming, as at this point in the second act. 'Subway Ride' leads into 'The Great Lover Displays Himself', where Gabey's dream-self appears. There are several key musical ideas used in this dance, which begins with a very rhythmic chordal section, and a descending trombone fanfare as the dream-self begins his seductive dance. The first real melody to emerge is based on a simple dotted rhythm, with some later syncopation with blue notes. At figure E the the 'Gabey's Comin'' music appears yet again, in a different rhythmic guise, and with some elaboration (see Example 1.5c). It is from these ideas that the piece is constructed, as shown in Table 1.4:

Table 1.4   Structure of 'The Great Lover Displays Himself'

Figure	Material	Bars	Key
	Chords	7	E
A	Trombone Fanfare	7	C
B	Dotted tune	6	C
C	Blues tune	6	C
D	Dotted tune	6	E
E	'Gabey's Comin'' motif	8	F
F	'Gabey's Comin'' motif	8	E
G	Chords	7	E
H	New York Fanfare	7	C
I	Dotted tune/blues tune	4+6	C minor
J	'Gabey's Comin'' motif	8	G
K	'Gabey's Comin'' motif	8	E
L	'Gabey's Comin'' motif	8	E
M	Chords	6	E
N	New York Fanfare and coda	8	E
O	New York fanfare	3	D

As can be seen from the table, the first few phrases are shorter and, especially in the seven-bar phrases, feel a little 'interrupted'; the sense of balance is only restored when the familiar 'Gabey's Comin'' music appears. The 'New York, New York' fanfare (the $\hat{5}$ $\hat{1}$ $\hat{2}$ $\hat{5}$ motif) heralds the arrival in Gabey's dream of the Master of Ceremonies from the nightclub he visited earlier, and he announces the battle between the Great Lover and Ivy Smith, the Pas de Deux, in which Ivy is the victor. As the whole of this section depicts the conflict between Ivy and Gabey, it is not surprising that music connected with the characters should be utilized, but it is significant that the only melodic material used is associated with Ivy; the main musical ideas are derived from the 'Miss Turnstiles' number, from the 'Allegretto di "Ballet Class"' section. Gabey's presence is only really acknowledged in the accompaniment, which echoes the rhythm of the accompaniment in the B section of the 'Lonely Town Pas de Deux'. The first four bars of the 'Ballet Class' phrase are rhythmically altered and ornamented with grace notes and arpeggios, and this is followed by a development of the same material. This music is repeated, and then there is a section based on the final four bars of the 'Ballet Class' music, which includes canonic imitation. The further musical idea in this number is more chordal than the other two segments; this section also includes a fragment of the descending chromatic phrase seen in 'Subway Ride', and will appear later in 'Some Other Time'. The actual structure of this section is a short rondo (Table 1.5):

Table 1.5   Structure of 'Pas de Deux'

Introduction		2 bars	Key of F
'Ballet class' music	A	12	F
'Ballet class' music	A	12	F
Canon section	B	12	A minor
'Ballet class' music	A	12	F
Chordal section	C	13	E
'Ballet class' music	A	12	F

This ballet sequence is significant as it is the only place where Gabey actually dances with Ivy, even if it is happening only in his dreams and through his alter-ego. His two friends have found their dates for the day, but Gabey has been denied his opportunity for romance. In the ballet, we see the outcome we, the audience, and he, Gabey, hope for, the fulfilment of his desires: '*On the Town*'s dream is really the just the climax of the story too short on time to show us what we need to see: the union of Gabey and Ivy. So we get the fantasy' (Mordden 1999, p. 126). The fact that Gabey never gets Ivy, never gets to spend any time with her or really gets to know her, keeps the dream intact: it is never spoiled by a real relationship. Gabey's romantic tendency was revealed at the very opening of the show when, in Scene 2, he declared that, rather than looking for a New York glamour girl, he wants someone special. Perhaps it is for the best that his idealistic wishes are left

Chapter 2
Trouble in Tahiti

'Mornin' Sun'

At the opening of Thornton Wilder's 1938 play *Our Town*, the Stage Manager cheerfully introduces us to Grover's Corner, describing it as a 'nice town, y'know what I mean?' (Wilder 1958, p. 7). His monologue provides a preface to the action that Wilder offers as 'an attempt to find a value above all price for the smallest events in our daily life' (1958, p. xi). Such concentration on the almost mundane, everyday aspects of life are an effort to 'capture not verisimilitude but reality' (1958, p. xi), can also be found in Bernstein's opera, *Trouble in Tahiti*.[1] In Bernstein's opening Prelude, a trio of singers echo the sentiments of Wilder's Stage Manager as they sing of the 'little white house' with its 'pretty red roof', and of the 'mornin' sun' which 'kisses the windows: kisses the walls … kisses the roof: kisses the doorknob' (Bernstein 1953, pp. 2–3). There is a cheerful naivety in both Wilder's play and Bernstein's Prelude that provides a positive, optimistic image of American life. This view was reflected in many of the musical films of the time, especially in MGM's *Meet Me In St Louis* (1944), *The Pirate* (1947) and *Easter Parade* (1948), and in the film version of *On the Town* (1949). These works were being produced in a decade that saw a country recently devastated by the Depression then followed by a world war, and provided a sense of detachment, an escape for a public desperate for a reminder of the healthy and happy lives promised by the American Dream.

Opposing the often jovial film-musical in the cinema was the *film noir*, dark thrillers where paranoia was rife, and people were trapped in webs of fear and intrigue. Although *film noir* was a manifestation of the public's nightmares, there is significance in the focus of the films, which show a shift towards an inner world: 'by the 1940s, horror lay close to home, in the veiled malevolence of trusted intimates, in one's own innermost thoughts' (Sklan 1994, p. 255). As political and social unrest combined with the perceived Communist threat from overseas, undermining the public's sense of wellbeing, doubts about the certainty of the American Dream crept in. There appears to be a focus on the reality beneath the façade of superficiality, and an acknowledgement that even in the country where

---

[1] Bernstein was certainly familiar with Wilder's play: his date book for 1949 states that he went to watch the 1940 film version on 1 September (box 321, LBC). He had a personal connection to the film, as the music had been composed by his friend Aaron Copland. Copland created a concert version of music from the film in 1944, which he dedicated to Bernstein (note on full score), who conducted the première of the new piece.

anything seemed possible for those willing to work not everybody could achieve the success they desired or deserved.

A further trend, based on a concentration on the specific rather than the general, appeared in the theatre. Here Tennessee Williams and Arthur Miller created works centred on unsuccessful or struggling characters, striving to regain some sense of dignity and happiness in oppressive environments (Wardle 1993, p. 209); these plays included *The Glass Menagerie* (1945), *A Streetcar Named Desire* (1947), *Death of a Salesman* (1949) and *The Crucible* (1953). In literature, social issues were also being dealt with, while the Second World War inspired novels dealing with military situations, including James Michener's *Tales of the South Pacific* (1947) and Norman Mailer's *The Naked and the Dead* (1948). The poem *The Age of Anxiety* (1946–47) by W. H. Auden dealt with characters searching for their identities and place in society following the conflicts, and Bernstein's Second Symphony (1949) is based loosely on this verse.

A more negative image of the American Dream is central to Marc Blitzstein's 1936–37 musical *The Cradle Will Rock*, a tale of the prostitution of various institutions and individuals, including the Church and the arts, to a single manipulative man. Blitzstein's ideas came about as a result of the Works Progress Administration, part of President Roosevelt's New Deal. It was commissioned as part of the Federal Theatre Project, to be directed by the rising star Orson Welles and produced by John Houseman, although the première has gone down in theatre history for completely different reasons. When federal backing was pulled, possibly when the strength of Blitzstein's pro-union story was revealed, the Maxine Elliot theatre was locked, and the performers and audience trekked uptown to a theatre that would allow them to put on the show. The musician's union also prohibited participation by the orchestra following the government intervention, so Blitzstein played the score on the piano, sitting alone in the middle of the stage.

This notoriety would have attracted Bernstein, who had first experienced Blitzstein's music when he watched *The Cradle Will Rock* on Broadway in 1938 (Burton 1994, p. 52), a performance which he found so inspiring that it provided the impetus for his own production in 1939 at Harvard, where he took Blitzstein's role as pianist. He then went on to give the world première of the fully orchestrated version on 24 November 1947, and conducted the first three performances of a five-week Broadway run in 1947–48 (Burton 1994, p. 176). *The Cradle Will Rock* was, without doubt, a definite influence on Bernstein during the creation of his next theatre work; it was not long after the 1947–48 production that Bernstein wrote:

> I have a basic interest in theatre music. Most of my scores have been, in one way or another, for theatrical performance, and the others – most of them – have an obvious dramatic basis … if I can write one real, moving American opera that any American can understand (and one that is, notwithstanding, a serious musical work), I shall be a happy man. (Bernstein 1982, p. 129)

Blitzstein's influence on Bernstein extended beyond the merely musical, as the older composer had attended the Harvard production and spent the afternoon talking to the young impresario; this meeting was the beginning of a long friendship between the two men, a relationship that was probably reinforced by the parallels in their lives. As Burton suggests, 'both came from well-to-do backgrounds. Blitzstein's father – also named Sam and also Russian-Jewish – had been a Philadelphia banker before the crash of 1929. Like Bernstein, Blitzstein was an excellent pianist' (Burton 1994, p. 54). They also shared an educational background, as both men had also attended the Curtis School of Music (Blitzstein was one of the first pupils in 1942: Gordon 1989, p. 20). The two men remained close over the years, and Blitzstein acted as advisor on the lyrics for the songs that Bernstein provided for the 1950 production of *Peter Pan* (Gordon 1989, p. 195). Bernstein was, in turn, a fervent supporter of the older composer, and when Blitzstein's opera *Regina* opened on Broadway in 1949 Bernstein wrote a salutary article for the *New York Times*. He not only praised Blizstein's new work, but also took the opportunity to discuss the future of the American opera, a future that he saw as emerging from the musical theatre.

Bernstein clearly had Blitzstein's work in mind as he planned his first foray into operatic composing. However, conducting engagements both in America and internationally took precedence for the following years, until 1951, when Bernstein took time from his busy schedule to devote to composing. Bernstein had originally intended to write 'big, loud pretty music for the American theatre' (Bernstein to Copland, in Burton 1994, p. 205), but instead he turned his attention to his own opera. Between *On the Town* and *Trouble in Tahiti*, Bernstein composed a number of other works, but the majority of these were small-scale pieces for chamber groups or soloists, although there were larger compositions such as the ballet *Facsimile* and his second symphony, *Age of Anxiety* (Table 2.1).

Table 2.1   Bernstein's compositions between *On the Town* and *Trouble in Tahiti*

1945	*Hashkiveinu*	choral piece
	Afterthought	solo voice with piano
1946	*Facsimile*	ballet
1947	*La Bonne Cuisine*	solo voice song cycle with piano
	Simchu Na/Reena	arrangements of Jewish songs
1948	*Brass Music*	solos and fanfare
	Four Anniversaries	piano solo
1949	*Two Love Songs*	solo voice with piano
	Age of Anxiety	symphony
	Prelude, Fugue and Riffs	piece for jazz band
1950	*Peter Pan*	songs and incidental music for play
	Yigdal	canon for choir

Another distraction from the task of composing his American opera was Bernstein's upcoming marriage to Felicia Montealegre Cohn. The composer had first encountered the Chilean actress at a post-concert party in February 1946 (Burton 1994, p. 145), and they had quickly fallen in love. They became engaged in December of the same year, but the engagement lasted for only eleven months, before collapsing under the strain of Bernstein's professional life and his sexual indecision (Burton 1994, p. 167). However, the separation didn't last, and the couple became re-engaged in August 1951; they married less than a month later on 8 September (Burton 1994, p. 212). Bernstein had begun work on his new opera prior to the wedding, whilst on retreat in Mexico in April (Burton 1994, p. 206), and he continued composition during his honeymoon. He was inspired by his new domestic situation: he wrote to Helen Coates in October 1951 'The days whizz by … *Trouble in Tahiti* is practically finished' (quoted in Burton 1994, p. 215). However, as will be observed, the subject of the opera appears a somewhat odd reflection of the wedded bliss of a newly married couple.

Although Bernstein was happily settling into married life, not everything was running as smoothly with his music, and by the following January he was lamenting the state of his opera: 'I have abandoned it, decisively. It just will not come … Something seems to have happened to the creative flow' (quoted in Burton 1994, p. 215). Fortunately, he had recently accepted an appointment as visiting music professor at Brandeis University, near Boston, and as part of his duties he had undertaken to direct their inaugural Festival of Creative Arts in 1952 (Burton 1994, p. 220). *Trouble in Tahiti* was to form part of the proceedings, so Bernstein now had a deadline to work to, and, as with so many, this motivation proved successful: he conducted the première on 12 June 1952 in the Adolph Ullman Amphitheatre at the University following a Symposium entitled 'An Inquiry into the Present State of the Creative Arts', which he moderated.

Bernstein's experience of opera in a professional environment was relatively small; since graduating from Curtis in 1939, he had been involved with productions of Britten's *Peter Grimes* (the US première in 1946, a student production at Tanglewood), the aforementioned *The Cradle Will Rock*, Copland's *The Second Hurricane*, Stravinsky's *Oedipus Rex*, and Paul Bowles's *The Wind Remains*.[2] Considering that *Trouble in Tahiti* was inspired by, and indeed dedicated to, Blitzstein, it may be reasonable to suggest that there may be some degree of similarity between the two works. However, in his usual way, Bernstein draws on a wide range of influences in the creation of his score, and so the musical link between *Cradle* and *Tahiti* is not strong; however, there are some elements common to both. The first is the negative view of American life, even though it appears on a different scale: that is, the corruption of a town compared with the breakdown of family life. The second concerns the structure and the number of scenes within each work. Both pieces were originally written as uninterrupted

---

[2]   Four of these operas were composed by members of the Nadia Boulanger circle: three of her students in Bowles, Copland and Blitzstein, and her friend Stravinsky.

works, although *The Cradle Will Rock* later acquired an interval (Block 1997, p. 366 n. 25). The Blitzstein work contains ten scenes, while *Trouble in Tahiti* consists of 12 (including the Prelude, Interlude, and short returns to previous scenes). By breaking the action down into such short divisions, Bernstein appears to be imitating Blitzstein rather than utilizing a more standard operatic act-based structure. In turn, it would seem that Blitzstein had been influenced by the structure of Weill and Brecht's *Die Dreigroschenoper* (1928), which he would later translate into a very successful English version. It was Brecht who had suggested that Blitzstein write *The Cradle Will Rock*, and the work was also dedicated to the older artist, who also championed criticism of society on stage, including in his *Aufstieg und Fall der Stadt Mahagonny* (1930). *Die Dreigroschenoper* consists of a Prologue, two interludes and eight scenes, totalling eleven separate locations or settings; a structure not derived from the original *Beggar's Opera*, the basis for Weill and Brecht's piece, as this is divided into three acts, but rather from Brecht's own writings for the theatre and his origins in German Expressionist drama. Both *The Cradle Will Rock* and *Trouble in Tahiti* combine the influence of *Die Dreigroschenoper* with the structure of Broadway shows, themselves derived from the short individual scenes or acts seen in vaudeville performances. This relationship is strengthened by the fact that both were produced at the Brandeis Festival, where Bernstein conducted the première of Blitzstein's translation of *The Threepenny Opera*, in addition to his own opera.[3] There is also a private joke included in the words of Bernstein's Prelude, as the scat section contains the words 'Skid a lit day. Skid a lit Ada Abarbanel: who but Abarbanel buys a visa' (Bernstein 1953, p. 9); this is a reference to Blitzstein's mother-in-law, Lina Abarbanell (minus the final *l*), a light opera singer who had settled in America in 1910 after emigrating from Berlin (Gordon 1989, p. 35 and p. 358). A final possible example of Blitzstein's influence is seen by Gordon in *Trouble in Tahiti* in its elements of social protest, 'against the depressing sexual division of labor that feminists would later criticize' (1989, p. 358); among the papers in the Leonard Bernstein Collection relating to the opera is a list that suggests Bernstein himself saw a separation in characteristics of men and women:

Women: They dream: They beautify themselves: They escape – They get analysed: They confide too easily: They need constant diversion.

Men: They are in order: They are strong: They can categorize: They organize: They go to the gym: They know where sex belongs.[4]

---

[3]   Bernstein was familiar with *Der Dreigroschenoper* before beginning work on *Tahiti*, as he had acquired a copy of the Lotte Lenya recording of the piece whilst at college in 1937 (according to an article dated 23 September 1976 that Bernstein wrote for the Kurt Weill exhibition at the Lincoln Center that year; box 90, folder 19, LBC).

[4]   It is unclear whether this list was made before or after work on the opera, and whether he is being sincere or satirical (box 72, folder 2, LBC), but there are clear links between the characteristics listed and elements of the story in the opera.

Despite Blitzstein's friendship with Bernstein, he was not overly impressed by all aspects of this new opera. In a letter to fellow composer David Diamond in March 1952, Blitzstein wrote: 'Lenny has been coming regularly to me with his one-act opera. It is lively musically, but dreary in subject' (Gordon 1989, p. 357).

In the plot of *Trouble in Tahiti*, it soon becomes clear that the optimism of the Prelude was an illusion, and real life takes a hold as the domestic arguments begin in Scene 1, a more authentic presentation of an everyday situation. Bernstein's opera follows the day of a married couple, Sam and Dinah, from a disagreement at the breakfast table, through their individual activities – Sam in the office and gym locker-room, Dinah at the psychiatrist's and in a hat shop after watching a movie – to their attempt at reconciliation that evening; see Table 2.2.

Table 2.2   Structure of *Trouble in Tahiti*

	Singers	Location	
Prelude	Trio	In front of curtains	
Scene 1	Sam and Dinah (and Trio)	Kitchen – breakfast time	
Scene 2	Sam (and Trio)	Sam's office	The sets for these two scenes were on stage simultaneously, allowing quick changes between.
Scene 3	Dinah	Psychiatrist's office	
Scene 2a	Sam	Office	
Scene 3a	Dinah	Psychiatrist's	
Scene 4	Sam and Dinah	Street – lunchtime	
Interlude	Trio	In front of curtains	
Scene 5	Sam	Gym	Simultaneously staged as above
Scene 6	Dinah (and Trio)	Hat shop	
Scene 6a	Sam	Front door of house	
Scene 7	Sam and Dinah (and Trio)	Sitting room – after dinner	

A trio of singers comments on the actions of the couple, in the manner of a Greek chorus; this group is described as being 'refined and sophisticated in a high-priced dance-band tradition'.[5] They appear at various points in the opera, always lauding the illusion of the perfect suburban life, and extolling the dreams of the couple. They sing in the manner of a radio trio, moving in parallel close-harmony and swing rhythms, full of superficial emotions and shallow aspirations. As previously mentioned, in the Prelude they sing of the delights of suburban living; in the Interlude they move on to sing the praises of the modern conveniences within the perfect home, and middle-class pastimes. Bernstein's depiction of this perfect lifestyle, contrasting sharply with what we have seen of the couple and

---

[5]   This description appears in Bernstein's 'Notes on Production', found at the front of the 1953 vocal score.

their relationship, is surely not sincere: 'As was consistently his way, Bernstein embedded a social message in *Tahiti* – in this case critiquing gender roles, consumerism, and suburban conventions of the boom immediately following World War II' (Oja 2005, p. 526).

Sam and Dinah's son, who is not seen during the opera, appears to be representative of Bernstein himself. Certainly, his own home environment was not always peaceful, and there is an autobiographical element in *Trouble in Tahiti*. The father shares the name of Bernstein's father, and the wife was at one point called Jennie after his mother,[6] although this was changed to Dinah, the name of his paternal grandmother. Shirley Bernstein, Leonard's younger sister, concluded that 'my mother and father were mismated, mismatched, both interesting and good people who should never have got married' (quoted in Burton 1994, p. 16). Shirley also talked of an incident when her mother asked her father for a quarter for her daughter, and 'he flew into a rage for no apparent reason. She was asking for money again; I guess that was at the base of it' (Burton 1994, p. 16). This, or a similar event, may have been the inspiration for the final part of Scene 1 where Dinah asks for money, to be refused, which is closely followed by Sam's brisk exit to work. The youngest Bernstein sibling, Burton, has described how another aspect of *Trouble in Tahiti* was based in reality: 'Dinah's suspicions about an affair that her husband allegedly had with his secretary, Miss Brown, sprang from a biographical incident. The malevolent wife of one of my father's employees once telephoned Jennie [Bernstein's mother] to hint that Sam was sleeping with a woman who worked in his office' (quoted in Peyser 1987, pp. 180–81). This focus on marital disharmony may be appropriate given the timing: Bernstein is needing to exorcise the past so that he can move forward with his own marriage.

The small number of characters in the opera (only Sam and Dinah are named) is to some extent dictated by the domestic situation portrayed, but may also have been influenced by a similar casting in *The Wind Remains*. Bowles's zarzuela-inspired opera, which Bernstein conducted in 1943, has only two singing roles, tenor and soprano (Burton 1994, p. 106). At the Brandeis première of Bernstein's work, the singers in the Trio took on the spoken roles of Miss Brown, Bill and the Analyst,[7] but these parts were deleted in the later revision of the opera. In the revised version, performed at Tanglewood two months later, only Sam and Dinah's voices are heard in the conversations, underlining the fact that we are observing their lives and experiences, and shutting out the rest of the world.

---

[6]   Among the papers in the Library of Congress there are several undated drafts of the libretto for *Tahiti*; in one the name of the mother is Jennie. More significantly, there is another draft where the name of the father is not Sam, but Paul (box 72, folder 21, LBC). A brief change of heart on Bernstein's part, perhaps?

[7]   These parts can be seen on a draft libretto of the opera (box 72, folder 21, LBC), and there is also a note on the programme for the Brandeis Festival performance: 'Various spoken parts will be taken by members of the Trio' (box 335, LBC).

The reason for Bernstein choosing such an intimate subject for his opera is not known, and the revelations of the inadequacies in his own home-life are a harsh way for him to treat his parents; Bernstein had a tendency to be cruel, usually unknowingly, in his frankness and his need to share opinions and passions with others. It is possible that Bernstein felt his own experiences would be easy for other Americans to empathize with, aiding the understanding he wanted others to have of his work. This self-portrayal continued in Bernstein's later opera *A Quiet Place*, a sequel to *Trouble in Tahiti* that takes up the story 30 years later. Bernstein's references to his own life continue, incorporated into the story of Sam and Dinah's family, as will be discussed in Chapter 8.

Motivic Techniques

The compositional techniques demonstrated in *On the Town* continue to be utilized in *Trouble in Tahiti*, for example the first vocal phrase in Scene 1 sung by Sam is an example of a recurring theme (see Example 2.1). Sam sings to his wife with barely concealed rage, accusing and reproaching her. The D–A–D–C pattern forms the basis of the opening scene's A section, and is manipulated through extension and development. The jagged melodic shape underlines the tension in the situation. As either Sam or Dinah pick another fault, we hear the 'conflict' figure each time the A section returns. This section is repeated several times, and as each eight-bar phrase progresses the couple's conversation peters out: the intervals in the vocal line also decrease, ending with a repeated E. The motif also appears at the end of the first B section, as it modulates from the D minor opening to B minor in the third repetition. The motif even finds its way into Sam's song in the next scene, and it is not unsurprising that it also occurs a few bars after his colleagues have inquired after Dinah, when Sam is agitated ('a slight frown', 'The frown again', [Bernstein 1953, pp. 32 and 36]). The mention of his wife reminds Sam of the morning's argument, and this thought creeps into the vocal line (see Example 2.2a).

Example 2.1 Conflict motif, scene 1

Dinah's song in Scene 3 begins with an inversion of this 'conflict' theme, and it is repeated several times in the melody. The D–A–D–C becomes A–D–A–B♭; the final descending major second changes to an ascending minor second, as Dinah describes her haunting dream, which is probably a consequence of the tension and hostility at home (see Example 2.2b). As Sam celebrates his handball victory in Scene 5, the motif returns in the ending of each of the three main verses, as (E–F♯)–G–D–G–F. His words here reflect the masculine, aggressive mood that he is in, changing for each verse, but always reflecting his competitive nature and his

Example 2.2 Appearances of the Conflict motif

(a) Scene 2, fig. 1 + 8
(b) Scene 3, fig. 1

desire to succeed. The motif finally returns when the music from Scene 1 is reused in the final scene, as the couple slowly begin to resolve their differences.

The phrase that can be considered the balancing motif, representing 'resolution', first appears in Scene 1, at fig. 7 (see Example 2.3).[8] The initial descending fourth is 'stretched' to a fifth and the whole phrase outlines a ninth. Although the full phrase contains seven notes, it is the first four that constitute the main motif, and it has been suggested that this resembles the 'Prize Song' motif from *Die Meistersinger* (Fanning 1988). Wagner's motif outlined is an octave, but I believe that Bernstein's lowering of the bottom note by a semitone to a D♯ is an important dramatic element.[9] In *Trouble in Tahiti* the phrase accompanies the words 'Try, Dinah, try to be kind', which is Sam's plea for communication, later echoed by his wife. The Resolution motif is then only heard again in the final scene, as the couple begin to resolve their problems, where the ascending tetrachord is extended to a seventh, imitating a phrase from the previous duet in Scene 4 (at fig. 6 + 8). Conrad points out that the last chord is a 'verticalization of the duet's theme' (1992b, p. 1202); it contains six of the seven notes of the extended motif, only omitting the

---

[8]   Jaensch labels this a 'Resignations-Motiv', which suggests a more negative tone for the phrase (2003, p. 188).

[9]   Similar figures can also be found in Stravinsky's *Oedipus Rex*, where it accompanies moments concerning the death of Laius, Oedipus' father, and his son's discovery of his true origins.

Example 2.3   Resolution motif, Scene 1

Example 2.4   Resolution motif, and final chord of *Trouble in Tahiti*

F♯ from the end of the phrase (see Example 2.4), suggesting that, by the close of the opera, there is some hope of reconciliation between the couple.

Bernstein's characteristic 4̂3̂1̂ *Urmotiv* appears twice in *Trouble in Tahiti*; both times are in Dinah's vocal lines. The first is in the verse of her Scene 3, and the second in the 'Movie' aria in Scene 6. This is significant as, by employing his characteristic motif in these situations, Bernstein is perhaps suggesting that, when she is on her own, Dinah's emotions are more genuine than her husband's, or than her own feelings when they are together. A further recurring phrase also appears in certain situations, although it is not used within developmental processes. As with the *Urmotiv*, this phrase is essentially a cadence figure, and occurs perhaps most significantly with the words 'quiet place' in Dinah's Scene 2 aria (see Example 2.5). This cadential figure is an elaboration of a standard 2̂–1̂ cadence (over a V–I harmony), with a 3̂ appoggiatura added onto the tonic in the melody line to create harmonic interest. The third degree of the scale now becomes an added sixth on the dominant chord. This device had been used before in Broadway

Example 2.5   Cadence 1 (ascending major second, descending major third), cadence 2 (ascending major second, descending minor third), cadence 3 (ascending minor second, descending minor third)

songs, for example 'Over the Rainbow', 'After You, Who?', 'Nice Work If You Can Get It', and 'A Ship Without a Sail'. Bernstein himself had used the phrase in *On the Town*, as the final cadence in 'Lucky to Be Me'. In *Trouble in Tahiti*, of the seven occurrences of cadence 1, four occur at the ends of phrases, and of these, three are on degrees $\hat{2}\hat{3}\hat{1}$. One of the other instances, which is in a central position in a phrase, ends on a note not the dominant or the tonic (Table 2.3).

Table 2.3　　Use of cadence 1

Scene 1	fig. 6+7	A little feel–*ing of home*	$\hat{2}\hat{3}\hat{1}$
Scene 2	fig. 1+1–2	*Oh, Mister Par–*tridge	$\hat{2}\hat{3}\hat{1}$
	fig. 1+3–4	*I'm perfectly fine*	$\hat{5}\hat{6}\hat{4}$
Scene 3	fig. 3+4	*Come with me*	$\hat{6}\hat{7}\hat{5}$
	fig. 4+8	A *quiet place*	$\hat{2}\hat{3}\hat{1}$
Scene 6	fig. 21+6–7	*ISLAND MAGIC*	$\hat{6}\hat{7}\hat{5}$
	fig. 23+8–9	It real–*ly is mine*	$\hat{2}\hat{3}\hat{1}$

(Italics indicate words accompanying notes of motif.)

All of these phrases include some element of hopeful imagination, as in the situation in 'Lucky to Be Me'; in some it is almost desperation. In Scene 1, the couple are arguing, and the motif is contained within 'outbursts', as they try to explain their frustrations and desires. In Scene 2, Sam is in the office, and is attempting to appear jovial and friendly towards people we can assume to be his colleagues, despite the furious row he has just had with his wife; twice he responds with a positive phrase, although the pleasantries are actually only aimed at boosting his own ego. Scene 3 is Dinah's visit to the therapist, whilst she describes her dream, in which she is called to a 'shining garden', a 'quiet place'. This use of the phrase is the most significant, as it associates the cadence figure with the most important concept of the opera: the 'quiet place', or situation of peace and contentment that both of them long to return to. The final two appearances of the figure are in Dinah's Scene 6 aria 'What a terrible movie'. Near the end of the aria, Dinah recalls the song from the movie she has just watched, a film called *Trouble in Tahiti*. As she remembers the song, the Radio Trio joins her in a beguine entitled 'Island Magic'. By this point in the aria, Dinah has become carried away in her description and is dancing emotionally around the stage. The movie has provided an escapist afternoon for Dinah, away from the arguments and stresses of home life, and it is within this context of imagined happiness that we hear the figure again.

The descriptive use of this phrase, cadence 1, can be underlined by the occurrences of two of its variations. The first of these, cadence 2, consists of the same ascending major second, followed by a descending *minor* third (see Example 2.5), which adds a disheartened feel to the pattern. This figure also appears in Scene 4, coinciding with the singers reflecting on the state of their marriage. A further example is sung by the Trio in Scene 7 just before Sam and Dinah finally sit down to try to work out their differences (Table 2.4). The scale degrees of these occurrences are ambiguous, and most happen when the tonal centre of the music is unclear. The second example is the only occasion where the figure is not at the end of the phrase, as the final word continues a descending D minor arpeggio. (In the first example, the final word is sung to repeated As, the last note of the cadence figure, and so can be seen as an extension.)

Table 2.4   Use of cadence 2

Scene 4	fig. 4+5–6	We're not so *very far* apart
	fig. 4+7–8	We like the same mov–*ies, the same* parties
	fig. 4+10–11	We have our *little child*
Scene 7	bb.7–8	*Wellesly Hills*

This version is also the 'contemplative' phrase that began the refrain of 'Lonely Town' in the previous show, emphasizing the words of the title.

A similar context surrounds the use of the second variation, cadence 3 (see Example 2.5), an ascending minor second followed by a descending minor third. This occurs twice during the Radio Trio items, and the remaining three times it appears to articulate something about the state of the couple's relationship. Although the final example is sung by Dinah in her 'movie' aria, when she is repeating the song that she has just heard, it is somehow reflective of her inner feelings towards Sam (Table 2.5).

Table 2.5   Use of cadence 3

Prelude	fig. J+8	*Ratty boo*	$\hat{6}\hat{7}\hat{5}$
Scene 3	fig. 1+4	A garden *gone to seed*	$\hat{2}\hat{3}\hat{1}$
Scene 4	fig. 6+7	All of *life to me*	ambiguous
Interlude	fig. A+8	*Lovely day*	$\hat{2}\hat{3}\hat{1}$
Scene 6	fig. 22+3–4	With the one I love *very near*	$\hat{2}\hat{3}\hat{1}$

Other variations on this second–third pattern are also utilized within the opera, but these three are the most frequently recurring. One further variant that does deserve mention is contained within the four-note vocal phrase that ends the opera. As Sam and Dinah leave to go to watch the movie that Dinah has already seen, the Radio Trio sings the words 'Island Magic'. The B–D–F♯–E phrase in the soprano part includes the retrograde of the cadence 1 motif, perhaps signalling some reversal in the fortunes of the couple. The lower parts also sing inversions of the phrase: the tenor a descending minor 3rd–ascending major 2nd; and the baritone sings a descending major 3rd–ascending major 2nd. This phrase also appears within the Scene 6 aria, with the same words. The dislocated repetition of this phrase at the work's end suggests a connection with preceding events and a reconciliation rather than the earlier song.

Single motif composition does not appear to have advanced, compared with the techniques used in *On The Town*, although in the opera there is the additional element of the emotional context, applicable as both words *and* music have been created by Bernstein.

Fugues and Canons, and Chromaticism

There are other interesting points regarding the techniques employed by Bernstein in the composition of his opera, the first of which concerns his use of fugal or canonic imitation. The initial, and most significant, moment when canonic imitation is used is during Scene 1, at the presentation of the Resolution theme. Although there is some very slight rhythmic variation, Dinah basically reiterates Sam's melodic line, an octave higher, and beginning one and a half bars later; in subsequent entries the gap between the melody and echo decreases until the final phrase is repeated after only a crotchet's space (Table 2.6).

Table 2.6   Canonic entries in Scene 1 of *Trouble in Tahiti*

Vocal entry		Delay in crotchets
'Try, Sam/Dinah, try to be kind'	fig. 7	6
'Help me to free you again'	fig. 7+4	2 ½
'Break down this/these wall/bars'	fig. 7+6	2
'Try, let us try'	fig. 7+9	1

As the entries get closer, and the couple end in harmony (a perfect fifth), it appears that they have made some progress towards a reconciliation, although it should be pointed out that they have not actually been singing *to* each other in this section; instead, we have been 'overhearing' their private thoughts. This echoing of melody occurs accompanied by only a pedal C♯, exposing the voices, and emphasizing the words at this point; the sparse accompaniment here gives the impression that it is the deepest emotions of the couple that are bared before us. This positive step is followed by an encouraging repetition of the Trio's refrain from the Prelude, singing once more of suburban bliss. As Dinah begins again, she makes an effort to be affectionate towards Sam, 'attempting warmth' (stage direction, Bernstein 1953, p. 23), but all the good work is undone ten bars later when Sam realizes that he cannot attend Junior's school play because he has to take part in the final of a handball tournament. Dinah perceives this as selfishness, and the advances that they had made are destroyed. When the Resolution theme reappears later in the same scene, for reasons that will be discussed later, it is heard only in the orchestra, and is not sung by the couple. For the moment, hopes of reconciliation are over.

When the music of this scene is reused in Scene 7, a more fugal treatment can be seen, as Dinah's first entry echoes Sam an 11th higher (but now beginning three bars later, rather than a bar and a half). Sam introduces a second melodic idea beneath Dinah's first entry, and on its repetition Dinah then echoes this music two crotchets later, the two entries overlapping in a brief stretto moment. The next entry brings the couple closer together, as they sing homophonically, a tenth apart, and finally, the section is ended in octave unison, by means of a further statement of the Resolution theme (see Example 2.6).

Further use of canonic techniques can be seen in Scene 4, as Sam and Dinah again consider the state of their relationship. Here the imitation is less strict, as Sam begins the repetition of Dinah's phrase at a distance of four bars, and a tenth lower. While the echo of the music occurs, Dinah has four bars of music that are not

Example 2.6   Scene 7, fig. 11

repeated by Sam, and the next phrase is repeated at two bars, but an octave lower. Sam's echo of the phrase is altered slightly, to bring about a synchronized ending of this section. Once again, the imitative writing underlines the fact that both Sam and Dinah are having similar thoughts, and the section ends with homophony, as they sing a tenth apart. This final homophonic section is then repeated as a coda in the last scene, and so the couple end in harmony, underlined by the *tierce de Picardie* (as Sam 'resolves' from C to C♯). Although it would be nice to think that this signifies a reconciliation, the couple still appear to be singing to themselves, rather than to each other, although their words are more positive, and there is a connection between the couple, as they 'look at each other for a brief instant' (Bernstein 1953, p. 116), before they leave to go to the cinema.

As with *On The Town*, where a number of the techniques used reflect those employed by Bernstein in other contemporary works, usually from a contrasting genre, this method of canonic composition can be observed in several of his pieces of the time: the ballet *Facsimile* (1946), the choral work *Hashkiveinu* (1945), and the third of his *Four Anniversaries for Piano*, 'For David Diamond' (1948). A further example of Bernstein's fugal writing can be seen very clearly in the middle movement of his *Prelude, Fugue and Riffs* (1949), with a fugue written for saxophones.

It is interesting that the first three of these examples have no other melodic accompaniment (the second has strings beneath), and perhaps more significant that, despite the contrasting genres of the pieces involved, all three are essentially two-voice textures, comparable with those in *Trouble in Tahiti*. This suggests an element of dialogue between the voices involved. The fact that Bernstein uses fugue and canon in *Trouble in Tahiti* appears to relate to the 'neo-classical' element of the opera, and a return to older, traditional technique, a return that he had begun in some of his other works.

A further aspect of *Trouble in Tahiti* that distances it from the sphere of the musical comedy is the opening clarinet figure, a three-bar phrase that encompasses all twelve tones of the octave (see Example 2.7). The first six notes outline two triads, ascending C major and descending G♭ major, which describe a shift through a tritone; perhaps this interval is a subtle indication of the tension and troubles to come in the opera, a foreshadowing of Bernstein's later use of the interval to underline a similarly tense atmosphere five years later in *West Side Story*.

Example 2.7   Prelude, bb. 1–3

(taking c as 1)   5   8   1   11   7   2   10   (11) 12 3   6 (8) 9   4 (3) (2) (8) (7)

This is not the first use of a highly chromatic tune by Bernstein, as demonstrated earlier in 'Presentation of Miss Turnstiles', where the theme contained 11 of the 12 notes within the octave, and a complete 12-note row can be found in 'The Dirge' in *Age of Anxiety*. In the symphony, as in the song from *On the Town*, the row is not treated serially – there are no retrogrades, inversions or retrograde inversions, and the row does not govern further aspects of the composition – but it is used as a basis for more traditional development. In *Trouble in Tahiti*, the clarinet row contains repeated notes, and it does not appear to have a thematic function but acts instead as a ritornello, appearing a total of seven times in this first movement. It provides a contrast to the smooth, conjunct movement and swinging, commercial sounds of the Trio that surround it in both the Prelude and Interlude. The chromaticism underlines the anxiety and conflict beneath the surface, dragging us back to reality from the Trio's dream of perfection.

Initially, the final four notes appear surplus to requirements, as all have arisen earlier in the row. However, after studying the second version of the row, which appears two bars later, their significance can be seen, as chromatic appoggiaturas on to D♭ and G♭ (see Example 2.8). In the second version of the row, the D♭ now appears as the last note in the row, in the bass part, preceded by an A♮ in the melody. Although it may seem that this note has been affixed merely to complete the row, it specifically acts as the dominant when the harmony moves to G♭ in the next bar, the beginning of the Trio's verse. This cadence figure is repeated in one more of the ritornello phrases (number 3), and in two other examples (numbers 4 and 6), where the final note of the phrase is the A, the D♭ can be seen in the bass part. In the remaining two reiterations of the ritornello, this pattern does not occur, as the key does not return to G♭, but instead these two examples end on an A♭ (a secondary dominant perhaps?). As can be seen in Example 2.8, there are two other characteristics that can be found in the ritornellos: the opening ascending arpeggio, which begins all the examples, and the section from the A to the A♭, which occurs in four of the phrases.

The manner in which Bernstein utilizes the row, with the repetition of notes at the end of each ritornello, emphasizes the fact that he is only employing those aspects of serial writing that he requires to create the sound that he desires at that point, frequently as a method of creating a dramatic atmosphere. Ultimately, he manipulates the chromaticism so that there is still a tonal drive behind it, underlined by the need for perfect cadences at the ends of his phrases.

Forms: Songs and Arias

Bernstein described *Trouble in Tahiti* as having its roots in the American musical theatre (Burton 1993, p. 7), and it would appear that some of the inspiration for the piece came from within the genre; but what discernable evidence to support this statement can be found within the opera? Stephen Wadsworth's later assertion that the opera is 'couched entirely in popular song form' (Wadsworth 1987) appears

Example 2.8 Ritornello phrases used in the Prelude

somewhat misguided. Bernstein was quite dismissive of the popular song in his own BA dissertation, as seen in the quotation in Chapter 1 (see p. 29), and, although the form may have advanced in the 13 years between his dissertation and *Trouble in Tahiti*, many aspects of Bernstein's description were still relevant. The standard form of AABA that Bernstein outlines can be found in his Prelude, but not in a purely Tin Pan Alley form. The opening movement of *Trouble in Tahiti*, sung by the Trio extolling the virtues of suburban life, has a double AABA structure, but its first A section is 13 bars long (following a seven-bar 12-tone introduction), and includes changes between ¢ and ¾ and a move from G♭ to a final cadence to G♮. In the second presentation of the form, the AA is a 'scat' style section sung by the girl of the Trio, with a clarinet obbligato similar to the chromatic introduction.

This is hardly Tin Pan Alley writing, despite the dance-band origins of the Trio and their vocal texture; Bernstein manipulates the popular materials at his disposal into something more intellectual. Elements of the vernacular still remain, and the B section could be considered a release due to its contrasting rhythmic and melodic ideas. This section also contains a familiar rising phrase in the bass part, an insertion which stretches the B section from an expected eight bars to a slightly more unusual nine bars (see Example 2.9).

Example 2.9   Prelude, three bars before fig. C, voices only

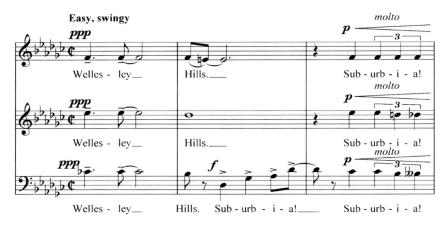

This fanfare is, of course, a quotation from *On the Town*, a reference to the chaotic metropolis, the 'hubbub' mentioned in the lyric: 'The audible reference to the *not*-suburban underscores the ironic quality of the Trio's anthem: all of the Trio's claims for the wonderfulness of suburban life are flatly contradicted by Sam and Dinah's misery' (Keathley 2005, p. 225).

The first scene in *Trouble in Tahiti* conforms to sonata form, reflected in the dramaturgy during the scene. Following a short introduction of five bars, the first subject is presented, beginning with the Conflict motif and accompanying an argument between the protagonists. This section ends with the words 'the subject is closed', an intellectual pun on Bernstein's part. There are two further repetitions of this music (A), each underlining a fresh disagreement between the couple, separated by an additional musical idea (B) as they reflect that this is the usual way for their day to start. This creates an AABA structure within the first subject area, but the harmonic patterns dismiss a popular song origin, and instead suggest that the form is derived from the narrative. The second subject area begins at fig. 5, as Dinah sings of her frustration at the situation that they are in, and the following idea in this section is the Resolution canon discussed earlier in this chapter. As the couple appears to make progress towards peace, the Trio enters and sings a phrase taken from the Prelude, this interruption taking the place of the development within the structure; it appears that rather than a musical development we are now

Example 2.11   Scene 3, fig. 3

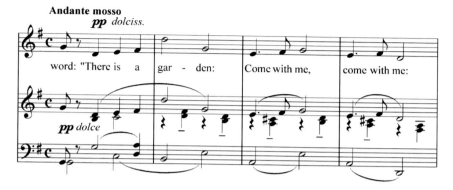

G major key signature, and a piano-based Opop[10] accompaniment that is
reminiscent of the accompaniment to 'Lonely Town' in Bernstein's earlier work
(see Example 2.11).

The first eight-bar phrase, which is quite simple and contains internal repetition
and development, is repeated with the same harmony, but with slightly altered
rhythms and a climatic melodic variation that are derived from popular song.
All of this is a considerable contrast to the surrounding music in this aria, which
contains changing time signatures, a more complex melodic line, unusual phrase
structures, and an accompaniment more clearly derived from a symphonic angle
(see Example 2.2b). As Keathley points out, the opening four notes are clearly
related to the 'Surburbia' motif, as they outline $\hat{5}\hat{1}\hat{2}\hat{5}$ (2005, p. 239). The structure
of the aria, including the ritornello, can be outlined as R–A–B–A¹–B¹.

The reason for the large contrast in the B section, which could be labelled the
'chorus', is dramaturgical: Dinah is describing her dream to the psychiatrist, and
the B section corresponds to the words that she hears in the garden in her dream,
beckoning her to a 'quiet place', a sanctuary.[11] The relative simplicity of the music
reflects the simplicity of her needs, and the calmness, happiness and almost childlike joy that the words bring to her. But the moment is brief, and as she goes on to
talk of the rest of her dream she once more becomes disillusioned. Dinah begins a
repetition of the B section at the end of the aria, but it is interrupted by a return to
Sam, and his music, in the office, as he confronts his supposed mistress. Dinah's
music becomes subservient to her husband's, as her personality is overpowered by
Sam's dominant nature. In Scene 3a, she continues the description of her dream,
and her music returns in an A²B form, some of the melody being taken by the

---

[10]   This is short hand for Oom-pah-oom-pah, or bass note – off-beat chord – bass note
– off-beat chord.

[11]   Keathley defines the difference between the A and B sections as the contrast
between 'Restless in Surburbia' and 'Resolution in the Garden' (2005, pp. 240–41).

orchestra as she leaves the psychiatrist and sings the 'chorus' as she walks home down the street, unaware that she is about to meet Sam.

Scene 4 is the central duet, and consists of three sections, the first two of which utilize the same accompaniment, featuring the melody of the B section of Dinah's Scene 2 'Garden' aria transformed into a waltz-like *gymnopédie*. The distinction between these two sections can be identified by the nature of their material. In the first section, Sam and Dinah are talking to each other having met by chance in the street at lunchtime, and then begin to walk off their separate ways. In the second section, they have stopped, and as they remain facing away from each other we hear their thoughts, the similarities between their contemplations being underlined by the imitative style of the phrases. This second section ends with the same plea as it began, the inner turmoil of the characters underlined by the A–G♯ discord in the voices. The third section of the song continues to disclose their individual thoughts, and the imitative writing now alternates between the earlier discussed fugato and canon, as they unconsciously echo the same sentiments. These reflections converge until they are singing together, and the orchestra then expands this idea to finish the duet with further material from Dinah's 'Garden' aria.

The Interlude that follows this duet is based on the same material as the Prelude, but is presented in a slightly shortened form. The clarinet introduction is shortened to three bars, but an additional three bars are added to this opening, music which first appeared at the close of the Prelude. There are two repetitions of A, followed by B, then a further reiteration of A, with the same ending as seen in the Prelude, but without the final clarinet figure and the closing vocal phrase (which has already been heard). Underneath the final two bars, the driving triplet rhythm begins which leads into Sam's aria in the next scene. As in the Prelude, the popular song form AABA can be seen, and the picture of suburban bliss is maintained, somewhat ironically after the lunchtime encounter we have just observed; the only things that seem to have changed are the names of the suburbs themselves.

Scene 5 contains Sam's second aria, as he exercises in the gym having won the handball final; once again in this half of the opera his song precedes Dinah's. As in his first aria, the music is in compound time, with a sense of drive in the rhythm that underlines Sam's competitiveness and determination to succeed. This song is strophic with three verses, but the third is 'interrupted' by a contrasting section halfway through. In each strophe, there is much repetition, both of words and musical phrases, emphasizing the prevailing energy of the beat, and a fanfare figure (a victory fanfare?), which recurs under the music both in this scene and in Scene 7. Through the verse a sense of tension builds, with a series of rising sequences, to a climatic E on the last word of the phrase. Between the sections there is a short bridge based on the introduction. The music of the first two verses is identical, which highlights the fact that the topic is the same for both: despite their best efforts some men will always be losers. The melody of the first half of the third verse is whistled by Sam as he admires himself in the mirror, and then we have the interruption, as Sam now expounds the virtues of 'the winner'. At the end of this section the rhythm shifts into a cross-rhythm for what can be seen as trumpet calls announcing the advent of the good old US navy to the rescue. (1953, p. 96)

Bernstein fuses popular song with his neo-classical tendency prevalent in the opera, by using the rondo structure. He had previously created a much simpler rondo in his *Rondo for Lifey* (1948), and it was a form regaining favour with composers who felt the influence of the classic traditions, including Stravinsky and Bernstein's teacher, Piston. Unusually, although it is used vocally in *Trouble in Tahiti*, Bernstein uses the form of an instrumental rondo, rather than the shorter rondò, an aria form used in the eighteenth century that usually consisted of only two sections, in an ABA form.

Scene 7, the Finale, is divided into two separate parts by a section of dialogue, but these are connected by the Trio's musical material, which occurs in both.[13] The first half is strophic, with four repetitions of the same material (the Trio accompanies Sam and Dinah as they repeat their music from Scene 1 in an attempt to begin conversation); the second, following the spoken section, begins with the same Trio music, but then moves on to the previously discussed fugato sections. During a second extended Trio section, Sam and Dinah sing imitative lines over the chorale accompaniment, creating an overall A–B–A¹–B–C structure, again a compound binary form, with a climatic coda.

It would appear that, rather than being based upon popular song, the majority of the arias, duets and ensembles that make up the opera hark back to earlier operatic models. This 'neo-classical' manner perhaps reflects the influence of Stravinsky and his *Oedipus Rex*, a work that Bernstein had conducted during his time with the New York City Symphony Orchestra (1945–47). The Prelude is perhaps the exception to this, although its function in the final scene as the chorale on which the duets are based aligns it with earlier influences.

So what inspired Bernstein, either consciously or subconsciously, in his manipulation of popular song forms, and in the juxtaposition of vernacular sounds with traditional structures? In his opera *Porgy and Bess*, Gershwin was accused of including hit songs, a charge he refuted by comparing his work with that of earlier composers: 'Nearly all of Verdi's operas contain what are known as "song hits". *Carmen* is almost a collection of song hits' (quoted in Block 1997, p. 66). However, a closer consideration of some of the numbers from *Porgy and Bess* reveals deviations from the popular song forms. 'Bess, You Is My Woman' begins predictably enough, with Porgy's opening eight-bar phrase, which is then developed and extended into an answering 12-bar phrase (A–A¹). However, when Bess takes up this music, and the key changes from B♭ to D major, there are changes, and the repetition of A¹ is interrupted by contrasting music ('I ain' goin''). This includes a shift from D major to D♯ minor, before a further fragment of the A melody, now beginning in F♯ major. The release of this song follows ('Mornin' time'),

13   This structure relates to the published finale. The differences between this and the original version, seen in the premiere, will be discussed later.

and it begin in this same key of F♯, but through modulation takes the music back to D major, for a repeat of Bess's music, but now with a contrapuntal vocal line. Following this repetition, there is a coda, completing the structure of A–A^1–A–A^2–B–A–A^2–B–coda. This form does not really resemble the AABA form of the popular song. Even in a song demonstrating such a structure, it is altered slightly, as in 'I Got Plenty o' Nuttin'', which has different-length phrases: A (9 bars)–A (11)–B (10)–A (16).

While it is not clear whether Bernstein was familiar with *Porgy and Bess* before writing *Trouble in Tahiti*,[14] he did know Blitzstein's *The Cradle Will Rock*, as previously mentioned. This show also demonstrates manipulation of forms, in one case for a specific reason. The song 'Croon–Spoon' is a parody of crooner's songs of the 1930s, and one aspect of this caricature is shown in the structure, with shortened phrase lengths: A (7 bars)–A (7)–B (6+6+2)–A (7+4). There are also deviations in the melody and the harmony, in order to satirize the 'idle rich' siblings that are performing the song. In his opera *Regina*, Blitzstein again used altered phrase lengths, this time in the number 'What Will it Be For Me?' This song is almost strophic, although with a contrasting section, but it is within the verses that the phrases are extended: A (5 bars)–A^1 (5)–B (4)–A (5)–A^1 (5)–B^1 (4)–C (6)–A (5)–A^1 (5)–B^2 (4)–D (10).

Apparently, despite Bernstein's comments regarding the origins of the opera's music, it is his classical training, and other works he knew, that influenced the forms and structures he has used. This has resulted in a 'highbrow' approach rather than the 'lowbrow' Broadway founded approach that Wadsworth suggests. Bernstein had set himself criteria for *Trouble in Tahiti*: 'It was meeting a challenge which I had set myself, to see if the American vernacular – both musical and linguistic – could be handled in something you could call an opera' (quoted in Burton 1993, p. 7).

Regardless of these aims, it could be said that Bernstein's intellectual temperament pushed this composition from the vernacular to high art; from Tin Pan Alley to opera. As would also be the case later with *Candide*, Bernstein's sense of music and drama produced sophisticated writing, contrary to his original desires and plans. Unfortunately, with *Candide*, it proved to be to the detriment of the public reception of the piece.

Forms: the Finale

Following the Brandeis première, Bernstein rewrote the closing of the final scene, before it was performed at Tanglewood in August of 1952. In both versions of this last scene, music from Scene 1 reappears, creating a connection between the

---

[14]   He certainly knew it before writing *Candide* two years later, as *Porgy and Bess* was included on the list of research materials for the seminars he gave at Brandeis University in 1954 (box 72, folder 31, LBC).

two scenes, and forming the basis for the Trio's chorale-like accompaniment. The relationship between the music from the first and last scenes can clearly be observed when Sam and Dinah's duet, also taken from the first scene, combines with the homophonic textures of the Trio. Dramatically, the reappearance of the music suggests a similar situation to that observed in the first scene: the couple is back at home, alone, and as soon as they start talking, they disagree – has anything really changed since the morning?

The first half of this final scene – the previously mentioned strophic section – contains two further references to earlier scenes, both in the orchestral accompaniment. A 'fanfare' motif from Sam's Scene 5 aria precedes his vocal entry, perhaps reflecting his previous determination and victorious emotions, as he hopes he can now begin reconciliation with Dinah; before Dinah begins the next duet section (at fig. 5), the 'Suburbia' motif from the Prelude and Interlude is heard. This underlines the ironic picture of domestic bliss that the Trio is singing about beneath the couple's developing argument. In the original version at this point, a visit to the cinema is suggested by Dinah, probably prompted by her trip earlier that day. The music from the argument scene is reused, but without the chorale backing, and with some rhythmic alteration. They actually appear quite cheerful at this point, as they discuss the film: '"A wonderful show!" / Look what it says / "Opened today / Trouble in Tahiti! / Glorious music"' (on manuscript, LBC). As Sam and Dinah leave the house together, the Trio again repeat their Prelude music, but this time in the rhythm from its first appearance, and they take on the characters of Miss Brown, Bill and the Analyst as they sing about going to watch the film as well: 'Hurry on down! / Hurry on down! / Got to get off / Off to the movies' (on manuscript, LBC). The orchestra ends the opera with an optimistic-sounding eight-bar coda (see Example 2.13).

Example 2.13 Scene 7, original ending from manuscript

The revised version of the Finale has a more restrained conclusion, beginning with the decision to go to the cinema. This is now spoken, meaning that the dramatic culmination of the piece is not sung – possibly influenced by a similar spoken section in Britten's *Peter Grimes*, at the tragic climax where Grimes is told by his friends that the only course of action left to him is to go and drown himself. There is a sense that now Sam and Dinah have stopped singing, they are finally confronting truths about their relationship:

> Sam: (*rises and tries again*) Look, Dinah ... maybe we ought to go out somewhere tonight. A movie, or...
>
> Dinah: (*still without changing*) We went out last night.
>
> Sam: But there's a different one tonight. Just opened (*consulting newspaper*). That new musical ... something about Tahiti...
>
> (*Dinah winces.*)
>
> Sam: (*coming to her almost tenderly*) How about it?
>
> Dinah: (*still toneless*) Sure. Why not. Anything. (*Rises with effort.*) I'll get my hat.
> (Bernstein 1953, p. 108)

This spoken section is followed by Sam and Dinah once more singing to themselves in the canonic Resolution duet, without the Trio. As they reach the first musical climax (fig. 12), the Trio's chorale which featured in the first half of the Finale rejoins the texture, and is accompanied briefly by a fragment of Dinah's 'Garden' refrain, as the couple begin to make their peace, and perhaps make the first steps towards their 'quiet place'. In this version of the ending, there is the feeling that they are putting off any serious consideration of the problems by going to watch an escapist film, and settling for the commercial fabrication of happiness. The Trio finishes with the motif mentioned previously, a reminder of the music from the film that the couple is going to see, and the 'island magic' they are settling for, in place of a real solution.

The second version of the Finale, with its less positive outlook, appears to be the more realistic, a more natural outcome to the day's events than the forced cheeriness of the original ending; the change in mood in the Brandeis production goes against the nature of the characters as demonstrated so far. The more tentative hopefulness of the revised conclusion, with a sense of resignation from Sam and Dinah, follows much more convincingly from the incidents seen through the course of the opera. They are essentially flawed characters, all too human in their actions and emotions: 'The simple truth about Sam and Dinah is that they are really only half-articulate. Their frustrations, observations, aspirations are told eloquently only in their music' (Burkat 1953, p. 98).

Trouble in Tahiti was quite different from *On the Town*, with sharp contrasts in subject, genre and construction; however, many compositional elements are common to both. Bernstein utilized contemporary sounds within the framework of traditional structures: the sound of the Radio Trio, the 'Island Magic' number and the main section of Dinah's 'Garden aria' are Broadway influenced but shaped in conventional aria and song forms. The relationship between Sam and Dinah is partly characterized by the use of fugues and canons, as their thoughts and wishes are similar, but rarely converge. The use of motifs has continued, now with the added emotional associations afforded by the fact that Bernstein also created his own text. A significant point, and one that helped shape the work, was Bernstein's desire to create an American opera, to contribute to a genre that he considered important, and perhaps the first sign that he felt his serious works may be overshadowed by his popular compositions. Despite these apparent concerns, his next theatre work would see a return both to musical comedy, and to the successful songwriting collaboration that had created *On the Town*: the lyricists Betty Comden and Adolph Green.

Chapter 3
Wonderful Town

'On your left, Washington Square'

The 1930s were vibrant and exhilarating years for the music scene in New York City. A wealth of musical diversity flourished, embracing the wide variety of ethnicities and social differences among the city's residents. Toscanini led the New York Philharmonic as principal conductor for successful seasons between 1929 and 1936, and the late 1930s saw Helen Traubel and Kirsten Flagstad singing Wagner at the Metropolitan Opera. The majority of both the popular songwriting and music publishing industries were established in New York, the former based around the by-now non-specific location of Tin Pan Alley. Radio City Music Hall opened in December 1932, and 1935 saw *Porgy and Bess* at the Alvin Theatre. Broadway witnessed many hit shows during the 1930s, including Jerome Kern's *The Cat and the Fiddle* (1931) and *Music in the Air* (1932), Cole Porter's *Gay Divorce* (1932) and *Anything Goes* (1934), Irving Berlin's *As Thousands Cheer* (1933), and Richard Rodgers and Lorenz Hart's *Jumbo* (1935), *On Your Toes* (1936), and *Babes in Arms* (1937). However, the music that appeared all pervasive during that decade, and which seemed to both inspire and define the people and ethos of the era, was jazz. Although its origins lay in New Orleans and in African music, the genre had gradually relocated from the south. Louis Armstrong and Jelly Roll Morton made their moves from Chicago to New York in 1928 and 1929 respectively (Schuller 1968, p. 246), joining other well-known jazz musicians and bandleaders such as Fletcher Henderson, Cab Calloway and Duke Ellington in what was now the jazz capital of the US. The city became a focus for the performance, recording and broadcasting of jazz, with the spotlight on Harlem.

Despite its origins and influences, the music being created in the Savoy Ballroom and the Apollo Theatre by the black musicians was not, for the most part, the music that was being heard by the rest of America. Segregation kept blacks and whites apart during the 1920s and early 1930s, and in an industry controlled by the white-dominated publishing and recording companies it was the white bandleaders and musicians who took the sounds they heard in Harlem and delivered them to an audience that may not otherwise have experienced jazz. As had so often been the case before this, and has also occurred since, 'the innovators were black; the imitators were white' (Nanry 1992, p. 188). But the music did not remain unchanged by the shift downtown; jazz was 'cleaned up' in its arrangements for the big bands, so it was 'familiar enough to be understood, yet novel enough to be new and exciting' (Nanry 1992, p. 188). In an effort to maintain original sound elements, some big bands employed black arrangers, such as Fletcher

Henderson who worked for Benny Goodman's band, until the time when black musicians could perform in the groups, or be recognized within their own bands.[1] This was perhaps an unusual working practice, but it was successful: 'spicing up familiar commercial, popular material with Harlem-oriented musical seasoning and selling it via a white band for a white musical/commercial audience' (Schuller 1989, p. 9). Discrimination eventually began to break down as the radio and record industries flourished, as although live performances could present racial barriers, these developing media were inherently colour-blind. Jazz, and the characteristic rhythmic traits that became known as 'swing', infiltrated society to such a degree that the years around 1932 became nicknamed the 'Swing Era', 'that remarkable period in American history when jazz was synonymous with American popular music, its social dances and its musical entertainment' (Schuller 1989, p. 4).

It is hardly surprising then, when offered a play set in the 1930s, Bernstein, Comden and Green found their imaginations stimulated, and they embarked on the task of creating songs and musical numbers for *Wonderful Town*. Originally Leroy Anderson and Arnold Horwitt had been engaged to produce the lyrics and music (Peyser 1987, p. 191), but their contributions had been considered unsuitable, and the creative team behind *On the Town* was approached to replace them. The show was based on the play *My Sister Eileen* by Jerome Chodorov and Joseph Fields, which in turn drew on the popular stories of Ruth McKenney. These articles had originally been published in *The New Yorker*, and were subsequently drawn together in a book in 1938. Two of McKenney's tales chronicling her exploits in the big city formed the basis for Chodorov and Fields's play: 'Mr Spitzer and the Fungus: the housing situation in Greenwich Village and how dismal it is', and 'Beware the Brazilian Navy: almost the worst thing that ever happened to us'. In transforming the stories into a drama, more characters were added and a plot developed to tie the two stories together, although Ruth was still central to the action, together with her sister Eileen. When the play opened on Broadway, on 26 December 1940, the infectious humour and mad-cap events impressed the critics, as demonstrated in Brooks Atkinson's review for the *New York Times*:

> The authors of 'My Sister Eileen' have served up the adventures in the form of crack-brained comedy without much rhyme or reason ... What is commonplace becomes incredible. The whole thing gradually develops into a nightmare of fabulous proportions. Thanks to Sister Ruth's acid-tongue and the neatly turned dialogue that has been written for her, 'My Sister Eileen' becomes a nimble-witted commentary on the humdrum foibles of Greenwich Village. (1940, p. 23)

It appears that the mood on Broadway at the time was more sombre, and that *My Sister Eileen* brought a little cheerfulness and happiness. As Atkinson pointed out in a later article on the show: 'The gloom that has been hanging over the dramatic stage longer than the oldest inhabitant can recall has finally been lifted ... Of the

---

[1]   Goodman himself integrated his own band in the late 1930s (Nanry 1992, p. 189).

lighthearted plays of the season, none has succeeded so completely as "My Sister Eileen"' (1941, p. X1). In light of the play's success, it is no surprise that it was later turned into a radio-show and film (Burton 1994, p. 224), and was considered a prime source for musical comedy. It was Chodorov and Fields who turned their successful script into a libretto for the upcoming Broadway version. One of the first changes to be made to the theatrical version was the expansion of locations: in the 1940 stage adaptation, all the action takes place in the studio apartment that is foisted upon Ruth and Eileen, the sisters from Columbus, Ohio; their landlord is now Mr Appopolous rather than Mr Spitzer. For the musical, other locations were added, and scenes that occurred off-stage before now took place in front of the audience: the girls' search for employment, the visit to the editor's office, the attempted interview of the Brazilian Navy cadets, the police station, and the final scene at the new setting of the Village Vortex.

The story begins as the girls arrive in New York, and seek employment in the big city, Ruth as a writer and Eileen as an actress (although the pretty younger sister attracts more propositions than job offers). After several rejections, Ruth's big break comes when she is sent to the Brooklyn Navy Yard[2] to interview the cadets, but they are more interested in dancing than in talking. The ensuing chaos results in Eileen being arrested but she charms the police into releasing her. Finally, just as the sisters consider returning to their old lives in Ohio, both of them find jobs, Ruth falls in love, and there is a suitable happy ending. As Chodorov and Fields were adapting their own material, there was a free looting of their own work, and a significant amount of the dialogue in the libretto of the musical is derived from the play, although some events were moved around within the narrative to provide a better flow of action, as can be seen in Table 3.1. Minor changes included the curious alteration of Mr Clark's first name from Chic to Chick, and a relocation of Wreck's education from Georgia Tech to Trenton Tech; a passing vendor sells Eskimo Pies rather than strawberries (but still refuses to take refundable milk bottles in exchange for giving the girls some food).

In the non-musical stage version, a strong comic element stems from the constant flow of people in and out of the girls' tiny studio apartment, and the situations that emerge from the collision of the two worlds, that of the provincial lives of the two sisters and the frenetic pace of the New York neighbourhood. This conflict of cultures played an important part in the original stories and reflected McKenney's outlook on the city; as Atkinson pointed out: 'Her attitude is one of wide-eyed innocence, as though the sisters were sane, intelligent and resourceful, but Greenwich Village completely mad' (1941, p. X1). This sense of madness is retained in the musical adaptation.

A film version made in 1942 starred Rosalind Russell, and the producers of the musical, Robert Fryer and George Abbott, had a contract for Miss Russell to star in their show. Unfortunately, due to Anderson and Horwitt's unsatisfactory contribution, the contract had only four and a half weeks left before it expired

---

[2] Also the location of the opening scene in *On the Town.*

Table 3.1   Structure of *Wonderful Town*

	Setting	Main events	Musical number	Location in *My Sister Eileen*
Act 1				
Scene 1	Christopher Street	Tour guide introduces setting and inhabitants. Ruth and Eileen meet Appopolous.	'Christopher Street'	
Scene 2	The Studio Apartment	Appopolous rents apartment to sisters. Visit by Fletcher. Invaded by drunks. Girls lament their situation.	'Ohio'	Act I Scene 1 I.2 I.1
Scene 2a	New York City	Dance pantomime of girls' attempts to get work in the city.	'Conquering New York'†	
Scene 3	The Street Outside the Apartment	Wreck moves in. Eileen discusses Frank.	'One Hundred Easy Ways'	I.2 I.2
Scene 4	Bob Baker's Office	Ruth takes her story to Baker.	'What a Waste' 'Ruth's Stories'	
Scene 5	The Street Outside the Apartment	Frank visits Eileen. Baker visits the apartment.	'A Little Bit in Love'	Act II (4)*
Scene 6	The Backyard of the Apartment	Mrs Wade spots Wreck. Violet visits. Chick arrives/Frank returns. Dinner party. Baker offends Ruth, and longs for love. Ruth receives phone call about Navy article.	'Pass the Football' 'Conversation Piece' 'A Quiet Girl'	II (1) II (2) I.2/II (5) II (3)
Scene 7	The Brooklyn Navy Yard	Ruth goes to visit Brazilian Navy cadets.	'Conga'	

Scene	Location	Description	Song	No.
Scene 8	The Backyard of the Apartment	Cadets follow Ruth back to apartment, still dancing.	'Conga Reprise'	II (6)
Act 2				
Scene 1	The Christopher Street Station House	Eileen has been arrested, but charms the policemen.	'My Darlin' Eileen'	
Scene 2	The Street Outside the Apartment	Baker visits Ruth. She has job advertising the Village Vortex.	'Swing'	
Scene 3	The Studio Apartment	Appopolous tries to evict the sisters. Chick's lies are revealed. Ruth realizes she likes Baker	'Ohio Reprise'	Act III III
Scene 4	The Street outside the Village Vortex	Baker realizes he likes Ruth.	'It's Love'	
Scene 5	The Village Vortex	Girls perform in Vortex. Ruth and Baker end up together.	'Ballet at the Village Vortex' 'The Wrong Note Rag' reprise 'It's Love'	III

* Numbers in brackets indicate order of events in Chodorov and Fields's play in Act II.

† For some reason, this dance appears to have been renamed at some point. In the vocal score for hire from Boosey & Hawkes, it is titled 'Conquering the City', and it is also called this by Gottlieb in both his 1964 dissertation, and the 1988 catalogue of Bernstein's works. It is called 'Conquering New York' in the new published vocal score, the Comden and Green published libretto, and also in the programmes for the tryouts at New Haven and the Broadway version at the Winter Garden. In this book, I will maintain continuity by always using the latter title for this number. Similarly, 'Ruth's Stories' is called 'Story Vignettes' in Comden and Green 1994, and in both the New Haven and Winter Garden programmes.

(Adolph Green, quoted in *Prelude, Fugue and Riffs*, Fall 1994). This placed the new team of Bernstein, Comden and Green under considerable pressure to create new material in time, but the idea of another show set in their beloved New York must have attracted the creative team's attention. Especially close to the team's heart was the location: Comden and Green had performed in the Greenwich Village club, the Village Vanguard (which was surely the model for the Village Vortex in the show), as part of their satirical group The Revuers. Green and Bernstein had shared an apartment on East Ninth Street for some time in 1939 (Burton 1994, p. 57), only a few blocks from Christopher Street and the Vanguard (on Seventh Avenue between 11th and Perry Streets). Once they had decided to take on the job, the trio locked themselves away to create the music and lyrics within the limited time available. It was probably at some point in this creative flurry that the title of the show evolved into *Wonderful Town*: this was a line from the movie version of *On the Town*, where the opening number's 'helluva town' was transmuted into 'wonderful town' for the silver screen (Peyser 1987, p. 190).

Despite all adversities, a score was produced in time for the New Haven tryouts, which opened on 19 January 1953. During these tryouts several changes were made, but perhaps the most significant addition was the song 'One Hundred Easy Ways to Lose a Man'. This number was written specifically for Rosalind Russell, at her request, as a song that would express her character, and be funny (Betty Comden, on Burton 1996); Comden and Green recall that Russell described the structure of the song as 'da-da-da-da-*joke*, da-da-da-da-*joke*' (Green, quoted in *PF&R*, Fall 1994).[3] The song itself was written whilst Miss Russell was unable to sing during the tryouts, due to a bronchial problem: 'we were in the hallway with the piano, and she was in her bed in the bedroom, and we sang it to her from the hall' (Comden, on Burton 1996). 'One Hundred Easy Ways' was firmly in place before the show transferred to New York, opening at the Winter Garden on 26 February (Gottlieb 1988, p. 8). The initial run lasted 559 performances (although Miss Russell was later replaced by Carol Channing), and there seems to have been a definite degree of appreciation for Bernstein's music: 'Wonderful Town – wonderful score – wonderful book, etc. etc. etc … There hasn't been anybody around like [Bernstein] since George Gershwin for jauntiness, tricky and intriguing modulations and graceful swoops with simple and pleasant melody' (Chapman in the *New York Daily News* 1953, quoted in Burton 1994, p. 226).

One obvious contrast with *On the Town* is the amount of narrative ballet in *Wonderful Town*: only 'Conquering New York' advances the story through dance, and this is by way of pantomime rather than classical dance. There are opportunities for dancing in 'Conga', 'Pass the Football', 'My Darlin' Eileen', 'Swing', 'Ballet at the Vortex', and 'Wrong Note Rag', but this is all spectacle dancing rather than narrative. This reversion to a less integrated approach could have been a result of the time limitations, or the desire to write a traditional musical comedy, or due to

---

3   This song replaced the more staid 'The Story of My Life', the title of which is a line from the Fields and Chodorov play that was also included in the libretto of the musical.

the fact that Jerome Robbins was not directly involved in the production.[4] In the absence of any symphonic dance music, Bernstein instead channelled his creative talents into producing pastiche items that represented and reflected the sounds of the 1930s in his 'wonderful town' of New York.

Pastiche: New York

Wonderful Town is a musical theatre piece written in the 1950s, but set squarely in the 1930s, and in this it contrasts with Bernstein's earlier shows as both *On the Town* and *Trouble in Tahiti* reflect the music of the time when they were written. To turn to a period-specific piece was a change for Bernstein, but provided a challenge that he rose to and revelled in, as Betty Comden explained: 'Lenny ran to the piano and played the famous Duchin vamp. The thirties gave us the musical style and that Duchin vamp opened the show' (quoted in Burton 1994, p. 224).

Although it had been suggested by Chodorov and Fields that the action should be updated to the 1950s, Comden and Green felt that the original 1930s setting was more exciting, and so it remained in the earlier decade (Burton 1994, p. 224). The year became even more specific, as in the opening song 'Christopher Street' a character, the Guide, sets the scene for the ensuing action: 'Ever since 1870, Greenwich Village has been the Bohemian cradle of painters, writers, actors, etc., who've gone on to fame and fortune. Today in 1935, who knows what future greats live in these twisting alleys? Come along' (Comden and Green 1997, p. 92).[5]

Despite the fact that writing to a specific time was a new venture for Bernstein, the actual subject period was obviously not unknown to him, as in 1935 he was beginning his freshman year at Harvard.

The method of defining a period through musical means is commonly achieved by employing pastiche. It is through identification of elements associated with the time that the atmosphere and manner of the setting can be established and maintained. The first pastiche technique found in *Wonderful Town* involves a degree of imitation, using recognizable elements of someone's songwriting style. Musically, the first song of the show opens with a very specific time-marker, and one associated with the city of New York: the Eddie Duchin vamp (see Example 3.1).

Duchin was a successful society bandleader in the 1930s, becoming well-known through his band's radio broadcasts from New York's Central Park Casino. His extravagant and showy piano playing is epitomized in his trademark vamp, distinctive in its chord progression and cross rhythms, which Duchin used as an

---

[4] He was brought in to fix some of the dances during the tryout stage, but his contribution remained uncredited (Burton 1994, p. 225).

[5] Although the references for quotations from the libretto cite Comden and Green, this is because the libretto is contained in a collection of their works. It should be remembered that the libretto for *Wonderful Town* was written by Joseph Fields and Jerome Chodorov, and the lyrics by Betty Comden and Adolph Green.

Example 3.1 'Christopher Street', bb. 1–4

introduction to some of his pieces and 'improvisations'. The libretto of *Wonderful Town* indicates the tone intended to be evoked by the phrase, describing it as 'a musical vamp in a style highly characteristic of the 1930s' (Comden and Green 1997, p. 92), while the music in the score has the additional style marking 'Molto "Duchino"'.[6] It is interesting that this vamp, which appears so representative of the era, also occurs briefly in the song 'One Wonderful Day' from Stephen Sondheim's early musical *Saturday Night* (1954). This is set in New York in 1929, a year when Duchin was active in the city in the Leo Reismann Orchestra. Although Sondheim did see *Wonderful Town* on Broadway before working on his musical, the reappearance of the phrase is purely coincidental,[7] and perhaps indicates the degree to which Duchin's sound is interwoven into the tone and music of the period. In the song that is introduced by this piano phrase, 'Christopher Street', the vamp goes on to provide the harmonic basis for the main verse section of the song, and the $\frac{6}{8}$ time signature also remains for a large part of the number.

The other song that borrows from a specific composer, rather than from a genre, is 'Wrong Note Rag'; within the framework of pastiche songs this is a 'second level' pastiche, as the characters in the 1930s recall a style from an even earlier era. This diegetic number, performed by Ruth and Eileen in the Village Vortex towards the end of the show, is described as a 'number they have known since their early childhood. They work in a deadpan sister-act style circa 1913' (Comden and Green 1997, p. 183). Despite being described as a rag, the main section of this song is more in the style of novelty piano music, a genre that was popular in the 1920s. As ragtime itself began to decline, composers and publishers sought ways to maintain the public's interest. A new style emerged, the novelty, which poked 'gentle fun at both piano ragtime and the player piano – two institutions without which the piano novelty could not have come to pass' (Riddle 1985, p. 285). The main proponent of novelty piano was Zez Confrey, who had appeared in Paul Whiteman's Aeolian

---

6   Mordden says that this is 'an apotheosis of the *secondo* vamp of the once-ubiquitous four-hand piano version of "Heart and Soul"' (1998, p. 97). While the chord progression does match that of the Hoagy Carmichael hit (which Duchin did record), the rhythmic pattern is pure Duchin, and it reappears at the beginning of many of his numbers, including 'Can't We Talk It Over', 'What Is This Thing Called Love', and 'Shine on Harvest Moon'.

7   Letter from Sondheim to the present author, 9 November 1998.

Hall concert where Gershwin's *Rhapsody in Blue* had been premièred (Schiff 1997, p. 58). Confrey's *Modern Course in Novelty Piano Playing* was the instruction manual for the style, which in part inspired Gershwin's *Rhapsody* (Riddle 1985, p. 286). Various ragtime rhythmic elements were absorbed into the new music: duple metre, stride bass patterns and secondary rag phrasing (Riddle 1985, p. 287), but the harmonic language demonstrated a development from that of its predecessor, and included unexpected key shifts and sudden 'tricks', reflected in the titles of the pieces, such as 'Dizzy Fingers', 'Stumbling', and 'Giddy Ditty'. Bernstein was certainly aware of novelty piano music, having heard 'Dancing Tambourine' by W.C. Polla when he was aged about ten or eleven, and he recognized Confrey as the 'greatest composer of [novelty songs]'[8] (*My Musical Childhood*, BBC 1986). 'Wrong Note Rag' reflects many characteristics of novelty piano music: the melody of the A section is very pianistic with its leaps and chromatic inflections; rhythmically, secondary rag patterns are used in the second half of each phrase, where groups of three beats within the ¢ time signature are underlined by the rising crotchet figures in the bass line (see Example 3.2). This section can be compared to part of Confrey's *Kitten on the Keys*, which also employs dotted quavers within secondary rag rhythms, and similar leaps in the melody. Bernstein's harmonic trick comes in the B section of the song, as the key jumps from B♭ to E major, the only preparation for this being the B♮, which initially sounds like a misplaced sharpened seventh (see last note of Example 3.2). It is also in this phrase that we hear the wrong note of the title: in the second and third bars the dominant pedal in the vocal line clashes with an A♯ in the counter-melody (the original tonic trying to reassert itself?). In this B section in 'Wrong Note Rag', we see the familiar ♪ ♩ ♪ ♪ ♩ ♪ rhythm of ragtime, but this is also subjected to secondary ragging in the third and fourth bars of the phrase.

Despite Bernstein's adherence to ragtime and novelty characteristics in this first section, he departs from these at figure E when he reaches the trio. At this point, the rhythms become smoother and foxtrot-like, over an oompah accompaniment. The start of the melody itself seems to be a parody of the love theme from *Rhapsody in Blue*, with D♮ jarring against D♯ in the accompaniment, although the ragtime element reappears at the end of the phrase. This section is almost incongruous, and ironic, and it seems to be a satirical swipe at the Gershwin piece, embedded in a caricature of novelty piano music.

Ragtime songs and music were mainly composed around the turn of the century, which means that when the sisters supposedly performed this act, in 1913, it had already become an evocation of an earlier sound; this is, however, a little too early for some of the novelty piano tricks that Bernstein injected into his number. By 1935, ragtime would have seemed dated and a little nostalgic, as it had been succeeded by jazz; when Eileen suggests that she sing 'Wrong Note Rag' as her debut at the Village Vortex, the manager Valenti says 'It's an oldie, but you'll

---

[8]   Although he did misremember Confrey's surname as 'Caffrey' (*My Musical Childhood*, BBC 1986).

Example 3.2 'Wrong Note Rag', bb. 5–12

never know it when I back you up with the licorice stick' (Comden and Green 1997, p. 178). Bernstein includes many aspects that he as a pianist would have been very familiar with, and although perhaps not a completely accurate pastiche of an earlier age, it is a successful parody of the genre, and is a very cheerful and rousing number.

In *Wonderful Town*, the second pastiche method employed is the inclusion of references to the popular dances of the time. By using rhythms identified with social dances, obvious time-markers are presented, for example the Charleston rhythm ($\frac{2}{2}$ ♩. ♪ ♩) with the 1920s. Bernstein, Comden and Green utilized this device to connect two of their songs in *Wonderful Town* to the city: 'Swing' and 'Ballet at the Village Vortex'. The first of these uses a term connected to the jazz music of the 1930s as a title. The concept of 'swing' is difficult to define clearly, mainly due to the diversity of music produced at the time under this banner, but the essence of the music is rhythm. The genre is suggested in the opening bars of the song with the percussion introducing a simple ♩ ♫ ♩ ♫ cymbal rhythm characteristic of the years concerned, as it is derived from the strict ♩ ♫ ♩ ♫ of the ragtime drummers (Collier 1986, p. 546). The accompanying introductory phrase, scored for clarinet, is very similar to the opening of the Prelude from *Trouble in Tahiti* (see Example 2.7), with comparable ascending and descending arpeggio figures, and characteristic 'blue' notes, the flattened fifth being used as a passing note in the descending phrases (see Example 3.3).

Example 3.3 'Swing', bb. 12–14

Following this introduction, 'swing' is immediately evident in the syncopated nature of the melody, presented over a crotchet-based accompaniment, a further characteristic of music from the 1930s. Although the bass line does not reflect the popular 'walking' style of the time, the first four bars of the accompaniment emphasize the second and fourth beats of the each bar, a clear swing element; this accenting occurs more strongly in the release section of the song. The chord progression of the main chorus section uses the expected chords of A minor, C major and E major, although there are frequently added-notes in the chords. There is an interesting sequence in the second half of the chorus, changing first from C major to E♭ major, with the key moving to A minor via parallel chords of A♭⁷ and G⁷, ending on a first inversion tonic chord (with added seventh). This rapid changing of keys disconcerted Miss Russell somewhat, as she informed a reporter that Bernstein enjoyed writing music that moved from key to key: 'a new one on each word!' (quoted in Burton 1994, p. 225). In 'Swing', a further aspect of recollection from the earlier era is heard at the beginning of Ruth's 'swing' lesson, where she repeats the phrases that the surrounding crowd sing, 'answering Cab Calloway fashion' (Comden and Green 1997, p. 170). Cab Calloway was a popular swing bandleader, who appeared with his orchestra in two cartoon films with the character Betty Boop. The first of these, *Minnie the Moocher* (1932), contained the song of the same name, which demonstrated Calloway's call-and-response scat singing, as the members of his orchestra echoed his nonsensical phrases. These lines included: 'Hi-de-hi-de-hi-de-hi', 'Oh, skip-bop-doop-bop-lay-de-doo!', 'Skee-bop-de-google-eet-skee-bop-de-goat!', and 'Skeet-dot'n-dot'n-dot'n-dot'n-dottee-oh!' (Lorenz 1999). Calloway's expressions are reflected in the lyrics for the call-and-response section of 'Swing': 'Whoa-ho-de-ho', 'Skid-dle-ee-oh-day', and 'Heedle-heedle-heedle' (Comden and Green 1997, p. 170). The preceding verse includes many slang words specifically related to jazz culture, as they originated before or during the 1930s: 'hep' (1908), 'jive' (1928), 'cat' (1932), 'dig' and 'solid' (1935), and 'groovy' (1937).[9] The only word that is out of place is 'square', which only entered the jazz vocabulary in 1944, as a description for a person with conventional views. The lyrics also include a reference to a song that was popular in 1935, 'The Music Goes 'Round and Around', played by Tommy Dorsey and his Orchestra (Visser 1997), in the line 'The jive is jumpin' and the music goes around and around' (Comden and Green 1997, p. 167). After the lesson in swing, Ruth delivers an advertising patter 'in a glaze-eyed hynoptic trance' (Comden and Green 1997, p. 170), and this spiel contains other references to the era; words 'reminiscent of lyrics from "Old Man Mose is Dead", "A Tisket a Tasket", and "Flat Foot Floogie"' (Laufe 1978, p. 171). The manner in which one idea leads into another suggests that Bernstein may have been involved in the creation of this section, as, along with Comden and Green, he loved word games and puzzles, and a similar section can also be found nearly 20 years later in the song 'Fraction' from *Mass* (see Chapter 6). 'Swing' contains allusions to: 'The Old Oaken Bucket' (traditional tune, lyric by S. Woodworth, 1818); 'Black is the Colour of my True Love's Hair' (traditional Scottish song); Hairbreadth Harry, a cartoon character in the *Philadelphia Press* from 1906 to 1940; 'I Dreamt I Dwelt in Marble Halls', from *The Bohemian Girl* by M. Balfe, 1843; 'Red Sails in the Sunset' (H. Williams and J. Kennedy 1935); and the Tarzan films. As can be seen, although many of the references are accurate in their time setting, some are a little premature, as they were only popular after 1935. Of course, Bernstein's aim was not to create a exact imitation of a swing piece, but to suggest the genre, and this he achieves successfully in this number, which evocatively reflects the concept and ideals of 'swing'.

The number 'Swing' can also be seen as being derived from the music of white bandleaders, despite the Calloway call-and-response section. The remaining New York pastiche number appears more closely linked to the sound of the black bands. The number at the beginning of the final scene, 'Ballet at the Village Vortex', is diegetic. The libretto describes the scene opening with the sight of the dancing inside the club: 'VALENTI leads the band with his clarinet as the crowd dances a slow, writhing jitterbug, packed tightly together like anchovies' (Comden and Green 1997, p. 182). The music accompanying this dance is in a 'blues' style, the jazz influence being immediately obvious in the harmonies below the brass melody (see Example 3.4).

What is noticeable however, is that these harmonies are too dissonant for the 1930s; the minor sound does not reflect the music of the white bands of the time. The majority of this section, which appears three times through the piece, only uses two chords, the two from the first bar. Both of these include added notes, which

---

[9]   All dates for words come from the *Oxford English Dictionary Online*, www.oed.com.

mentioned at any point). In the directions at the beginning of the play, the time setting indicated is 'Only yesterday' (Chodorov and Fields 1941, p. 5); as the play had premièred in 1940, there is no problem with the use of the dance. In the original story by Ruth McKenney, 'Beware the Brazilian Navy', the main dance is the rumba, performed in the Village Barn when the admirals follow Ruth and Eileen as they go for something to eat – the admirals pay the orchestra to keep playing (McKenney 1938, p. 223). It is the addition of the date that causes the problems with the use of the conga as a time marker, and, although it is spoken text, it lies within a song, and so was probably added by Comden and Green; one can hardly blame the collaborators for their enthusiasm for such an energetic dance. As is the case with 'Swing', the main point of the number is to produce a lively spectacle, and such a minor mistake is unimportant when the visual and musical impact of the number is considered. The lyrics of 'Conga!' contain encyclopedic references to the era, as previously seen in 'Swing', including mentions of government agencies (NRA and TVA), famous performers and sportspeople (Major Bowes, Mitzi Green, Dizzy Dean, Leopold Stokowski and Helen Wills), and authors and diplomats (John Steinbeck and Charles G. Dawes). Bernstein had actually used recycled music in 'Conga!', as the phrase shown in Example 3.5 was first used in his music for *The Peace* in 1940, where it was used in the finale of Scene 3 (Gottlieb 1964, p. 270); it was also briefly employed in *On the Town* as the scene change music for the Congacabana.[12]

The opening of Act II musically transports us to a different shore, with the Irish song 'My Darlin' Eileen'. There is some clue to the origins of this song in the score,[13] where it states that the music is 'based on an Irish Reel'. However, there is a puzzle posed by this statement, by the marking at fig. D which gives the tempo as 'Allegro (like a reel)'. Reels are generally in $\frac{4}{4}$, while this number is in $\frac{6}{8}$, the time signature associated with the jig. The tune that this song is probably based on is known by various names; 'Haste to the Wedding', 'The Small Pin Cushion', 'Carrick Fergus', 'Trip to the Dargle' and 'The Capture of Carrickfergusby'.[14] There are small variations in these tunes, but the basic melodic shape is the same in all. When it is compared with the tune for 'My Darlin' Eileen', marked similarities can be seen, and in fact Bernstein's contribution appears quite small (although he will have added the harmony). It is possible that Bernstein heard similar tunes on a visit to Ireland in 1950 when, following his debut with the Concertgebouw Orchestra in Holland, he flew to County Donegal with his brother and sister to stay with an American friend who had estate on the west coast. In a letter to David Diamond, Bernstein relates that he had been very active: 'I've hunted deer, fished

---

[12] Jaensch notes that the conga is used in *On the Town*, but does not recognize that it is the same music that is later heard in *Wonderful Town* (2003, p. 173).

[13] In *Bernstein on Broadway*, p. 123. The note is not present in the Boosey & Hawkes hire vocal score of *Wonderful Town*, nor is it in the 2004 published vocal score.

[14] Information found at The Fiddler's Companion (www.ceolas.org/tunes/fc) and in Fleischmann (1998).

and danced "The Siege of Carrick" all night' (quoted in Burton 1994, p. 203). Apparently his host, Henry McIlhenney, 'had taken his guests below stairs to join the domestics in an evening of Irish reels' (Burton 1994, p. 203).

The actual performance of 'My Darlin' Eileen' also owes something to the traditions of Irish performers that had developed in New York over the years. Initially, Irish characters in minstrelsy and melodrama were the object of ridicule and cruel humour. The image of the hard-drinking, violent, emotional Irishman was gradually toned down, as 'by the 1850s there were enough Irish and Irish Americans active in the business (as well as in the audience) to soften the images presented in the songs and jokes and to make them more positive and sympathetic' (Williams 1996, p. 65). Irish performers found success in the entertainment industry in New York, some of the most famous being Harrigan and Hart, Maggie Cline and the Four Cohans. In a city populated by large groups of immigrants, sketches and songs produced by representatives of one such group were well liked:

> What they saw were characterizations, often comic and grotesque, of people whose original homes and homelands lay far beyond the boundaries of the city, all striving, not just to survive, but to 'make it' in an environment that was at once alien and mesmerizing, grim, dirty and, at the same time, glittering with the promise. (Williams 1996, p. 127)

One Irish singer taken to heart by the American public was John McCormack, a lyric tenor who, in addition to performing at the New York Metropolitan Opera during the 1910s and 1920s, was also well known for his renditions of Irish traditional tunes. His association with such music more than probably led to the indication in Chodorov and Fields's libretto that in 'My Darlin' Eileen', the police chief Lonigan should sing 'à la John McCormack' (1997, p. 161).[15] The presentation of the policemen as Irish is also significant, and corresponds to an important social detail of the era, as joining the police was seen as a good way to ascend the social ladder and escape immigrant poverty at the time. As a result of this, 'during the latter half of the nineteenth century the Irish dominated New York City's police force' (Williams 1996, pp. 138–9).

'My Darlin' Eileen' also demonstrates its Irish roots with its lyrics: the longing to return to the homeland and the concept of the colleen. Both were popular subjects for Irish songs at the beginning of the twentieth century, featuring in songs such as 'My Wild Irish Rose' (1897), 'When Irish Eyes Are Smiling' (1912), 'The Daughter of Rosie O'Grady' (1917) and 'Plain Molly O' (1891). The sentimentality of these songs highlighted a trend for nostalgia that had already existed in Irish songs for several decades, and 'the association of the colleen with mother and Ireland reveals the way in which the images of the Irish were moving

---

[15]   In the 2004 vocal score the performance indication is 'in Irish Tenor style' (Bernstein 2004, p. 127), rather than naming a specific singer; perhaps this is because McCormack was no longer well known.

away from the city in American popular music after the turn of the century' (Williams 1996, p. 221). Bernstein, Comden and Green have combined a number of characteristics to produce a song that portrays an image of the Irish that would have been immediately recognizable to the audience of the 1950s.

'Ohio' is the remaining song that brings to mind a location outside of New York. This is called a 'hill-billy' lament by Atkinson (1953a, p. 22), and there is certainly a country feel to the song, evoked by the bass line, with its lazy swung rhythm. However, yet again Bernstein exploited existing music, whether consciously or unconsciously, to provide the melody for 'Ohio'. This was picked up on by Blitzstein, who was obviously not impressed: 'when he calmly grabs the Brahms 2nd Piano Concerto for his "hit", called "Why-oh-why-oh-why-oh, why-did-I-ever-leave-Ohio?"', I gaga (I mean gag)' (quoted in Gordon 1989, p. 364).[16] Despite this, the actual sound that Bernstein creates for the lament of the two sisters does sound very provincial, compared to the urban sounds of New York, and nicely contrasts the origins of the pair and the situation they now find themselves in. There are definite parallels between this song and the Andrews Sisters' version of Cole Porter's 'Don't Fence Me In', recorded in 1944 with Bing Crosby: the cowboy feel, both with triplet or dotted rhythms, and the female harmonies. It is undocumented as to whether Bernstein knew the Porter song, but as it was a very successful number it is most likely that he did.

The mix of genres and styles within *Wonderful Town* creates the effect of a vaudeville show, and there are hints of the vaudeville format in the structure of the 1953 piece. George Gottlieb, a booker for vaudeville in New York, outlined the first act thus (Kislan 1995, pp. 45–47): 'a dumb act to start (animals or dancing), an act to settle the audience, a comedy dramatic sketch, a rousing number and a big dance number to close'. 'Conga!' is certainly the closing dance number, with the other 'acts' appearing as 'Conquering the City' (ballet), 'Ohio', 'Conversation Piece' and '100 Easy Ways to Lose a Man'. The second half fits less strictly within the vaudeville mould, although it does contain an Irish act in 'My Darlin Eileen', a full stage act in 'Swing', and the big finale in 'Wrong Note Rag'. The seven numbers that do not fit directly into Gottlieb's scheme still reflect items that could have been found on the vaudeville stage: the three types of ballad in 'A Little Bit of Love', 'A Quiet Girl' and 'It's Love'; the male comic wiseguy acts of 'What a Waste' and 'Pass That Football'; and the melodramatic sketch of 'Story Vignettes'. 'Christopher Street' would have provided an introduction to the evening's proceedings. This format reflects a style of entertainment that was in decline in

---

[16]   A further link between the Brahms and the Bernstein lies in the piano duet of Moszkowski, *Aus Aller Herren Länder*. The piece in a German style includes a section that closely resembles the melody of the Brahms, although in straight quavers, and also includes similar harmony to the Bernstein version, notably the subdominant chord with double appoggiaturas above. It is not unreasonable to consider that, at some point in his piano lessons, Bernstein would have encountered the Moszkowski duets. (Similarity between the duet, the Bernstein and the Brahms pointed out to me by S. Banfield.)

the 1930s, as the Depression and advances in motion pictures began to take their toll on live performances. Comden and Green had certainly seen vaudeville shows as children,[17] and their own shows as the Revuers had maintained some of the comic traditions of the earlier style. Three years later, in his *Omnibus* television programme on 'American Musical Comedy', Bernstein spoke on the importance of the revue show, and its influence on the form of musical comedy:

> Musical comedy has learned a lot from revues. It has learned to treat its book in the manner of a variety show; it has learned to take variety and unify it. This is one of the great secrets of our magic formula: to give the audience a continuous and convincing story, yet to have them leave the theater feeling they have also had a rounded evening of fun – dancing, comedy scenes, emotional singing, gay singing, pretty girls – the works, but somehow all cleverly integrated into a good story. (Bernstein 2004, p. 180)

Whether it was a conscious or an unconscious decision that led to such a layout in *Wonderful Town*, the variety of styles of music certainly mirror the diversity of music heard in New York in the 1930s.

Trunk Music

As in *On the Town*, where he had introduced melodic ideas drawn from his juvenile works, Bernstein used music composed prior to the writing of the show in *Wonderful Town*, despite the opinion of one New York journalist: 'Mr Bernstein had the notion that he could use stuff hidden away in a bottom drawer, but it didn't turn out that way' (Taubman 1953, p. 11). This fact is not surprising considering the time limitations placed on the composer during the writing of his second show. The practice of using 'trunk' music – that is, music that remained initially unused or in the composer's 'trunk' following its composition, or reuse of melodies and music in different shows – was certainly not new. A good example of this is George and Ira Gershwin's song 'The Man I Love'. This number was, as Ira Gershwin details in his book (1978, p. 5), first written early in 1924, and was then incorporated into the show *Lady, Be Good!* later that year. However, after a week in the Philadelphia tryouts, the song was cut from the show, as its 'sweetness and simplicity in style do not make for the vociferous applause given dancing duets and novelty numbers' (Gershwin 1978, p. 5). The song appears in *Strike Up the Band* (1927), and, although it remained in the show, the show did not remain on the stage, lasting less than three weeks pre-Broadway. 'The Man I Love' was next entered with some lyric alterations into *Rosalie* (1928), as a number for Marilyn Miller – once again, failing to make it through the tryouts. Following three abortive attempts, the song remained contextless, but gained popularity regardless, as 'it

---

[17]   Letter from Green to the author, 13 July 1999.

has since led a fairly active and respectable life, thanks ... to dozens of recordings and uses in motion pictures' (Gershwin 1978, p. 6).

Jerome Kern also used trunk music, understandably as he composed at a time when shows were produced at an alarming rate: Kern had music included in ten shows in 1915, in four the following year, and in seven in 1917 (Suskin 1992, pp. 26–37). Even with Kern, some songs struggled to find a suitable home: one of his best-known numbers, 'Bill', was originally used in 1918, in *Oh, Lady! Lady!!* (from which it was cut), and in 1919, in *Zip, Goes a Million* (Suskin 1992, p. 55), before re-emerging in 1927 in *Show Boat*, where it now seems to have always belonged.

Returning to Bernstein, the most significant piece of inserted music in *Wonderful Town* was *Prelude, Fugue and Riffs*, a number employed as the 'Courtroom Ballet' that opened Act II (Gottlieb 1964, p. 270). The piece had originally been written four years earlier as part of a series of commissions for Woody Herman and his band that already included Stravinsky's *Ebony Concerto* (1946). Bernstein's piece was never paid for, and so remained on the shelf until the opportunity arose for its use in *Wonderful Town*, its jazz sounds and ensemble-based arrangements fitting in well with the sounds of the 1930s created for the show. Unfortunately, the ballet was subsequently cut prior to the New York opening of the production, possibly because it held up the action at the opening of the second act;[18] it was eventually premièred in full by Benny Goodman in 1955 as part of Bernstein's *Omnibus* programme, 'The World of Jazz' (Laird 2002, p. 69).

Whilst Stravinsky's *Ebony Concerto* sounds like a serious composer adapting jazz techniques and applying them to his own music, Bernstein's work flows more naturally and convincingly as an example of big-band writing. He used a standard band set-up: solo clarinet, two alto saxophones, two tenor saxophones, baritone saxophone, five trumpets, four trombones, piano, string bass and percussion (kit player plus xylophone, vibraphone, wood block and timpani). These forces were divided between the three movements, beginning with the brass, plus drum kit and bass, in the opening 'Prelude'. This movement contains two contrasting sections, again equivalent to the two elements discussed in Chapter 1, described by Gottlieb in this piece as 'the "hot" versus the "blue"' (1964, p. 237): faster, rhythmic music with changing time signatures, juxtaposed F♯s/F♮s and syncopation, balanced by slower music with an emphasis on a blues-style melody. The 'Fugue' is written just for the five saxophones, beginning with a disjointed first subject, which contrasts with a more lyrical second subject, reminiscent of Stravinsky's clarinet melody in the first movement of his *Ebony Concerto*. The two groups of instruments play together, and are joined by the piano, solo clarinet and tuned percussion players in the final 'Riffs' section. Here, Bernstein gradually increases the texture by layering the melodic material, beginning with new phrases on the clarinet and piano, and reintroducing the first fugue subject and the blues section from the previous movements. The music intensifies until a five-bar section is reached; this is

---

[18] Suggested by Cris Alexander, a member of the original Broadway cast (Klain 1994/5, p. 37).

repeated 'as many times as seems psychologically right (that is, to an "exhaustion point")' (score note to *Prelude, Fugue and Riffs*, Bernstein 1950, p. 31), the aim being to sound like an improvisation or jam session.

Despite the fact that the piece as a whole was cut from *Wonderful Town*, its influence can be heard in the remaining numbers. 'Conquering New York', the first-act dance pantomime, contains two figures derived from the earlier piece. These are a rapid ascending figure in the central section of the dance, marked 'Subway' (score note),[19] which is a clarinet figure taken from the 'Riffs' movement, and a descending fifth phrase which comes from the 'hot' section of the 'Prelude'. The reiteration of these phrases would have created a link between the two dance/ballet sections, both of which concern the people of the city. The number 'Conversation Piece' features a distinctive vamp phrase, representative of the tension and unease of the characters involved, as they struggle to make polite conversation at a party (see Example 3.6). This phrase was originally heard in the 'Prelude' section of the *Prelude, Fugue and Riffs* (bb. 44–53), and also reappeared in the 'Riffs' finale (bb. 244–52). Within its context in the 'Courtroom Ballet', this vamp may have been used to depict the 'drunks' included in the character list of the ballet (New Haven programme[20]). The final link with *Prelude, Fugue and Riffs* came in the first version of the show's opening number, 'Three–Point–Two', which started with the music of the 'Fugue'.

A song transplanted from another show was 'Lallapalooza', again a victim of a pre-Broadway cut from *Wonderful Town*. This was its second ejection, as it was also removed from *Peter Pan* (1950), the show it was originally composed for, during the tryouts. Bernstein shelved the song before attempting to introduce

Example 3.6 'Conversation Piece', bb. 1–4

---

[19]   The marking 'Subway' can be found in vocal score available on hire from Boosey and Hawkes. It has been removed from the new edition of the published vocal score.

[20]   Included in the Comden and Green Collection in the New York Public Library.

it into the later show, as a number specifically for the character of Appopolous, the 'lovable landlord of Christopher Street' (Comden and Green 1997, p. 93). Originally this character had no songs, but Bernstein decided that he should have a number, and a singer, Henry Lascoe, replaced the original actor, Harold Huber. The music for 'Lallapalooza' was inserted, with new words talking about the good aspects of the apartment that the sisters were looking at,[21] but then the song was dropped before reaching Broadway[22] (Cris Alexander, quoted in Klain 1994/5, p. 37). There is an indication in an early script of *West Side Story*[23] that Bernstein also thought about inserting the number into his latest show, but fortunately this idea was soon dropped. 'Lallapalooza' never made it into a Broadway show, and remains unpublished.

Of the songs that form a canonical part of *Wonderful Town*, two are based on previously composed music. The chorus of Wreck's solo 'Pass That Football' shares music with an earlier song, 'I Can Love a Woman'. This connection, pointed out by Gottlieb (1964, p. 269), is underlined by a manuscript of the earlier lyrics in the Library of Congress dated c.1947. Although these lyrics are typed, and no author is mentioned,[24] the metre of these earlier words matches the Comden and Green lyric for 'Pass That Football'. The second song is 'A Quiet Girl', the chorus section of which reuses the music of a composition called 'Jamie's Lullaby' (Gottlieb 1964, p. 270). This song was written on 27 October 1952, following the birth of Bernstein's first child, Jamie, on 8 September. Although the lullaby has less musical material than the later version, it can clearly be seen as the source for 'A Quiet Girl' (see Examples 3.7a and b).

Marc Blitzstein, in a letter of 1953, suggests that Bernstein had actually borrowed both title and melody from his works: 'I don't mind when he swipes from me (he has a number, "Quiet Girl", which title I used years ago; but instead of writing *that* song, he has written another of mine: a lullaby I wrote for *No for an Answer*)' (quoted in Gordon 1989, p. 364). In addition, Drew proposes (1955, p. 79), that the B section of 'Quiet Girl' is actually based on a section of Copland's *Billy the Kid*, 'Billy and his Sweetheart', which Bernstein certainly would have known. Thus the majority of music within this song comes from other sources, rather than from Bernstein's own pen.

As previously mentioned, 'Conga!' was also based on a former composition, meaning that five songs that remained in the show, and three that were cut, included previously composed music. Further 'borrowing' occurs in the chorus section of 'What a Waste', although this cannot be labelled as 'trunk' music, as Bernstein is not drawing on his own music. The two-bar descending scale appears to be heavily influenced by Aaron Copland's 'Buckaroo Holiday' from *Rodeo* (1942), a

---

[21]   The positioning of the song in the tryouts, between the opening and 'Ohio', suggests that it would be sung to the girls, encouraging them to take the apartment.

[22]   Lascoe remained in the cast, despite having no songs to sing.

[23]   Undated script in box 73, folder 10, LBC.

[24]   Box 71, folder 38, LBC.

Example 3.7   Comparison of 'Jamie's Lullaby' and 'A Quiet Girl'

(a) 'Jamie's Lullaby', bb. 1–8, from manuscript
(b) 'A Quiet Girl', bb.13–20

piece that Bernstein was certainly familiar with. This 'borrowing' can also be seen in the previously discussed 'Ohio', although in that case the composer was not a personal friend of Bernstein.

Although Bernstein brought pre-composed music to the collaboration, the songs themselves, as dramatic wholes, did not pre-exist. The lyrics and context of each number, aspects that form an integral part of the song as a functioning item within a musical theatre work, were all created specifically for *Wonderful Town*, as pointed out by Adolph Green in connection with that show: 'All composers have melodies they've written that turn up later. But you can't do that with the lyrics' (letter to the present author, 13 July 1999).

Fifths

A motivic device employed by Bernstein in *Wonderful Town*, and identified by Gottlieb (1964, p. 22), is the use of the interval of a fifth.[25] Gottlieb pointed out this as the opening interval in 'It's Love' and 'A Little Bit in Love', and its appearances within phrases in 'What a Waste' and 'Conversation Piece' (1964, p. 23); however, the motif is more specific, and it features in more songs. It is also significant that the two notes outlining the interval are always the tonic and dominant, $\hat{1}$ and $\hat{5}$. The interval is heard as a tonic to dominant leap at the beginning of 'What a Waste',

---

[25]   This connection is also noted by Rice: 'a good deal of the score of "Wonderful Town" … is based on various permutations of the simple interval of a fifth' (1958a, p. 58).

where it forms the basis for the introduction, and this opening is then reprised at the start of 'A Quiet Girl' and 'It's Love' (see Examples 3.8a–c).

Example 3.8 Appearances of the tonic–dominant motif

(a) 'What a Waste, bb. 1–2
(b) 'A Quiet Girl', bb. 1–2
(c) 'It's Love', bb. 1–4

These three songs are sung by Baker, and follow the course of his relationship with Ruth, from his first, rather harsh, words to her ('What a Waste'), to the slow realization of his feelings towards her ('A Quiet Girl'), and in the final statement of his affection ('It's Love'). In this last example, Eileen has to encourage Baker to confront his emotions, and as he does the interval he sings to the words of the title changes from being a repeated note to an octave, and then to the perfect fifth that resounds with his passion. The verse of Baker's first song ('What a Waste') contains descending fifths, from dominant to tonic, which mirror the ascending intervals seen in the introduction, as each person's talent (and passion) is explained. This music is also used as the verse in 'Pass The Football', the reappearance perhaps suggesting that Wreck's education, which he describes to this melody, was also a waste of time, although tempered by his contribution to the game he loves. The ascending $\hat{1}\hat{5}$, together with words associated with romance, also appeared in Ruth's cut song 'The Story of My Life', as she sings of 'any story that is filled with love, and joy, and hope'.[26]

The retrograde of this phrase, a descending fifth ($\hat{5}\hat{1}$), is the interval that begins Eileen's 'A Little Bit in Love', as she sings about a man she has recently become

---

[26] Lyrics from script for *By Bernstein*, box 89, folder 31, LBC.

acquainted with, standing 'all starry-eyed' (Comden and Green 1997, p. 122)[27] (see Example 3.9a). Eileen restates her first phrase at the opening of 'Conversation Piece', to attempt to open the discussion by exhorting the pleasantness of the situation (which includes the presence of one of the objects of her affection) (see Example 3.9b).

Example 3.9   Appearances of the dominant–tonic motif

(a) 'A Little Bit in Love', bb. 3–4
(b) 'Conversation Piece', bb. 11–12

Later in 'Conversation Piece', both ascending and descending fifths are employed in its main verse. Although the piece is in G major, the first four bars are harmonized with the dominant chord, so D and A are $\hat{1}$ and $\hat{5}$ above this. There is also a slight variation on the motif, with the addition of the G♯ as a tritone, which 'resolves' upwards onto the dominant, in a phrase that foreshadows the start of 'Cool', from Bernstein's later musical (see Example 3.10).

Example 3.10   'Conversation Piece', bb. 15–18

A further example of the motif can be found in the dance pantomime 'Conquering New York'. This is very similar to a repeating pattern in the 'Riffs' section of Bernstein's *Prelude, Fugue and Riffs*, and also resembles an earlier phrase in the 'Prelude', the reasons for which have already been discussed. It is at the opening of the dance in *Wonderful Town* the $\hat{1}\hat{5}$ pattern is seen, but here it outlines a descending fourth, rather than a fifth (see Example 3.11a). This alteration could be related to the fact that the number is not directly about any of

---

[27]   Eileen sings a short reprise of the same song only two pages later, referring to a different young man, 'with the same starry-eyed look as before' (Comden and Green 1997, p. 124).

the characters, but is instead relating their early experiences in the city. The fanfare at this point was also present in the original opening number, 'Three–Point–Two', and in this example, the notes are clearly seen as $\hat{1}$ and $\hat{5}$ (see Example 3.11b).

Example 3.11 Appearances of the descending fourth figure

(a) 'Conquering the City', bb. 2–5
(b) 'Three–Point–Two', from manuscript

In 'Conquering New York', the flattened seventh (E♭) is included in the key signature, despite the fact that the music is clearly in F major for the opening 11 bars of this piece.

All but two of the occurrences of the fifth motif within *Wonderful Town* are sung (the exceptions being in 'Conquering New York'), and the majority of these are sung by Eileen or Baker. It is perhaps significant that their songs are either about love, or directed to the potential object of their affection. In 'Conversation Piece' Eileen is trying to enliven a party including two of her admirers; in 'What a Waste' Baker is advising Ruth, who will shortly become the love of his life. Wreck's 'Pass That Football' may also be seen as a love song, as he sings about his passion for the game; and in 'The Story of My Life', Ruth is bemoaning the fact that the good things in life, including love, seem to pass her by.

This emotional context is perhaps a continuation of the motif's appearance in the two previous shows. The main 'New York, New York' theme from *On the Town* ($\hat{5}\hat{1}\hat{2}\hat{5}$) consists of two interlocking ascending fifths (E–A–B–E), and certainly denotes admiration, if not love, of the city. In *Trouble in Tahiti*, the Resolution motif, which signals the re-awakening of Sam and Dinah's feelings for each other, begins with a descending fifth, though not dominant and tonic in this context (see Example 2.3). This interval had played an important part in Bernstein's other preceding compositions, often being placed significantly within the themes of works, such as his songs and chamber music, as well as a ballet.[28]

Bernstein's *Urmotiv* occurs within three songs in *Wonderful Town*, as pointed out by Gottlieb (1964, p. 35): 'A Quiet Girl', 'What a Waste' and 'Conga!' (see

---

[28]   These other works include three movements of his *Brass Music* (1948), *Facsimile* (1946) and *Afterthought* (1945).

Example 3.7 for the first of these). It is interesting that, of these three numbers, two were written prior to work beginning on the show and later inserted. This leaves 'What a Waste' as the only song written specifically for *Wonderful Town* that demonstrates use of the motif. Perhaps the emotions being portrayed in the show were too superficial for Bernstein, even at a subconscious level, to attach his *Urmotiv* to them, except in a song mourning the wasting of natural talent.

The return to musical comedy in *Wonderful Town* gave Bernstein the opportunity to demonstrate his skill in writing pastiche, recreating the sounds of the 1930s and earlier: swing, blues, Latin American and Irish music, hill-billy ballads and novelty piano pieces. In contrast to the preceding musical theatre works, the song forms used in this show are those of Broadway and Tin Pan Alley, not the highbrow structures seen in *Trouble in Tahiti*, and in the dances of *On the Town*. This may be due to the fact that *Wonderful Town* is a traditional musical comedy, with none of the aspirations of integration and organicism of *On the Town*; the intellectual approach of the earlier show is lost, compounded no doubt by the very short time allowed for the creative processes. Despite this consideration, Bernstein still employs motivic techniques, creating connections between songs and indicating character development, although now there is only one principal motif: the interval of a fifth.

Bernstein's operatic tendencies, suppressed in this show, would resurface in his next work, as he moved away from the sounds and conventions of Broadway – in *Candide*.

Chapter 4

Candide

'Look at the view! Mountains and flowers!'

The decade before *Candide* had been a difficult one for both Broadway and Hollywood, as a highly charged political atmosphere led to strong anti-Communist feelings. America perceived a threat from across the Atlantic, as the Soviet Union consolidated Communist rule in Eastern Europe between 1945 and 1948. To the west of the States, on the other side of the Pacific, the danger came from Communist North Korea, fighting against pro-Western South Korea from 1950. Intervention by the US in the Korean War was a specific attempt to halt the spread of Communism, although American involvement did not have an altogether positive effect on the outcome. However, the battle was also being fought on home soil, and tensions had been rising since the 1930s, when the breakdown of the capitalist dream and the stock market crash had led to the Great Depression, denting people's belief in the American Dream. Workers turned to unions for support and socialist ideals attracted many followers, which worried the established authorities, particularly the Catholic Church (Jenkins 1997, p. 232). It seemed that the freedom of the American public was under threat from foreign concepts and beliefs, and those who sympathized with socialist principles found themselves under suspicion. Unfortunately, the entertainment industry contained many with left-wing, if not specifically Communist, sympathies, and found itself under scrutiny in 1947 and 1951 (Wollen 1992, p. 45). The House Un-American Activities Committee (HUAC) subpoenaed individuals to question them on their political activities, and to pressure them into naming Communist Party members, past or present. Alongside this, groups arose that acted as self-regulation organizations; these groups would 'blacklist' suspected leftists, and force them to clear their names by denouncing Communism, and often by naming others to be blacklisted (Wollen 1992, p. 46). Several high-profile Hollywood and Broadway personalities were called to hearings by HUAC, including Jerome Robbins and Elia Kazan, both of whom 'named names' in order to clear themselves (Myers 1998, p. 83 and p. 86). Betty Comden and Adolph Green had both been named in a hearing in February 1952, and two other members of their Vanguard Revuers group, Alvin Hammer and Judy Holliday, had appeared before the Committee, although both had avoided giving any names (Wollen 1992, p. 49). In 1952 the writer and playwright Lillian Hellman was subpoenaed to appear, following the jailing of her lover Dashiell Hammett for refusing to accept the authority of the Committee. Hellman declined to comment on anyone's politics but her own, and wrote a letter to HUAC stating this:

I am ready and willing to testify before the representatives of our Government as to my own opinions and my own actions, regardless of any risks or consequences to myself. But I am advised by counsel that if I answer the committee's questions about myself, I must also answer questions about other people and that if I refuse to do so I can be cited for contempt … I cannot and will not cut my conscience to fit this year's fashions, even though I long ago came to the conclusion that I was not a political person and could have no comfortable place in any political group. (Quoted in Moody 1972, pp. 236–7).

Within the artistic community, several people demonstrated their reaction to the Committee inquisitions through their work, including Arthur Miller and Elia Kazan. Miller drew parallels between the Salem witch trials of the seventeenth century and the McCarthy hearings in his play *The Crucible* (1953): the women in Salem are accused following allegations from people whose motives are not questioned, and are unable to protest their innocence against the weight of religious bigotry and narrow-mindedness. There is a sense of the course of action being unstoppable once it has been set in motion, as the hangings go ahead despite the opposition of the judges, a reflection of the relentless progress of the McCarthy trials in the fervently anti-Communist atmosphere of the time, and the terror it created. In *On the Waterfront* (1955), Kazan and Budd Schulberg tell the story of one man standing up to the dominance of crooked bosses in the docks of New York, saving himself by testifying before the Crime Commission to expose the labour racketeering at the waterfront. As both Schulberg and Kazan appeared before the HUAC trials and 'named names', their film is seen by some as a defence of their behaviour; these actions initially deterred Bernstein when he was approached to write the music for the film, but he was won over when he saw the drafts, and he then spent three months composing the music (Burton 1994, p. 236).

For Lillian Hellman, the theatre had always offered opportunities for the presentation of moral and political issues, beginning with her first play in 1934. *The Children's Hour* told the tale, based on a true story, of two heterosexual teachers who are falsely accused of a homosexual relationship by an embittered pupil, who is readily believed by a society too willing to accept the lies. As the consequences of the incident take a hold, tragedy follows: the school that the two women run is closed, one loses her fiancé, and the other kills herself. In her dramas, Hellman frequently illustrated the struggle of the individual against the pressures of the world, particularly against the corrupt and greedy. Special attention was reserved for people who subjugated others, and those who 'stand and watch them do it' (quoted in Moody 1972, p. 351). The former category included Hellman's adaptation of Anouilh's *The Lark* (1955), the story of Joan of Arc, and one example of the latter was *The Little Foxes* (1939), which detailed the disintegration of a family caused by greed. Hellman's antipathy towards Hollywood was compounded when she was blacklisted in 1948 due to her political beliefs, which made the studios very reluctant to hire her; the situation lasted until the 1960s (Phillips and Hollander 1965, p. 66).

The McCarthy witch-hunt left its mark on Hellman, and part of her response can be seen in her libretto for *Candide*. It is interesting that both Miller and Hellman, who were staunchly opposed to the HUAC trials, set their tales in the past, distancing the action from the real events, and locating their allegories in 1692 and 1756 respectively. This contrasts with the approach taken by Kazan, who had capitulated to the Committee, and who set his defence in modern-day New York, utilizing the parallel story of the union troubles on the docks. It was Hellman who approached Bernstein with the idea of collaborating on a musical version of Voltaire's 1759 novella *Candide* in the autumn of 1953, and public announcement of the project came in February 1954, in the *New York Herald Tribune* (Burton 1994, p. 236). The pair had been considering a collaboration as early as 1950, but in a letter to his sister Shirley in April of that year Bernstein says that he has 'written Lillian to count me out'.[1] The nature of this work is unclear, although it is known that Hellman and Bernstein had thought about working on an opera on the life of Eva Peron, but this project had fallen through (Burton 1994, p. 236). The composer clearly felt the same way as Hellman, and saw *Candide* as a way of reflecting the mood of the time: 'Puritanical snobbery, phony moralism, inquisitorial attacks on the individual, brave-new-world optimism, essential superiority – aren't these all charges levelled against American society by our best thinkers? And they are also charges made by Voltaire against his own society' (Bernstein 1956, p. 3).

By the end of summer 1954, the first act of *Candide* had been sketched out, but Bernstein had also been occupied by a different piece, *Serenade* (for solo violin, harp, percussion and strings), a request from Isaac Stern (Burton 1994, p. 238). In fact, between February 1954 and 1 December 1956, when *Candide* finally opened on Broadway, Bernstein had also composed incidental music for Hellman's *The Lark* and for *Salome* (a production of Oscar Wilde's play), a song called 'Get Hep!' for Michigan State College, and a great deal of the music for his next show, *West Side Story*. He had also conducted productions of Bellini's *La Sonnambula*, and Puccini's *La Boheme* at La Scala, and had written and appeared in five *Omnibus* broadcasts on television: 'Beethoven's Fifth Symphony', 'The World of Jazz', 'The Art of Conducting', 'The Role of the University in American Life' and 'The American Musical Comedy'.[2] In addition to the pressures of other work, there was also a dilemma about finding a suitable lyricist for *Candide*, as people came and went. The original lyricist, John LaTouche, withdrew in January 1955, and Bernstein himself considered taking on the task (Secrest 1995, p. 203), before realizing the size of the job, and the impossibility of fitting it around his other commitments. It was in December 1955 that Richard Wilbur became the final member of the team, and he worked through the summer and autumn of

---

[1]   Letter in LBC, dated 17 April 1950, reproduced on Library of Congress website, http:hdl.loc.gov/loc.music/lbcorr.00320.

[2]   The last of these was actually after nearly all the work on *Candide* had been completed, broadcast on 7 October 1956.

1956, creating new lyrics and revising existing words (Burton 1994, p. 257); further lyrics were also provided by Dorothy Parker. Ultimately, the gap between inception and early work to the Broadway premiere of *Candide* was almost three years, a stark contrast to the five-week period spent on *Wonderful Town*.

In *Candide*, Gottfried Leibniz's theories appear embodied in the teachings of the character of Pangloss, who purports that this is the 'best of all possible worlds' (Voltaire 1947, p. 20). Leibniz was born in 1646, 48 years before Voltaire, and his writings became associated with those of the 'optimistic' philosophy of the time:

> Now as there is an infinite number of possible universes in the ideas of God, and as only one can exist, there must be a sufficient reason for God's choice, determining him to one rather than to another.
>
> And this reason can only be found in the *fitness*, or in the degrees of perfection, which these worlds contain, each possible world having the right to claim existence in proportion to the perfection which it involves.
>
> And it is this which causes the existence of the best, which God knows through his wisdom, chooses through his goodness, and produces through his power. (Leibniz 1973, p. 187)

Voltaire opposed these views, mainly in the light of two natural disasters that occurred 30 years after Leibniz's death: an earthquake in Lima in 1746, and another in Lisbon in 1753 that killed thousands of people. He could not reconcile the calamities with the Optimist doctrine, and he articulated these views in his *Poem on the Disaster of Lisbon* in 1756 (Budd 1946, p. 9). The story of *Candide* continues Voltaire's criticism of Optimism, as in the face of the terrible tragedy and misfortune that befalls the characters, one character maintains that all is happening for the best, and his optimism remains in the face of disaster, despair and all manner of deaths. The novella follows the eponymous hero, Candide, through his many travels with his teacher, Pangloss, as he strives to find his sweetheart, Cunegonde. On his journeys he meets and re-meets many characters, including an Old Lady, Cunegonde's brother Maximillian, their maid Paquette, the Governor of Buenos Aires, a pessimist called Martin, and a servant called Cacambo. The tale moves through many countries and over two continents, and despite misadventure, and the fact that the main characters cheat death a ridiculous number of times, the major players in the story conclude their exploits living happily together, which Pangloss states is a direct result of all their intervening troubles:

> There is chain of events in this best of all possible worlds; for if you had not been turned out of a lovely mansion at the point of a jackboot for the love of Lady Cunegonde, and if you had not been involved in the Inquisition, and had not wandered over America by foot, and had not struck the Baron with your

sword, and lost all those sheep you brought from Eldorado, you would not be here eating candied fruit and pistachio nuts. (Voltaire 1947, p. 144)

One focus of Hellman's interest in Voltaire's story was a scene in Lisbon, which contained an *auto-da-fé* with hangings and burnings, the gory events being mounted in an attempt to prevent a further earthquake. Candide and his tutor Pangloss are arrested and presented before an inquisition 'one for speaking and the other for listening with an air of approval' (Voltaire 1947, p. 36), their sentences dispatched with alarming haste. Voltaire's ridiculing of the Catholic Church, the pillorying of their ruthless investigation techniques and sense of justice, offered an opportunity for Hellman and Bernstein to make a similar judgement on their present social climate; in Bernstein's words:

> The particular evil which impelled Lillian Hellman to choose *Candide* and present it to me as the basis for a musical stage work was what we now so quaintly and, alas, faintly recall as McCarthyism – an 'ism' so akin to that Spanish Inquisition we just revisited in the first act [the Lisbon scene] as to curdle the blood.[3]

Hellman's interpretation of this scene will be considered in some detail later in this chapter.

The creative processes involved in producing Hellman and Bernstein's *Candide* appear prolonged and complex, with the protracted collaboration time, changes of personnel and other distractions, but these pale in comparison to what happened to the operetta after the first production. There was always the feeling that something was not quite right with the piece as a whole, usually attributed to the heavy-handed nature of Hellman's book, which exchanged Voltaire's wit and levity for a dry satirical take on the story, and subsequent versions attempted to correct this. Hellman herself admitted that she found the collaborative nature of creation associated with the musical theatre overwhelming:

> I went to pieces when something had to be done quickly, because somebody didn't like something, and there was no proper time to think it out. I couldn't go away for a month to decide whether it was right of wrong … In looking back at *Candide*, I realized that I panicked under conditions I wasn't accustomed to. (Quoted in Dramatists Guild 1970, p. 129)

Bernstein collaborated on a further six interpretations of *Candide* – London 1959, Los Angeles 1966, Chicago 1967, San Francisco 1971, New York City Opera 1982 and Scottish Opera 1988 (Burton 1994, p. 259). Of these, the last two are the most significant, as they attempted to create a definitive version, and are

---

[3] This is taken from one of Bernstein's spoken sections during the 1989 concert performance of *Candide*; text included in a leaflet with the video.

also the productions that exist on recordings. There was another important staging of *Candide* in 1973, without Bernstein's direct involvement, produced by Harold Prince at the Chelsea Theatre in Brooklyn. For this version Hugh Wheeler created a completely new libretto (as Hellman refused to allow her libretto to be altered), Richard Wilbur and Stephen Sondheim revised the lyrics, and the score included songs from 1956 that had been discarded before the original production. These alterations resulted in the first successful version of the show, running for 740 performances. Prince's aim in this version was to create a 'less "important", more irreverent production' (Prince 1976, p. xii); the result was a circus-inspired show, with the audience seated in between performance areas, which were joined by runways and bridges. The orchestra was also divided into four groups, distributed throughout the space in the Chelsea Theatre, at Bernstein's suggestion (an echo of the quadrophonics at the opening of his *Mass*?). This integration brought the performers and the story closer to the audience, in contrast to the 1956 version. As Prince explained: 'One of my major objections to the 1956 production was that it was dominated by ideas rather than characters, which made it cerebral, kept at arm's length. This new production must embrace the audience' (Prince 1976, p. xiii).[4] Although this new show restored some of the fun into Voltaire's tale, there were still some compromises made, as the one-act structure and lively pace meant that some of the musical items from 1956 were cut, including 'What's the Use' and 'Eldorado' (Prince 1976, p. xiii). But the discarded music refused to stay unheard, and in 1982 *Candide* resurfaced yet again, this time in a venue that some of the critics in 1956 had felt would be more appropriate: the opera house. Wheeler expanded his own shorter, lively account and developed it back into a two-act tale that was again directed by Prince, who described the production as a response to the increasing level of crossover between opera and musical:

> The Broadway musical, racing ahead for so many years, is experiencing a lull primarily because of prohibitive costs but also because of the need for finding new directions. Opera, identified during these same years as a kind of museum artifact, is suddenly revitalized – new audiences, new works, a renewed interest in it as theater. (Prince 1985)

---

[4]   The 2003 Birmingham Opera Company production of *Candide*, directed by Graham Vick, had similar aims of connecting audience and performers: the opera was performed in a disused factory in the city, with different scenes being performed in different areas, and with the audience walking around to view the action (although the orchestra remained static on a balcony above the main area). Occasionally the boundaries were blurred further, with the cast walking among the spectators. There were several interesting aspects to the production, including a tank appearing for 'Alleluia', the sheep from Eldorado flying down a 'death-slide' from a raised balcony, and the last scene being located in a sado-masochism club rather than a casino. (Present author was a member of the chorus for this production.)

This element of intersection between opera and musical describes the position that *Candide* had always occupied, falling between the two stools. The enlargement of the libretto created opportunities for the music that had not appeared in 1973, and for other music to be used for the first time. This production played 34 sold-out performances over three seasons at the New York State Theater, a large number for such a staging.[5]

And yet Candide had not finished evolving. Bernstein was still not completely happy with the piece, and John Mauceri, the musical director from 1973 and 1982 who had been responsible for restoring a lot of the original score to the Opera House version, also felt that improvements could still be made.

> Something had gone out of *Candide* after 1971 and the composer wanted it back ... Leonard Bernstein's music has always been about one thing: exploring the differences among people and pleading for tolerance to allow us to live in peace and happiness. This *Candide* had turned into one long joke. The heart, the tears and the faith all clearly part of Voltaire's reason for writing *Candide* were nowhere to be found in the post-Hellman versions. Also the music was all out of order. (Mauceri 1988)

Unfortunately, Hugh Wheeler died before he could adapt his libretto yet again, and the task fell to John Wells. Together with Jonathan Miller, he fashioned a further version that restored many of Voltaire's ideas and which placed the musical items back where they had originally been: the 'Venice Gavotte' returned to Venice and the 'Paris Waltz' and 'Glitter and Be Gay' were both back in Paris. Wells worked with Bernstein in an attempt to create the show that the composer had perhaps always wanted: 'From our original discussions it became clear that what L.B. wanted was more Voltaire. He wanted Candide to sing his lament over Cunegonde's body ... He wanted more of Voltaire's original text' (Wells 1991, p. 3). This version, which Bernstein then conducted in a concert performance in 1989 shortly before his death, marks the final stage of *Candide*'s journey under Bernstein's guidance, and the fact that it is this version that he chose to commit to a recording (and video) emphasizes the importance that the composer placed on this last adaptation.

The number of different versions, some with new words, added songs and altered orders, has resulted in a multitude of items that have, at some time or another, formed part of *Candide*, as demonstrated in Table 4.1.

---

[5] This production was been revived in the same venue, and again by the New York City Opera, for a run of nine performances in March 2005. It is interesting that Tommasini of the *New York Times* criticized the production for its lack of intimacy – 'I only wished that this mostly delightful production ... could be played in a much smaller auditorium than the 2,700-seat New York State Theater' (review from *The New York Times* online, 10 March 2005, www.nytimes.com/2005/03/10/arts/music/10cand.html).

Table 4.1   *Candide* listings – all items listed for 1956 version; some very short instrumental passages and reprises in other productions have been omitted

1956	1973	1982	1988
Broadway	**Chelsea**	**New York Opera House**	**Scottish Opera**
Overture	Overture	Overture	Overture
			3a. Westphalia Chorale
	17. Life is Happiness, Indeed	17. Life is Happiness, Indeed	17. Life is Happiness, Indeed
1. The Best of All Possible Worlds	1. The Best of All Possible Worlds	1. The Best of All Possible Worlds	1. The Best of All Possible Worlds
			25. Universal Good
2. Oh, Happy We	2. Oh, Happy We	2. Oh, Happy We	2. Oh, Happy We
2a. Wedding Procession, Chorale and Battle Scene			
3. Candide Begins His Travels		3. Candide Begins His Travels	
3a. It Must Be So	3a. It Must Be So	3a. It Must Be So	3a. It Must Be So
		2a. Westphalian Fanfare, Chorale And Battle Music	2a. Westphalia Fanfare
			2a. Westphalia Chorale
			2a. Battle Scene
3b. Candide Continues His Travels			17a. Candide's Lament
			24. Dear Boy
			26. Storm Music
			23. Earthquake Music
3c. Entering Lisbon			
4. Lisbon Sequence			4. Auto–da–fé
4a. Fanfares			

1956	1973	1982	1988
4b. Earthquake			
5. It Must Be Me	19. O Miserere		3. Candide Continues His Travels/ It Must Be Me
6. Paris Waltz Scene			6. Paris Waltz Scene
7. Glitter and Be Gay	7. Glitter and Be Gay	7. Glitter and Be Gay	7. Glitter and Be Gay
7a. Paris Waltz Reprise			
		23. Earthquake Music	
		24. Dear Boy	
	4. Auto-da-fè (What a Day)	4. Auto-da-fè	
	17a. This World	17a. Candide's Lament	
8. You Were Dead, You Know	8. You Were Dead, You Know	8. You Were Dead, You Know	8. You Were Dead, You Know
9. Pilgrims' Procession			
9a. Pilgrims' Exit			
11. I Am Easily Assimilated	11. I Am Easily Assimilated	11. I Am Easily Assimilated	11. I Am Easily Assimilated
9b. Governor's Fanfare			
10. My Love	10. My Love	10. My Love	
11. I Am Easily Assimilated			
	20. Barcarolle		
	9. Alleluia		
12. Quartet Finale		12. Quartet Finale	12. Quartet Finale
13. Quiet			
14. Candide's Return from Eldorado	14. Eldorado (instrumental)	14. Ballad of the New World	
14a. Eldorado			
		10. My Love	10. My Love
			13. Quiet

continued

Table 4.1   *concluded*

1956	1973	1982	1988
		20. Barcarolle (The Old Lady's Tale)	9. Alleluia
		9. Alleluia	14. Introduction to Eldorado
			14a. Ballad of Eldorado
			28. Words, Words, Words
	21. Sheep's Song	21. Sheep's Song	
		6. Governor's Waltz	
15. Bon Voyage	15. Bon Voyage	15. Bon Voyage	15. Bon Voyage
		13. Quiet	
15a. Into the Raft			
15b. Raft to Venice			
	22. Constantinople	22. Constantinople Underscore	20. The Kings' Barcarolle
			15c. Money, Money, Money
			29. We Are Women
15c. Venice Gambling Scene			
16. What's the Use		16. What's the Use	16. What's the Use
16a. Venice Continued			
17. Venice Gavotte			17. Venice Gavotte
			30. Nothing More than This
17a. Return to Westphalia			17a. Candide's Lament
			25. Universal Good
18. Finale: Make Our Garden Grow	18. Make Our Garden Grow	18. Make Our Garden Grow	18. Make Our Garden Grow

Notes to Table 4.1

The Westphalia chorales share the same music.

The 'Lisbon Sequence' and 'Auto-da-fé' utilize some of the same music, but with changes between versions. See section later in this chapter.

The 'Paris Waltz Scene' and the 'Governor's Waltz' are the same waltz.

'Pilgrims' Procession' shares the same music as 'Alleluia'.

The 'Venice Gambling Scene' is the same as 'Money, Money, Money'.

'Return to Westphalia' uses the same music as 'Candide's Lament' and 'This World', although the last two contain lyrics.

'Life is Happiness, Indeed' reuses the music of 'The Venice Gavotte'.

The 'Barcarolle' was written for the 1956 version, but was cut prior to opening, and has the same music as 'The Kings' Barcarolle'.

'O Miserere' has the same music as 'It Must be So, 'It Must Be Me' and 'Candide Begins/Continues His Travels'.

'To the New World' shares music with 'Ballad of Eldorado'.

The Entr'acte of the New York Opera House version borrows the 'Into the Raft' music of 1956, and is not the same as the 1988 Entr'acte.

The two 'Earthquake' music segments, from 1956 and 1982/1988, are different.

Other points: 'Dear Boy' was written for 1956, but cut prior to opening; 'We Are Women' was composed for the 1959 London production; 'Sheep's Song' has the same music as an unconnected song, 'Lonely Men of Harvard', which in turn is based on 'Fernando's Lullaby', a different song cut from the 1956 *Candide* (e-mail to author from Charlie Harmon, 11 May 2000); 'Universal Good' was originally part of Candide's aria 'Get You Up', which was cut before the first performance.

In order to narrow down the amount of material considered, and provide a focused discussion, this chapter concentrates on the music written for the 1956 production, with some mention of other music when relevant; there is one section that looks at the evolution of the Lisbon Scene through four of the incarnations of the operetta/opera. This is because the show which appeared on Broadway in 1956, despite changes that had to be made due to outside pressures, nevertheless reflects the original objectives of both Bernstein and Hellman. Subsequent productions did not use Hellman's libretto, and so an essential part of the first version, however successful or unsuccessful, is detached from *Candide*. Of course, it is impossible to isolate Bernstein's intentions amongst those of the other collaborators, but perhaps, through the various manifestations of the show in which he had some influence, Bernstein managed to reassert some of his original ideas that may have been subverted by the process of collaboration that dictated the form of the first production. The full score of *Candide*, based on the Scottish Opera version, states that 'this score incorporates the composer's final intentions regarding *Candide*' (score, front-pages), but one cannot help thinking that had Bernstein lived longer he would have felt drawn back to this work for further refinement.

The fact that *Candide* ended up in the opera house is not surprising when Bernstein's compositional intentions are considered. In 1954, while he and Hellman were working on the show, Bernstein taught a series of seminars at Brandeis University, based on this work (Gottlieb 1997, p. 5). From the notes he made prior to these seminars, the direction he hoped the piece would take are clear, as under the subtitle of 'music' he lists the following points: 'opera, operetta, singspiel, comic opera? How much, in relation to dialogue? Style? (Style of lyrics?) "Weight"'.[6] There seems no indication of a Broadway influence, and the operatic aims are underlined by the list of works that he intended to study, and probably use within his teaching: *Porgy*, *Carousel*, *Fidelio*, *Carmen*, *Orpheus* or *Perichole*, *Don Giovanni*, *Magic Flute*, *Rake's Progress*, *Regina*, Britten, Verdi, Puccini, Wagner. Although Bernstein had already completed an opera in *Trouble in Tahiti*, that was an American opera, and in this new work he was turning to the Old World for his inspiration, the result of which creates a survey of European, and some New World, musical styles. Wells recognized Bernstein's passion for the old traditions, and the reasons behind it:

> he loved Voltaire's old European jokes. L.B.'s roots were deep in Europe: he spoke German, Italian and French well enough to be able to mimic accents and turns of phrase, and a lot of his best stories were about the same society Voltaire had satirized, adjusting now to the political changes of the late 20th century. (Wells 1991, p. 3)

---

[6]   Notes for seminar on *Candide* in Box 72, folder 31, LBC,

Hellman's plot begins, as does Voltaire's, in Westphalia, where we are introduced to the principal characters and to the teachings of Pangloss, embodied in song. As Candide and Cunegonde's marriage ceremony begins, the Hessian army invades and seems to kill the Baron, his daughter (Cunegonde), her brother Maximillian and their teacher (Pangloss). Candide sets off into the world alone, and finds himself in Lisbon just before the famous earthquake. He is reunited with Pangloss, who had miraculously escaped death at the hands of the Hessians; unfortunately the teacher is sentenced to death by the Inquisition, and killed again at the end of the scene. Our hero travels to Paris where, following a ball, he discovers Cunegonde is still alive, although she is now a courtesan. Candide murders her two lovers, and the pair escape together with an old lady who has been attending Cunegonde. They join a group of pilgrims journeying to the New World, but unfortunately the trio is sold into slavery in Buenos Aires. Here Candide meets Martin, a pessimist played by the same actor playing Pangloss, but who is philosophically the antithesis of his old teacher. Maximillian reappears as an officer serving the Governor of Buenos Aires, and is reunited with his sister. However, he refuses to let his sister marry Candide, so our hero commits his third murder and dispatches her brother. Cunegonde is taken under the 'protection' of the Governor, and Candide escapes again, this time setting off for the mythical Eldorado, the land where Martin had lived until being sent away for being miserable in such a wonderful and pleasant place. The first act ends with Candide bemoaning his separation from his beloved, Cunegonde explaining that she will only endure the Governor's attentions in order to protect her sweetheart, the Old Lady celebrating their new-found comfort, and the Governor resolving not to wed Cunegonde as the passion always dies after marriage.

Act II opens still in Buenos Aires, where Cunegonde and the Old Lady are bored with their opulent lifestyle, and the Governor is tired of their constant complaining. Candide returns to reclaim his love, laden with riches from Eldorado, but she has been packed off on a cotton boat, together with the crone. The Governor sells Candide an unseaworthy boat for an exorbitant price, and as it sinks into the sea, our hero is left on a raft with Martin. The pessimist is dragged into the sea by a shark, but Pangloss reappears once more, having escaped from pirates who just happened to be in the vicinity, and the pair travel on to Venice. Cunegonde and the Old Lady are working in a gambling house, and Candide and his teacher arrive searching for the women. The young lovers meet again, but not under favourable circumstances: both are masked and Cunegonde is attempting to steal Candide's remaining gold. Disgusted by the behaviour she has been reduced to, he leaves, followed by the now unemployed Cunegonde, the Old Lady and Pangloss, who has lost all his money in the casino. They return to a ruined Westphalia, and find Maximillian alive once again. Candide dismisses his travelling companions as liars, complainers and shirkers before again asking Cunegonde to marry him, although his hopes and optimism have been tempered by his experiences: 'What we wanted, we will not have. The way we did love, we will not love again. Come now, let us take what we have and love as we are' (Hellman 1957, p. 141). All that is left for them to do is make the best of the situation, and to turn to a more practical approach to life. In Voltaire's final words: 'il faut cultiver notre jardin' (1964, p. 108).[7]

Sevenths and Octaves

The opening of the Overture trumpets one of the intervallic motifs used in *Candide*, distinctive in its use of the minor seventh resolving upwards to the octave (see Example 4.1). This phrase, which opens the whole show, is drawn from the first song,[8] 'The Best of All Possible Worlds', in which Dr Pangloss, a teacher of 'metaphysico-theologo-cosmolo-nigo-logy' (Voltaire 1947, p. 20), presents a lesson to his pupils at the castle at Thunder-ten-tronckh. He inquires whether his pupils have 'any questions?', and the rising musical line naturally echoes the enquiring nature of the text. The flattened seventh in the phrase, appearing on the notes D–C♮–D in the song, helps the motif to serve as a modulatory figure in the music, which moves from D major to its subdominant G major.

Example 4.1 'Overture', bb. 1–2

Pangloss's lesson in love and happiness is followed by a demonstration of his teaching illustrated by the marriage of Candide and Cunegonde, although the happy ceremony is interrupted by the outbreak of war. The musical figure returns, slightly rhythmically altered, as a fanfare in the 'Wedding Procession' that precedes the nuptials. It would appear that the motif is associated with Pangloss, but this proposal is frustrated by the fact that there are no references to it in the final song in which he sings, 'The Venice Gavotte'. It is also absent from in 'Dear Boy', a song for the character that was cut before the show reached Broadway but which was reintroduced in later versions. The motif would seem to be connected to the philosophical ideas presented by Pangloss, rather than with the Doctor himself. Jaensch suggests that it is associated with their home, as he labels it the 'Westphalia Fanfare' (2003, p. 117). However, the figure is also employed twice in the Lisbon scene, reappearing in a slightly varied form. It is first heard during the 'Lisbon Sequence' beneath a syncopated melody, as the local crowd prays for mercy during the earthquake. Later in the same scene, fanfares are heard during the

[7] 'We must go and work in the garden' (Voltaire 1947, p. 144).
[8] In the 1956 version. In some of the later productions, the song was moved; see Table 4.1.

but the consequent is extended by a further rising second, a pattern which could be seen as a kind of inversion of the original four-note motif, with an extension of the reaching phrase. As already seen in his earlier works, Bernstein has used simple variation and development techniques again to produce a musical phrase from an intervallic cell.

The motif next appears in the 'Quartet Finale', in the section sung by Candide, a development of the music from the 'Paris Waltz'. The rhythms have been ironed out, and the music changes character from a light-hearted dance to a melancholy love song as the hero contemplates leaving Cunegonde again (see Example 4.6). This music then forms the accompaniment for Cunegonde's own verse, which follows, although the first descending interval is altered from a tone to a semitone (C–C–B♮–A) so that the figure fits in the new key of C major. Placing Candide's music beneath that of his sweetheart reinforces the sentiment of Cunegonde's words. Later in the second act, the basic four-note motif recurs in 'Return to Westphalia', as the characters finally journey back to where they started, the place where the optimism and hope began.[10] The motif appears six times in this instrumental number, and there is also one appearance of the extended ascending pattern B♭–B♭–C–D.

Example 4.6 'Quartet Finale', bb. 1–4

The final number in the operetta, 'Make Our Garden Grow', also begins with the motif, here presented in a slower tempo and with added suspensions (see Example 4.7). The impression of 'reaching' extends even higher in this introduction, as in the varied second phrase the music ascends two tones above the octave leap (b. 4). The key here is deceptive though, as there is a G pedal that could be considered the dominant, taking into account the earlier occurrences of the motif. However, Bernstein changed the tonal context here, and it is the final note of the phrase, the B, that is the dominant. The music 'lifts' into the unexpected key of E major for the first verse, and the first vocal phrase is a development of the motif, with a tonic added within the octave leap: $\hat{5}\hat{1}\hat{5}\hat{4}\hat{3}$. It is here that the emotional connotation of the $\hat{4}$ can most clearly be felt, as the note 'pulls' to resolve onto

---

[10] In Voltaire's tale, the adventure ends not in Westphalia, but in Turkey, and Cunegonde's brother is sent to Rome rather than remaining with the others.

Example 4.7 'Make Our Garden Grow', bb. 1–9

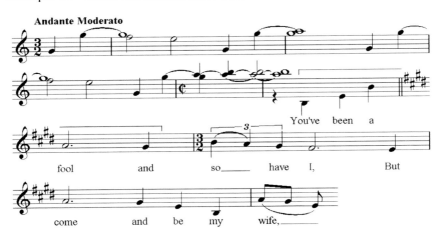

the $\hat{3}$. Within this version of the motif in the song, the appoggiatura effect is emphasized by the parallel third below the A in the accompaniment (the F♯), which forms a seventh that resolves down onto the tonic.

The motif appears in a less prominent position in 'You Were Dead, You Know', developing out of a figure in the melody of an ascending sixth / descending second (G–E–D). In Cunegonde's line at the end of the verse, this evolves into G–G–F, with Candide singing the original phrase beneath this as harmony. This fragment of the motif is heard three times, and then in the final vocal phrase the voices repeat their penultimate notes (the octave Gs), while the orchestra plays the F, using this as a springboard into the first phrase of the 'Paris Waltz Scene' music.

The aforementioned 'Return to Westphalia' originally contained lyrics and was called 'Candide's Lament', but this form of the song was cut before Broadway. In the 1982 New York Opera and 1988 Scottish Opera versions the vocal line of the song was reinstated, and in each case occurs near the beginning of the show, before the other songs containing the motif (see Table 4.1). This was clearly meant to be its original position, as indicated in an audition précis for *Candide*,[11] and thus it is important that the first appearance of what John Mauceri calls the 'Cunegonde theme' (1988), contains the simplest version of the motif; in the subsequent presentations, the motif is more extended and developed. Mauceri's label also underlines the motif's dramatic function and its link to Candide's love for Cunegonde. 'Candide's Lament' is sung by the hero when he first believes his beloved is dead; the 'Paris Waltz' is heard just before we discover Cunegonde's true fate; 'You Were Dead, You Know' is sung by both characters as they are briefly reunited; in the 'Quartet Finale', Candide is bemoaning being separated once more from Cunegonde; and they are finally reunited and reconciled to their less than

---

[11]   Box 74, folder 11, LBC.

perfect lives in 'Make Our Garden Grow'. In the same way that the interval of a fifth accompanies the development of Baker and Ruth's relationship in *Wonderful Town*, so the 'Cunegonde' motif follows her relationship with Candide. That the 'Cunegonde' motif should be a variation of the 'optimism' motif indicates that Candide sees his happiness as being dependent on his being with Cunegonde – his optimism derives from his love. In fact, the music for 'Candide's Lament' was written before work on *Candide* began, in the form of one of Bernstein's short piano pieces (see Example 4.8).

Example 4.8 'Cesarina Riso', bb. 1–4, from manuscript

This piano piece is dedicated to Cesarina Riso, a pianist and friend of Bernstein, and was written on paper left over from *Wonderful Town* (the show name is printed on the bottom). It then became one of a set of *Six Children's Pieces*, before then being 'Ilana – the Dreamer' in a collection called *Six Sabras*. As this final version was written on Israeli music paper, this suggests that the piece may have originally been written between September 1953, the opening of *Wonderful Town*, and November 1953, which was the next occasion he journeyed to Israel before beginning work on *Candide* in 1954.[12] If this is the case, it was among the first music written for the show, which may account for the repeated use of the motif within the show.

There are marked similarities between the motifs in *Candide* and those of Bernstein's contemporary works, which involve ascending sevenths, octaves or ninths, followed by a step up or down. This comparison is not surprising, considering the interwoven nature of the composition processes, as outlined earlier in the chapter. The 'optimism' and 'Cunegonde' motifs can be compared to a theme from *On the Waterfront*, two fragments from the opening phrase of *Serenade*, the opening phrase from 'Somewhere' from *West Side Story* and a phrase from the first music heard in *Salome*. Each of these occurs within a romantic context: in *On the Waterfront*, the theme is representative of Edie and Terry's relationship; *Serenade* is based on Plato's *Symposium*, which itself is a paean to love, the first

---

[12]   Gottlieb points out that Bernstein was also in Israel in 1948 and 1950, and so it could also have been written after any of these visits. He suggests that the piece could have existed as the anniversary piece for Cesarina Riso and as the *Sabra* at the same time, rather than the former being converted into the latter (2003, p. 9). As the manuscripts are not dated, it is unlikely we will ever know the real date of composition.

movement being described by Bernstein as 'a lyrical oration to Eros, god of love' (programme notes, in score 1956); 'Somewhere' is one of the principal love songs in *West Side Story*, despite not being sung by either of the main romantic characters; in *Salome* it is lust rather than love that drives forward the tragedy, both that of Herod for his step-daughter, and that of Salome for Jokanaan. According to Larry Kert, who played Tony in the original *West Side Story*, 'Somewhere' was written at around the same time as *On the Town* (quoted in Peyser 1987, p. 239), so this was probably the first of these pieces including such a motif to be composed. Bernstein received the draft of the first four scenes of the Romeo and Juliet show in April 1949 (Burton 1994, p. 144), but work on the project began in earnest in August 1955, after the completion of *On the Waterfront* and *Serenade*. Perhaps the song had remained in his subconscious throughout the creation of the other pieces, and resurfaced later.

Bernstein's *Urmotiv* is only found in one number in *Candide*, the concluding 'Make Our Garden Grow' (see Example 4.7). In the original version of the show, this can be considered to be the only depiction of genuine emotion amongst the parody, satire and melodrama. Indeed, the sincerity of the final chorus, together with *Candide*'s 'It Must be So' and 'Eldorado', appears somewhat at odds with the remainder of the score (Mordden 1998, p. 179). The fact that Bernstein reserves his characteristic motif for the closing number indicates the importance that he places on the sentiments it embodies: the hope for a better future. This is not the mindless optimism of the opening of the story, but a confidence and expectation tempered by their experiences, outlined by the speech Candide makes prior to singing the first verse of 'Make Our Garden Grow':

> We will not think noble because we are not noble. We will not live in beautiful harmony because there is no such thing in this world, nor there should be. We promise only to do our best and live out our lives. Dear God, that's all we can promise in truth. (Hellman 1957, pp. 141–2)

Rhythm, Parody and Pastiche

Rhythm

An important aspect of *Candide*, one that distanced it from Bernstein's earlier popular musical theatre works (not including *Trouble in Tahiti*) and aligned it with his orchestral and 'highbrow' compositions, is the rhythmic language that he employed. As Laird explains, Bernstein's rhythmic characteristics include 'the regular use of unusual or shifting meters in a regular pattern, in slow, medium, and fast tempos; [and] movements in which irregular rhythms are notated through such devices as rapidly shifting meters, groups of two and three eighth notes in irregular groupings, and rich use of syncopation' (2002, p. 22). However, in the Tin Pan Alley and Broadway-derived songs of *On the Town* and *Wonderful Town* he had avoided such complexities and employed simpler metres, as was fitting for the genre. Even though *Candide* was destined for Broadway, it was always going to be atypical within the usual offerings seen there, especially when Bernstein's compositional intentions are considered. By employing the more complex rhythms that he usually reserved for his more serious music, Bernstein found a way of creating a distinction between his musical comedies and this new comic operetta. This can first be seen in the Overture, where the second subject is presented in patterns of ¢ and $\frac{3}{2}$ (see Example 4.9a); this is the melody from 'Oh, Happy We', the rhythm of which Laird describes as seeming 'at the same time out of place and curiously right' (2002, p. 23). In the song, however, the tune is presented in $\frac{7}{4}$, with the rhythmic values in diminution (see Example 4.9b). It is unclear why Bernstein felt it necessary to alter the division of the bars in the Overture, as he certainly never tried to avoid such time signatures in his other orchestral writing: the second movement of his *Jeremiah* symphony used metres of $\frac{3}{8}$, $\frac{4}{8}$, $\frac{5}{8}$, $\frac{6}{8}$, $\frac{7}{8}$, $\frac{8}{8}$, $\frac{3}{4}$ and c in various patterns and sequences.

Example 4.9 Rhythmic comparison of 'Overture' and 'Oh, Happy We'

(a) 'Overture', bb. 83–8
(b) 'Oh, Happy We', bb. 4–5

A similar method of rhythmic division as can be seen in the Overture can also be observed in the 'Pilgrims' Procession' (see Example 4.10). The vocal phrases in the main sections are written as eight bars of alternating $\frac{3}{2}$ and ¢, and this music is obviously related to the 'Overture' and 'Oh, Happy We', both rhythmically and melodically, with similar descending patterns. There is a sense that the religiosity of the song, emphasized by the Bach-style chorale nature of the melody, is corrupted by the interruption of the phrase caused by the 'removal' of the last minim beat. This is perhaps an omen of the fate of the pilgrims, their mission cut short by being sold into slavery by the captain of the ship taking them to the New World. There is also some foreshadowing of the 'Procession' music in the

Example 4.10 'The Pilgrims' Procession', bb. 21–4

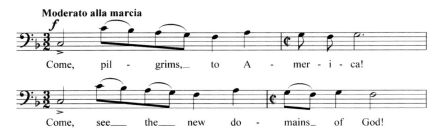

instrumental introduction to this piece, where there is a reversed pattern of ¢ $\frac{3}{2}$ ¢ $\frac{3}{2}$, followed by six bars of ¢.

The 'Venice Gambling Scene' also has repeating patterns of time signatures, following the Croupier's opening cry, of $\frac{2}{4}$ $\frac{3}{8}$ $\frac{3}{4}$. The 'Ballad of Eldorado' is written in $\frac{5}{8}$, although there are brief excursions into $\frac{3}{4}$ and $\frac{7}{8}$ at the end of each verse, but Bernstein manipulates the beat in different ways within the song. In the first verse the five beats are subdivided into 3+2, while the contrasting middle section sees the beat divided into 2+3. To a lesser extent, the technique is used in 'Return to Westphalia', where the first four bars alternate between $\frac{3}{4}$ and c, but this is not a consistent feature within the number.

As well as his use of quintuple and septuple time signatures, Bernstein 'disturbs' the natural metre of the music in *Candide* by employing strong cross-rhythms. Strikingly in 'Bon Voyage', the ¢ metre is juxtaposed by phrases in $\frac{3}{2}$ and $\frac{3}{4}$ (indicated on the score). The insecure pulse reflects the dubious nature of the Governor's offer of an unsafe boat to Candide, an act outlined in the song.

In the coda of 'Glitter and Be Gay', and also in the corresponding section of the 'Overture', the music takes an unexpected turn, as Cunegonde's 'four-square' crotchet-based melody is accompanied by a $\frac{3}{8}$ bass line. This underlines the contradiction between the words, as Cunegonde sings of her supposed 'dreadful shame' at her imposed lavish environment and her beautiful ornaments, and the character's true feelings about her present situation. Bernstein also incorporates a Spanish feel to the music, and there exists a rhythmic resemblance to part of *España* by Chabrier, which included juxtaposed duple time over a triple-time metre, the reverse of 'Glitter and Be Gay'; other influences on this song will be discussed in the subsequent section of this chapter.

A secondary use of cross-rhythms occurs in 'Best of All Possible Worlds', at the end of the verse, accompanying and emphasizing the title words. The fact that the rhythm of these words is at odds with the pulse of the music suggests that Pangloss's espousal of Leibniz's theory may not be the best course of action, a point that is proved to be true by the end of the adventure. There is also a hint of Cole Porter in the hemiola, which is reminiscent of the first number in his *Kiss Me, Kate* (1948), 'Another Op'nin', Another Show'.

Bernstein also exploited the shifting and unstable characteristics of the unusual time signature in his music for *On the Waterfront*. The *Presto Barbaro* section, which embodies what Bernstein calls the element of violence (programme notes, in Gottlieb 1964, p. 232), uses alternating bars of ¢ and $\frac{3}{4}$ with a rhythmic ostinato that accentuates the fluctuating pulse. In the film, the music accompanies the opening shots, showing the first scenes of the waterfront itself, and of Johnny Friendly, the union leader. Terry Molloy, an ex-boxer who runs errands for Friendly, is seen at night walking from the pier to a tenement block, as 'the music takes on a dangerous quality, with particular urgency in the lower strings' (Burlingame 2003, p. 136). The musical tension mounts as Molloy tricks his friend Joey Doyle into going onto the roof where Friendly's henchmen are waiting, and the music abruptly ends as Doyle is thrown from the top of the building.

In Bernstein's violin concerto, *Serenade*, the allegro of the first movement begins with a repeating $\frac{3}{8}$ $\frac{2}{4}$ pattern (subdivided $\frac{7}{8}$ phrases?), while the third movement contains a $\frac{2}{4}$ $\frac{5}{8}$ sequence (overall a $\frac{9}{8}$ figure, but with quavers divided into 4+5 rather than 3+3+3). Bernstein's music for *The Lark* includes many changes of time signature, including a repeating $\frac{6}{8}$ $\frac{3}{4}$ rhythm that would later reappear in *West Side Story*, but not in a way that regularly subdivides an odd number of beats. The only song in the set with consistent changes is the 'Requiem', with the three-bar phrases in $\frac{6}{8}$ $\frac{5}{8}$ $\frac{6}{8}$.

The employment of metres in five and seven, and such consistent use of cross-rhythms were methods employed by Bernstein to ensure a difference between his American popular-song-based Broadway shows, and this European-derived operetta. These unusual and vibrant rhythms reflect the influences of jazz and Latin American music as previously discussed in connection with his other shows, and had been used in his music as early as *The Birds* in 1938. In addition, however, there is a further rhythmic stimulus seen in *Candide*, a neo-classical tendency to disrupt the flow of the music. Bernstein used rhythmic twists to disrupt the classical line, so that where the music of the 'Overture' would be expected to be in two four-bar phrases in ¢, the fourth and eighth bars are both cut short by a minim beat, creating bars of $\frac{3}{2}$. This rhythmic distortion is common in neo-classicism, as it manipulates the balanced and measured phrases of classical music. In *The Rake's Progress*, one of the pieces Bernstein studied whilst writing *Candide*, Stravinsky was quite free with his rhythms, changing time signatures and odd accents within phrases; the opening of Act I begins with music that uses time signatures of $\frac{2}{4}$, $\frac{3}{8}$ and $\frac{3}{4}$. Another neo-classical piece that employed these twists is Prokofiev's *Classical Symphony*, where the first movement includes shortened phrases that cause the music to 'jolt' into the next section. With both Prokofiev's and Bernstein's music, there is the sense of the composer 'fooling' the audience, disrupting the predictability of the expected musical line and interrupting the natural order. So, although Bernstein embraced old styles and traditions, he combined them with more modern ideas to create his unique sound, so that the music is on one hand familiar, but also fresh and exciting on the other.

Pastiche and Parody

In the previous chapter, pastiche in *Wonderful Town* was discussed, placing the show firmly in the 1930s. To what extent does Bernstein employ this technique in *Candide*, considering the range of styles and genres of music used within the show? As we already know, pastiche is the use of music to define and maintain a specific period in time, or a geographical location. The inclusion of music for an ironic or comic effect, by implication or by ridicule, is not pastiche but parody. In *Candide*, as in *Wonderful Town*, there are two main types of derivative writing: the use of locale-specific dances and using recognizable elements of another composer or style. In terms of locations, Voltaire's 1759 novella *Candide* is picaresque in nature, moving through many countries and across oceans. Hellman's 1956 libretto reduced the number of settings from 13 to five, resulting in the action taking place in Westphalia, Lisbon, Paris, Buenos Aires and Venice, and then returning to Westphalia. However, the music presented in each city is not usually native to the specific country. A Schottische appears on the wrong side of the Atlantic in Buenos Aires, a Gavotte is heard in Venice, and Viennese waltzes occur in Paris and Venice. The setting of 1759 may also appear a little early for a waltz to appear, but Bernstein stated that in the creation of *Candide* the time span was extended, a reasonable action when all the travelling in the story is taken into account. According to Bernstein, 'we are concerned with periods ranging from 1750 to 1830. In this show we play hopscotch with periods, jumping around in style' (1956, p. 3). Regardless of this, each of the items is a well-crafted piece of music based on clear stylistic characteristics, but each functions as a parody rather than pastiche, as they serve no defining purpose in their placing. Only two numbers occur in their 'natural' settings, and of these only one is also temporally correct. 'I Am Easily Assimilated', set to a distinctive tango rhythm, does feature in one of the Buenos Aires scenes; however, the eighteenth century is approximately 100 years too early for such a dance. The only consistent pastiche item is the 'Chorale' in the first scene, set in the Castle Thunder-ten-Tronck in Westphalia: following a procession, the loyal subjects of the Baron sing the chorale as they begin the wedding festivities. The music of this chorus item is based directly on the verse of 'Best of All Possible Worlds', where Pangloss had anticipated the marriage, and announced the 'happy celebration'. The melody of the earlier song becomes the soprano line in a Bach-style harmonization, subtly changed to sound more suitable and solemn. The lengths of phrases and the positions of pauses match those of the first half of Bach's setting of 'Ein' feste Burg ist unser Gott', and the 1982 New York Opera House version of *Candide* juxtaposed the words of the German chorale on to Bernstein's music. Although the part writing is characteristic of chorales, there are unexpected turns in other elements of the piece. The texture builds gradually, expanding first from unison octaves to two-part harmony, with soprano and alto lines echoed at the octave by tenors and basses. Next there are three vocal lines (tenors tacet), before expanding to full four parts for the final two phrases (see Example 4.11). The texture only affects the harmony in the second

Example 4.11 'Wedding Procession, Chorale and Battle Scene', bb. 7–16

phrase, where the doubling results in second inversion chords, very atypical for Bach. In the subsequent phrases there are several anachronistic chords: half-diminished seventh chords, tonally ambiguous chords containing clashes, and very uncommon cadences, ending on unusual triads. This appears to be a further example of neo-classicism: using the basic outline and style of the chorale, but combining this with Bernstein's own harmonic ideas.

As seen previously in *Wonderful Town*, Bernstein again creates pastiche items by using familiar elements of a specific composer or composition. One song in *Candide*, 'Glitter and be Gay', is particularly subjected to this kind of comparison. This is frequently labelled as a parody of the Jewel song, 'Ah! Je ris de me voir', from Gounod's *Faust* (Secrest 1995, p. 208).[13] Despite sharing subject and sentiment – jewels and love of them – the two songs have little else in common. 'Glitter and Be Gay' begins in the same $\frac{3}{4}$ metre as the Jewel Song, but moves

---

[13] For example, Schwarte lists the aria's influence as 'bravura coloratura aria, "Jewel Song" from Gounod's *Faust*, *Valse Triste*, Satie's *Gymnopédies*, Jitterbug, Galop, Lehár and Strauss' (1995, p. 579).

into $\frac{4}{4}$ on two occasions, with an intervening return to triple time. The changes underline the structure of the song: A–B–A^1–B–coda, a two-tempo rondo, with a faster closing cabaletta section in the style of a Rossini aria. This is comparable with the A–B–A^1–coda form of Gounod's piece, although the latter contains no major changes in tempo, and certainly no alternating time signatures. However, the florid coloratura writing of Bernstein is definitely not derived from the *Faust* aria. The arpeggiated nature of some of the figures instead suggests the influence of the Queen of the Night's aria in *Die Zauberflöte*, but the ornamented melodies of Bellini were perhaps a more probable source of inspiration. In February and March of 1955, Bernstein had taken time out of his work on *Candide* to conduct Bellini's *La Sonnambula* at La Scala in Milan, with Maria Callas in the title role (Burton 1994, p. 243). Florid lines can certainly be found frequently in the lines of the principals, some of which are comparable with phrases in Bernstein's song. There is also some similarity with the melisma in Rosina's aria from *Il Barbiere di Siviglia* 'Contro un cor che accende amore'.

Secrest draws a parallel between 'You Were Dead, You Know' and the light-operetta music performed by Nelson Eddy and Jeanette MacDonald (1995, p. 208). Although there are some 10th harmonies in 'Indian Love Call' from *Rose Marie*, the music is stylistically very distant from 'You Were Dead, You Know'. It appears more likely that the main influence for Bernstein's duet comes from his experience of Bellini's score, pointed out by Burton: 'when the lovers are reunited for the surrealistic duet "You Were Dead, You Know", they warble in thirds and sixths in the best *bel canto* style, remembered from *La Sonnambula*' (Burton 1994, p. 260). Candide and Cunegonde only sing together for 12 bars out of the 78 of the song, but when they do they sing in parallel 10ths, and there is a section in one of the duets in *La Sonnambula* that bears a strong resemblance to some of Bernstein's writing: in Bellini's aria 'Son geloso' there is a short unaccompanied cadenza-like passage, similar to the end of 'You Were Dead You Know' in that the lovers sing separately, and then join together for a final flourish.

A resemblance has been suggested between Pangloss's catalogue of women in the 'Lady Silly, Lady Frilly' section of 'Venice Gavotte' and Count Danilo's list of the girls at Maxim's in *Die Lustige Witwe* by Lehár (Sutton 1995, p. 396) but there is no correlation in the music for the two songs. More interesting is the similarity of the music of one of Lehár's songs 'A Melody in Waltz Time', with that of 'Paris Waltz', where both share a descending opening phrase, and a sense of cross-rhythm. The actual melody of Bernstein's waltz resembles more closely the waltz from *Der Rosenkavalier*, especially the octave jump in the second phrase.

'Oh, Happy We' incorporates something of the joy and excitement of Papageno and Papagena's duet in *Die Zauberflöte*, as both songs tell of the anticipated happiness to come. However, unlike their earlier counterparts, there is no place where Candide and Cunegonde sing in 3rds (10ths), betraying the difference in the views they hold on marriage. The Mozartian pair also sing together in harmony for most of the song, as they share a single vision of their future, while when the opportunity arises for Bernstein's lovers, they end up singing in canon, their music being slightly unsynchronized, just as their opinions are.

Another influence mentioned by Bernstein's commentators is that of Gilbert and Sullivan,[14] perhaps a surprising element to be found in the work of an American composer who, up to this point, had written his theatre works under the influence of Tin Pan Alley. However, as Burton points out, Bernstein had been involved in amateur productions of the work of the British pair during his youth: *The Mikado* and *HMS Pinafore* with the Sharon Players in 1935 and 1936, and *The Pirates of Penzance* at Camp Onota in 1937. It appears that the music from these productions stayed with Bernstein, and shaped his contributions to *Candide*. Perhaps the most obvious is the use of the chorus in 'Best of All Possible Worlds' and 'Dear Boy'; Schwarte also hears the echo of Sullivan in 'The Ballad of Eldorado', 'Bon Voyage' and the later addition 'Life is Happiness Indeed' (though, interestingly, not in the 'Venice Gavotte', on which the latter is based) (1995, pp. 579–80). In the first of these songs, 'Best of All Possible Worlds', there is repetition and variation of solo material by the chorus. In the former, the final four lines of Pangloss's verse are repeated by the chorus, the first couplet being transposed up a 4th (from F♯ to B), while the second is sung at the same pitch as Pangloss's presentation. In 'Dear Boy', a further number for Pangloss, the refrain is extended and completed by tenors and basses, who sing music developed from the first two bars of the refrain. This technique, where the chorus echoes the sentiments and music of the soloist, appears frequently in Sullivan's operettas, and there are examples in the three shows Bernstein knew. There is also a further example of the chorus 'echo' device in the 'Ballad of Eldorado', where they have simple contrapuntal phrases at the end of each verse section.

The 'Venice Gavotte' also utilizes a compositional technique that appears briefly in *Pinafore*: in 'Sir Joseph's barge is seen', the men of the ship sing one melody, followed by another sung by the ladies. Then, for eight bars, both tunes are juxtaposed, with the basses singing an ostinato in fifths beneath. This resembles the melodies that Bernstein creates in the 'Venice Gavotte', although more complex than Sullivan's writing, where two melodies are sung separately at first, and then placed in counterpoint to each other. An earlier example of this technique was written for *On the Town*, but it was cut before reaching Broadway. 'Say When' and 'I'm Afraid It's Love', to be sung by the two couples Claire and Ozzie, and Chip and Hildy in two separate apartments on the stage, were written in a way that allowed them to be sung together.[15]

It is interesting to consider whether Bernstein's experience of *Pinafore* influenced him to write the 'Barcarolle' which was cut from the original production,

[14] Burton 1994, p. 260; Gräwe 1989, p. 54; Jaensch 2003, p. 104; Myers 1998, p. 94; Schwarte 1995, pp. 579–80; Secrest 1995, p. 208.

[15] On a manuscript of 'Say When' in the Library of Congress, the melody of 'I'm Afraid It's Love' can be faintly seen on a stave over the chorus, where it was written before being later erased.

as Sullivan had written a similar piece for a hidden chorus of ladies in his operetta. The six deposed kings who sing the number in *Candide* were, in Voltaire's novella, all at a meal in an inn. However, the kings were transferred to a galley in Hellman's book, thus opening the opportunity for a barcarolle.

The song 'Quiet' can also be considered a parody. This number begins with a 12-tone row, which is also used in transposition (P2 and P11), and inversion (I1 and I11) (see Example 4.12). The lyrics of the song tell of the boredom that the Old Lady and Cunegonde are experiencing in the palace of the Governor of Buenos Aires, with the chromaticism reflecting the anxiety and tension of the situation. The use of such music demonstrates Bernstein's feelings about serial music, and he had obviously made his opinions clear, as Gottlieb describes the song as an 'inside joke of a twelve-tone row in a song about boredom' (1997, p. 5).

Apart from the tango, all the music that is parodied is European, underlining the influences on *Candide*, and also emphasizing the origin of the story itself.

Example 4.12 'Quiet', bb. 1–3

Evolution of a Scene

The degree of metamorphoses that *Candide* underwent over the years can be characterized by the changes that took place in one particular scene: the Lisbon sequence. This depicts the earthquake of 1746, and is a fictional *auto-da-fé*, carried out to appease Nature and prevent further disaster. As already discussed in this chapter, this scene reflected Hellman's and Bernstein's opinion of the political atmosphere in the US at the time. Through its various incarnations, this sequence has been subjected to more alterations than other section of the work, with musical ideas coming and going, being combined and recombined, and with changes in dialogue, characters and the progression of events.

In the original 1759 story, Voltaire's scene is quite short, and opens after the earthquake. Pangloss and Candide are arrested, imprisoned for a week, and then brought out in sacrificial cassocks and paper mitres. They are to be punished, along with 'a Basque, convicted of marrying his godmother, and two Portuguese Jews who had refused to eat bacon with their chicken' (Voltaire 1947, p. 36). There is no actual inquisition or trial in Voltaire's tale, and following the burning of the other

At last we can be cheery,
The danger's passed us by.
So chant a Dies Irae!
We've hung the bastards high.

We've had a nice fiesta,
The heretics are dead.
It's time for our siesta,
So let's go home to bed.
                    (Hellman 1972, p. 631)

When Wheeler and Prince reshaped the scene for the 1976 Chelsea version, they looked at both Hellman and Voltaire's renderings for their inspiration, and also delved into Bernstein's trunk of unused music. In this new account, the earthquake now occurs before our pair reaches Lisbon, and Pangloss and Candide are brought back together following a shipwreck and are quickly arrested for heresy by agents of the Inquisition. They are brought to the market place where the crowd is now gathering specifically to witness the *auto-da-fé*. The market music 'Look at this, look at that' is lyrically transformed into 'What a day, what a day, For an auto-da-fé' (Bernstein's original lyrics for the same music). Instead of the Arab and Casmira arriving in the market, Wheeler introduces a young girl representing Our Lady of Opporto, who does not sing, but is brought in to suitably Spanish/Latin-American tinged music. The Grand Inquisitor enters, and we now have two inquisitions that are sung rather than spoken, between which the crowd sing 'What a lovely day, what a jolly day, what a day for a holiday!': a flippant portrayal of their bloodthirsty desire for public executions. The music halts briefly for Pangloss and Candide's hearings, and they are swiftly sentenced to hanging and flogging respectively. The music restarts for the punishments, and what had been the crowd's prayer for themselves in 1956 becomes an accompaniment for Candide's beating. The scene ends with a reprise of 'What a Lovely Day' before Pangloss's final speech. His 'dying' words are now even more ridiculously optimistic, considering his situation: he praises the invention of the rope and the noose, and extols the wonder of the neck, leading to the natural conclusion of his hanging.

As Wheeler was also responsible for the libretto for the 1982 Opera House staging, the general shape of this adaptation of the scene is very close to the preceding version. However, as the time restraint of having only a single act was removed, other music could be interpolated and restored in the new adaptation. The first additional section came near the beginning, following the 'market' music. Here there is a section of another song cut from the 1956 performances, 'Ring Around a Rosy'. A fragment of the music from Bernstein and LaTouche's satirical take on the progress of syphilis around the world had briefly appeared in the 1973 version, but here the song is refashioned and new words created by Sondheim. Instead of relating the journey of a disease, the section now reinforces the gory curiosity of the gathering crowd, as they look forward to the upcoming torture. Following the market section, Bernstein reuses some of the Casmira's music from 1956, her laughing phrases now given to Cunegonde and the Old Lady, who just happen to be in the crowd. There are also some sections added to the end of the sequence, extending the prayers of the 'faithful'.

In the final version, Wells, Mauceri and Bernstein trimmed down some sections while expanding others. In the 1988 Scottish Opera edition, we hear all of the 'Ring Around a Rosy' song, now with the original lyrics. The questionable justification for a syphilis song in an inquisition scene is that Pangloss protests that he cannot be executed as he is too sick to die (Wheeler 1989, p. 24); in Hellman's 'definitive text', Pangloss sings 'Dear Boy', his other syphilis song, as an answer to Candide's question of why he is so scarred and wretched. Music that has been removed includes the Casmira's laughing music, and some extra music that had added in 1982 for the entrance of the Madonna. The sections of music and their various combinations are laid out in Table 4.2.

Table 4.2   Structure of the Lisbon scene (labels indicate musical sections, not lyrics)

Pre-Broadway*	1956	1973	1982	1988
	Introduction	Introduction	Introduction	Introduction
What a Day	What a Day	What a Day	What a Day	What a Day
Hurry	Hurry	Hurry	Hurry	Hurry
What a Day x 4	What a Day	What a Day	What a Day	What a Day
Hurry	Hurry			Hurry
What a Day x 4	What a Day x 2			What a Day
Hurry	Hurry			Hurry
What A Day	What A Day			What a Day
		Ring Around a Rosy (instr.)	Ring Around a Rosy	Ring Around a Rosy (full version)
		What a Day	What a Day	What a Day
			Hurry	
			What a Day	
Arab exotic recit.	Arab exotic recit.			
	Presto		Presto	
Crowd/Laughing	Crowd/Laughing		Crowd/Laughing	
Crowd/Laughing	Crowd/Laughing		Crowd/Laughing	
Exotic recit.	Exotic recit.			
Crowd/Laughing	Crowd/Laughing			
Crowd/Laughing				
Exotic recit.	Exotic recit.			
Crowd/Laughing				
Crowd/Laughing				
Exotic recit.				

Pre-Broadway*	1956	1973	1982	1988
Crowd/Laughing				
	Presto			
Exotic recit./	Arab and Crowd			
Laughing				
Dialogue				
Dear Boy				
Fanfare				
Dialogue – Earthquake and Inquisition	Earthquake			
			Ohs	
			Madonna Music	
			Hurry	
			What a Day	
Inquisition				
What a Lovely Day				
Fanfares		Fanfares		
		Spanish Music		Spanish Music
		What a Day		What a Day
		Fanfares	Fanfares	Fanfares
Inquisition		Inquisition	Inquisition	Inquisition
What a Lovely Day		What a Lovely Day	What a Lovely Day	What a Lovely Day
Inquisition		Inquisition	Inquisition	Inquisition
		What a Lovely Day	What a Lovely Day	What a Lovely Day
			Spanish Music	
What a Day,			What a Day,	
What a Day			What a Day	
What A Lovely Day			What a Lovely Day	
		Dialogue	Dialogue	
	Ohs	Ohs	Ohs	Ohs
	Pray for Us	Pray for Us	Pray for Us	Pray for Us
	Instrumental and Fanfares	Instrumental and Fanfares	Instrumental and Fanfares	Instrumental and Fanfares
	Pray for Us		Pray for Us	Pray for Us
Dialogue				
What a Lovely Day		What a Lovely Day	What a Lovely Day	What a Lovely Day

* This plan is derived from the lyrics alone, in Hellman 1972, pp. 623–32; some sections intended to be purely musical may be missing.

With the changing political atmosphere, it is unsurprising that this scene has changed over the years. What began as a biting criticism of the McCarthy witch-hunt has been transformed into a display of the public desire for retribution and entertainment. It is the crowd that bays for blood before the Inquisition has even started, and the frenzy in the market place appears to be a circus centred on the *auto-da-fé*. Mordden says that 'The musically richer Lisbon sequence we see today is more fun: it shouldn't be. It's silly; in 1956 it was brutal' (1998, p. 181). However silly it seems, it should be remembered that in 1956 the public was all too familiar with the HUAC trials and the political atmosphere. Today these events are but a distant memory, and public perception has changed. The antics of the crowd in the later versions of *Candide* presage the developments in 'reality' television and shows such as *Big Brother*, where arguably the audience is waiting for the humiliation of those taking part, in a voyeuristic manner that relates to the desire for entertainment seen in the Lisbon sequence.

The Overture and Instrumental Music

The Overture to *Candide* is slightly unusual as it is constructed in sonata form (a further nod to the neo-classical influence?), although treated to typical Bernstein variations within the structure. It opens with a fanfare style presentation of the 'optimism' motif; it has also been touched upon that the second subject is based on 'Oh, Happy We', and that the cabaletta section of 'Glitter and Be Gay' forms the basis for the coda. To put these extracts into the context of the Overture, the overall structure is laid out as follows (see Table 4.3).

It should be noted that drafts of the Overture exist in which there is extra material that was later cut. These additions would alter the structure, so it is significant that this is how Bernstein decided to ultimately present his piece. This is one of the items in the operetta that has not changed since the 1956 première. It is in an unusual structure, a sonata form with no development,[16] although there are other works that use the same form. It is found more usually in slow movements, as seen in Haydn's string quartet, Op.50 No.5, Mozart's Symphony in E♭, K. 543, and Brahms's Symphony No. 4, or in finales, as distinguished in Mozart's String Quartet in E♭, K.428/421b and Brahms's Symphony No. 1 (Webster 2001, p. 697).[17] The structure is also employed in several overtures, including Beethoven's *Die Geschöpfe von Prometheus* and Mozart's overture to *Le Nozze di Figaro*, the second of which Bernstein was certainly familiar with, as he had conducted

---

[16]   Mordden suggests that the Overture is in rondo form (1998, p. 178), but this would be a very atypical rondo: A–A–B–C–A–B–C–D–A–B–C.

[17]   Bernstein had conducted two of these pieces, the Mozart Symphony in November 1945, and Brahms's Symphony No. 1 in January 1945, and April and July 1956 (from programmes in, boxes 335 and 336, LBC.).

it in March 1944.[18] This also has three melodic subjects, no development, and quotations of earlier music within the coda (see Table 4.4).

The only contrast between the two pieces can be seen in the harmonic structure. In his recapitulation, Mozart presents all of his themes in the tonic key of D major, whereas Bernstein maintains the relationship between his first subject themes by keeping the Battle music in the dominant key of B♭; the second subject material in *Candide*'s overture is recapitulated in the tonic key, as expected in sonata form.

Table 4.3   Structure of Overture to *Candide*

Bar 1	Key of B♭	Exposition	Introduction	'Optimism' motif
7	E♭		1st subject I	
19			'intro'	
24			1st subject I	
47	B♭		1st subject II	Battle music
64	D		bridge	Based on 1st subject I
83	B♭		2nd subject	'Oh, Happy We'
134	E♭	Recap.	'intro'	
139			1st subject I	
161	B♭		1st subject II	Battle Music
178	E♭		2nd subject	'Oh, Happy We'
206				General pause
207		Coda		Cabaletta 'Glitter and Be Gay'
255			'intro'	
261	D		1st subject I	
271	A♭		1st subject II	Battle music
279	E♭		2nd subject	

Table 4.4   Structure of Mozart's Overture to *Le Nozze di Figaro*

Bar 1	Key of D	Exposition	1st subject I	Quaver pattern
59	A		1st subject II	Longer notes
107	A		2nd subject	Alberti bass
135			Bridge	
139	D	Recap.	1st subject I	
173	D		1st subject II	
220	D		2nd subject	
236	D	Coda		Includes fragment of 1st sub. at bb. 256–63

---

[18]   Programme box 335, LBC.

Bernstein's coda also moves to the slightly unusual key of D major, and the more closely related A♭ major, in the coda, before finally returning to the tonic for the final reappearance of the 'Oh, Happy We' music. Unlike Mozart, but in keeping with Broadway tradition, Bernstein utilizes music from within the show: the identification of the 1st subject II theme as part of the music from the 'Battle Scene', and bb. 207–30 of the development as derived from Cunegonde's laughter in 'Glitter and Be Gay' leaves only the 1st subject I theme unlabelled. Gottlieb states that the fanfare leads directly into music from the 'Battle Scene' (1964, p. 238). The initial ascending 'flourish', based loosely on an rising arpeggio, can be found at b. 65 of the 'Battle Scene', but the subsequent music does not match the following melody in the Overture (see Example 4.13a and b).

Example 4.13 Comparison of 'Overture' and 'Battle Scene'

(a) 'Overture', bb. 11–13
(b) 'Wedding Procession, Chorale and Battle Scene', bb. 68–71

There is a certain amount of correlation between the ascending Overture phrase and the melody of the second subject, 'Oh, Happy We', where the first note of the phrase is also approached by an ascending figure. Although the phrases share melodic outline, an ascending tenth phrase, and a descending fifth, the ascending second is major in one example and minor in the other, and there is no conclusive link between the two. However, as Bernstein carefully drew the rest of the Overture material from the songs within the show, it seems strange that this subject theme should not also be from a song. One possible explanation is that, as the Overture was probably written after the rest of the songs in the operetta, Bernstein had this melodic variation in his mind before writing the piece, and it derives from the 'Battle Music' in the manner of a variation.[19] This 'backward' process of thematic development is similar to that seen in the *Jeremiah* symphony,

---

[19]   Suggested by Charlie Harmon, email to present author, 11 May 2000.

where the first movement themes are derived from ideas in the previously composed third movement.

Other Instrumental Music

Considering the amount of ballet music in *On the Town*, and dances in *Wonderful Town*, it is interesting that of the remaining instrumental numbers in *Candide* there is only one is a separate dance, the 'Paris Waltz Scene'. The other pieces exist to facilitate scene and location changes, or as underscoring for onstage action. Some of these items use music from elsewhere in the operetta, the first of these being the 'Wedding Procession', which, as previously discussed, is based on the 'optimism' motif. The melody of the next instrumental item, 'Candide Begins His Travels', anticipates that of the following song, Candide's solo 'It Must Be So', and there is also a short 'Candide Continues His Travels' after the song, again utilizing the same material. The former of these, with its melancholy nature and arpeggio-based melody, bears a strong resemblance to 'We shall be there with him' from Britten's *Peter Grimes*, a piece which, as already noted, Bernstein was very familiar with. In Bernstein's instrumental version there is the added aspect of a canon, which is similar to Britten's version, although his echo is in inversion.

The fanfares at the Inquisition in Lisbon are extracted from the previous number, the 'Lisbon Sequence'. As previously mentioned, the clashing tones and semitones indicate the hostility and tension in the scene, as Pangloss and Candide are about to be hanged. The subsequent earthquake, which saves Candide from the noose, is accompanied by a dissonant chord, which has the notes of a B♭ minor chord in the upper parts, clashing with E♭, A and E♮ in the lower.

The pieces that make up the Raft Sequence – made up of 'Into the Raft' and 'Raft to Venice' – are scene change items (indicated by directions on the vocal score). The first piece begins with music derived from the Governor's earlier song 'My Love'. This is quite appropriate, as it is as a result of the Governor selling Candide an unseaworthy ship that the hero comes to be on a raft at this point. The music then moves to oscillating chords, mimicking the roll of the ocean, moving from C major to other chords that are quite distant, including E♭ minor and A♭ minor. The 'Raft to Venice' music continues the rocking motion of the vessel, here swinging between D minor and other chords. There is also a 'Governor's Fanfare' in the first act. This is before the song 'My Love', and is based on the music of the song that it precedes.

Of the other instrumental items, the 'Battle Scene' has already been mentioned in relation to the Overture. The 'Paris Waltz', discussed within its motivic context, is actually quite an extended number, being some 140 bars long. It does not contain the seven or eight different melodies usually found in a Viennese waltz, but there are three clear themes, which are linked. The first melody (Example 4.5), A, leads to the second, through the repetition and development of a fragment of the final phrase, an E–F–E♭ figure (see Example 4.14a). The chromaticism of the second theme, and the altered bass line, with a crotchet rest on the downbeat of the first six bars, distinguish it from the opening melody. The A melody returns, and is then followed by C, another theme based on the same motif as B, with a further alteration in the bass line, with the off-beat chord lasting a minim rather being played as two crotchets (see Example 4.14b).

Example 4.14 'Paris Waltz Scene'

(a) bb. 42–5
(b) bb. 98–101

Both of these themes are further examples of Bernstein's neo-classicism, with unexpected notes creating a jarring effect within a familiar rhythm and structure. The A theme reappears at the end of the piece, but is transformed into $\frac{5}{4}$ time, a final twist in Bernstein's unusual waltz. The 'Return to Westphalia', another item mentioned earlier, is a simple piece based around the 'Cunegonde' motif and a further scalic theme: the simplicity of the music contrasts with the sounds of the preceding Venice gambling house, leading into the final scene in the ruins of their Westphalia home.

The remaining instrumental piece, 'Candide's Return from Eldorado', is rather unusual. It is essentially in an A–A[1] form, the second half acting as underscoring to dialogue. The music of A seems quite different from the rest of the music in *Candide*, although certain associations do exist. There is an element of the seventh–second relationship within the two melody lines, although here it is a major seventh in both cases (see Example 4.15).

The first phrase contains a seventh–second figure, but in a new configuration, seen as A♯–C♯–B, while the answering melody ornaments the figure. This number is also the odd-one-out in the instrumental pieces, with a key signature of sharps, as opposed to the 'flat' keys of all the other items. The contrast may be due to the fact that it appears related to a section from another song, 'Get You Up', which was cut before the show reached Broadway. This was Candide's final aria, where

Chapter 5
West Side Story

'When you're a Jet, you're a Jet all the way'

When Bernstein moved to New York in 1942, he sent a card to Helen Coates back in Boston that said 'I have come to the Big City, finally, to seek my fortune' (in Burton 1994, p. 100). By 1957, Bernstein had certainly gone a long way towards achieving his goal. Following his debut conducting the New York Philharmonic only a year after arriving in the city, Bernstein's relationship with the orchestra had strengthened and flourished. After working with them on a more or less regular basis for 13 years as both assistant and guest conductor, he was named as co-conductor for the 1957–58 season, sharing the appointment with Dimitri Mitropoulos, who was preparing to leave his post as the Philharmonic's musical director (Secrest 1995, p. 222); Bernstein was later offered the position, to commence in October 1958. The negotiations for the job coincided with the work Bernstein was doing on his new show, *West Side Story*, and the contract was signed on the same day as the initial run-through of the new material. Bernstein's excitement at the day's activities, both contract and play-through, is clearly evident from the letter he sent to his wife Felicia that night: 'I signed the Philharmonic contract. Big moment ... We ran through today for the first time, and the problems are many, varied, overwhelming; but we've got a show there, and just possibly a great one'.[1] The musical director's job marked a pinnacle for Bernstein as a conductor, an appointment made all the more significant as he was the first American-born conductor of the prestigious orchestra. The blossoming of his relationship with the New York ensemble, and thus his association with the city as a whole, was reflected in the number of compositions in which Bernstein demonstrated his affection for the city. His enthusiasm for the hustle and bustle of New York life can be heard in the music he composed for the ballet, musical comedies and film that had their locations in the city: *Fancy Free, On the Town, Wonderful Town* and *On the Waterfront*. The poem by W.H. Auden *The Age of Anxiety*, which inspired Bernstein's symphony of the same name, also begins its action in the metropolis, in a 3rd Avenue bar. As Burton points out: 'no composer sang of an urban landscape in so many moods or with such intensity' (1995, p. 488). The culmination of this 'New York period' can be seen in *West Side Story*. But perhaps as Bernstein attained the highest echelons of the New York Philharmonic, he felt he had completed his tribute to the city and that he had paid his dues. *West Side Story* was the last chapter in the New York

---

[1]   Letter dated 3 August 1957; reproduced on Library of Congress website: http://hdl.loc.gov/loc.music/lbcorr.00060.

saga, and the city would not feature in his subsequent works, either as a location or as a direct inspiration. The piece also marks an approximate halfway point in Bernstein's compositional output, despite being less than a third of the way through his professional life.

Of Bernstein's works for musical theatre, *West Side Story* has been the main focus of scholarly writing, predominantly as a result of the perceived symphonic nature of the composition, and the integral part the dances play in the action. Chapters, articles and books devoted to the show have all appeared, and biographies of the members of the collaborative team behind it describe the background and history of the show.[2] Bernstein himself detailed parts of the creative process, from the initial idea in 1949 to the Washington première in 1957, in his retrospective '*West Side Story* log', excerpts of which are published in his book *Findings* (1982). However, not all aspects of this account may be accurate, as demonstrated by the recollections of the collaborators during a discussion in 1985 (in Guernsey 1985, pp. 40–54). As Bernstein himself stated: 'All of us recall events slightly differently, and that's as it should be, because we are very subjective people in our objective way' (in Guernsey 1985, p. 41). As the focus of my book is the musical content of the shows, and also as so many other accounts are available, I will not go into great detail regarding the background, but will provide an outline of events, based on available records. Jerome Robbins first suggested to Bernstein that they work together on a show based on the Romeo and Juliet story in 1949, having been approached by a friend who was playing Romeo asking how he might play the role. Originally, the warring families of the tale were to be Jewish and Catholic, the title initially being *East Side Story*, and Bernstein was excited at the idea of a tragic story being told through the medium of musical-comedy. Despite a meeting with a third collaborator, the playwright Arthur Laurents, plans were put on hold until 1955, when work began more seriously on the project. Stephen Sondheim joined the team as lyricist, and the recent gang trouble in a Mexican neighbourhood in Los Angeles prompted a change in the plot to a conflict between rival groups of Puerto Ricans and 'Americans', two groups that featured in contemporary New York society.[3] Bernstein's work on *West Side Story* was temporarily interrupted by the *Candide* project, and it was less than ten months after the opening of Hellman

---

[2]   Musical and analytical studies are included in Bauch 2003; Block 1997; Gottlieb 1964; Gräwe 1987; Jaensch 2003; Mellers 1964; Mordden 1998; Stempel 1988; and Swain 1990. Biographical and historical accounts can be found in Banfield 1993; Burton 1994; Garebian 1995; Guernsey 1985; Ilson 1989; Laurents 2000; Myers 1998; Peyser 1987; Prince 1974; and Secrest 1995 and 1998. Simeone 2009 looks at both the historical background and the musical details of the show.

[3]   Peyser quotes Laurents as saying that he suggested the blacks and Puerto Ricans in New York (1987, p. 229), and there is further one reference to this from Laurents, who said that he had a letter from Cheryl Crawford, the original producer, saying 'she wanted to see how the neighborhood changes from immigrant Jews to Puerto Ricans and blacks' (quoted in Guernsey 1985, p. 46).

Shakespeare's	Romeo and Juliet	Laurents's	West Side Story	Main musical numbers in West Side Story
3	Friar Laurence's cell. Romeo tells him of Juliet, asks the Friar to marry them.	6	The drugstore. The rumble is planned. Tony tells Doc about his feelings for Maria.	'Cool' (Riff and Jets)
4	A street. Romeo sends nurse to get Juliet.			
5	Orchard. Nurse brings Juliet			
6	Friar Laurence's cell. Romeo and Juliet's marriage.	7	Bridal shop. Tony and Maria's make-believe marriage.	'One Hand, One Heart' (Tony and Maria)
Act III				
1	A public place. A fight. Deaths of Mercutio and Tybalt.	8 & 9	The neighbourhood and under the highway. Preparing for the fight. The rumble takes place. Deaths of Riff and Bernardo.	'Tonight' (Maria, Tony, Anita, Riff and Bernardo) 'The Rumble' (instrumental)
2	Orchard. Juliet is in love. Nurse tells her of Mercutio's death.	**Act II** Scene 1	The bedroom. Maria is in love. Chino tells her of Bernardo's death. Tony arrives and stays with Maria. (Dream sequence.)	'I Feel Pretty' (Maria and Girls) 'Under Dialogue' and 'Ballet Sequence' (instrumental)
3	Friar Laurence's cell. Romeo hides.			
4	Capulet house. Paris is to marry Juliet.			
5	Orchard. The morning. Romeo leaves Juliet following a night together.			
Act IV				
1	Friar Laurence's cell. Juliet receives poison.			

continued

Table 5.1   *concluded*

Shakespeare's	*Romeo and Juliet*	Laurents's	*West Side Story*	Main musical numbers in *West Side Story*
2	Capulet house.			
3	Juliet's room. She takes the poison.			
4	Capulet house.			
5	Juliet's room. Find her 'dead'. Comedy from musicians	2	Another alley. Jets meet up. Comedy.	'Gee, Officer Krupke' (Jets)
		3	The bedroom. Tony leaves Maria, who is confronted by Anita.	'A Boy Like That'/'I Have a Love' (Anita and Maria)
Act V				
1	Mantua. Romeo hears that Juliet is dead.			
2	Friar Laurence's cell. Message from Juliet has gone astray.	4	The drugstore. Maria's message goes wrong as Anita is abused.	'Taunting Scene' (instrumental)
		5	Cellar. Tony hears that Maria is dead.	
3	Churchyard. Romeo finds Juliet and kills himself. She awakes and also kills herself. Two families are reconciled.	6	The street. Tony finds Maria but is shot by Chino. Maria breaks down. Two gangs are reconciled.	'Finale' (Tony and Maria)

is that adults such as Doc, Gladhand, Schrank and Krupke do not sing at any point in the show. This mirrors a similar situation in Gershwin's *Porgy and Bess*, where the white outsiders, who are not part of the society of Catfish Row, do not have sung words, and do not converse in the recitative Gershwin created for the others. Both Bernstein and Gershwin created musical languages for the main groups of the story, and those who do not belong to those groups, the adults in one case and the whites in the other, are excluded from the musical action. Not only are the gangs separated from the adults in the story, they are also alienated from each other by virtue of their differing origins. The issue of ethnic distinction had concerned Sondheim when he was first asked to join the collaboration, specifically the matter of writing for Latin-American characters. This concern almost prevented him from taking the job, as he told Oscar Hammerstein II: 'I can't do this show ... I've never even known a Puerto Rican' (Burton 1994, p. 255). Hammerstein managed to convince the young lyricist that this was an opportunity too good to pass up. The older writer had considerable experience of such a situation, as some of the musicals he had written with Richard Rodgers had focused on differing cultures, and each society needed a specific style of language. In *South Pacific* (1949), and *The King and I* (1951), Hammerstein had created words with nuances of speech that added to the characterization of people from the Pacific islands and Thailand respectively, although from an outsider's point of view. Prior to these works, in *Show Boat* (1927), Hammerstein had delineated between the language of the white show-folk and the African-American slaves and servants.

The tragic plot at the heart of *West Side Story*, and the social issues it confronted, were presented on the stage in a form of realism that Broadway was not familiar with at that time, what Laurents described as 'a lyrically and theatrically sharpened illusion of reality' (1957). Although the introduction of music, singing and dancing into any situation lifts it out of actual everyday experience on to a level of abstraction, there is still a sense that the intolerance and hatred that lead to the violence and murder are reflected in the theatrical elements in a way that makes them believable. However, to me at least, the expression of the harsh truth of gang warfare seen in the 'Prologue' and 'The Rumble' is then undermined by the inclusion of the dream ballet in the second act, by stepping out of the already elevated 'real' world into fantasy. According to his '*West Side Story* log', Bernstein appreciated something of this dilemma: 'Chief problem: to tread the fine line between opera and Broadway, between realism and poetry, ballet and "just dancing", abstract and representational' (1982, pp. 145–6). It is the final concept that is under question here, with the action of the conflict being temporarily displaced by the visions of the lovers. The dream ballet Robbins and Bernstein had created for *On the Town* gave the audience the opportunity to see in dream-form what they were denied in 'reality' by the time constraints: Gabey and Ivy together. However, in *West Side Story*, Tony and Maria have that time together (there is the definite implication that the couple have spent the night together after the rumble), and so this is not the function that the dream ballet is fulfilling. What the illusion does show is the 'somewhere' that the lovers long for, the place that will allow their love to grow and flourish without the interference of the outside world, where the young people can live together in peace. In contrast with Gabey's daydream, which could have become reality if only he had more time to spend in the city, Tony and Maria's is an unachievable dream, underlined by the fact that it rapidly turns into a nightmarish re-enactment of the fight from earlier that night. Fate will always be against the two, whether in the shape of the hatred of gangs, the altered message, or Chino's bullet, and so the dream is stating the obvious: the lovers would like to escape, but cannot, being confined by the city and the gang culture that surround them. It is significant then that the 1961 film version of the show does not include the dream ballet, but instead has Tony and Maria singing 'Somewhere' themselves (rather than the girl in the dream) before sinking down onto the bed together (Lehman 2003, pp. 96–7); on the screen, the representation of reality is not interrupted by fantasy, and in my opinion, although the omission of such beautifully crafted music is a shame, the story does not suffer too much for the absence of the sequence.

One aspect of the show that is often discussed is the lack of music at the dramatic climax: when Tony has been shot and Maria is both grieving for him and confronting the two gangs whose enmity resulted in his death. Her final speech is spoken, rather than sung, a detail seen as a shortcoming by some critics. Bernstein himself wanted to compose music for this point:

> It cries out for music. I tried to set it very bitterly, understated, swift. I tried giving all the material to the orchestra and having her sing an *obbligato* throughout. I tried a version that sounded just like a Puccini aria, which we really did not need. I never got past six bars with it. I never had an experience like that. Everything sounded wrong. (quoted in Burton 1994, p. 275)

The decision was therefore made to leave the words as spoken text, although the climax of Bernstein's earlier *Trouble in Tahiti* was also without music. It seems that the dramatic apogee of *Peter Grimes* was influencing Bernstein once again, even if subconsciously. Although Maria does not die at the end of *West Side Story*, she has certainly been emotionally shattered by the preceding event, a point noted by Richard Rodgers, as remembered by Jerome Robbins; 'We had a death scene for Maria – she was going to commit suicide or something, as in Shakespeare. [Rodgers] said, "She's dead already, after this happens to her"' (quoted in Guernsey 1985, p. 43). There is a sense that the tragedy that has befallen Maria is so monumental, so devastating, that it has carried us past an emotional level that music can express, into a darker place. On another level, the fact that Maria can no longer express herself in song removes her from the ranks of the gangs and other young people, and places her among the adults of the show, those excluded from the musical action: the tragedy has caused her to grow up very quickly.[5] Maria's

---

[5]   This point was noted by a student of mine in an essay written about the show. Unfortunately, as it is university procedure for essays to be submitted anonymously, I cannot personally credit the person in question.

survival is the catalyst for the end of the bloodshed, and a new start for members of the gangs, endowing her with a new maturity and responsibility: 'By letting Maria live, the creators of *West Side Story* allow her to assume the authority previously delegated to the patriarchal figures of the Capulet and Montague families and to inspire a reconciliation between the Sharks and Jets' (Block 1997, p. 258).

The significant coverage of most aspects of *West Side Story* leaves little room for new thought and study, but, despite this, the following aims to look at some elements of the show from a fresh viewpoint.

Tritones and Fifths

The motivic unity of *West Side Story* has been discussed by many Bernstein scholars and critics, particularly in the extensive analyses by Block and Swain, and much has been written regarding the use of the tritone as a significant motif within the show. As Gottlieb points out (1964, p. 26), the tritone is usually found in conjunction with the perfect fifth, or its inversion the perfect fourth – the *diabolus in musica* being offset by the purity of the perfect interval. Bernstein's use of the fifth within important motifs creates a link between his 'New York' shows, as it features in the *On the Town* New York fanfare motif (constructed of two interlocking ascending fifths), and is also significant in *Wonderful Town*. The interval continues to play an important role in *West Side Story*, and it seems that for Bernstein there is a link between the fifth and the urban sound of the city, as in *Candide* he moved away from this interval, instead utilizing patterns based on the seventh. In *West Side Story*, one place where the fifth is utilized is at the beginning of the refrain of 'Maria', which is a pertinent place to begin discussion as it was amongst the first music to be written for the show (Gussow 1990, p. 5) (see Example 5.1).

Example 5.1 'Maria', b. 9

Bernstein himself noted the significance of this phrase, and specifically its importance within 'Maria':

> ['Maria'] had those notes. I think that was the kernel of the piece, in the sense that the three notes of 'Maria' pervade the whole piece – inverted, done backward. I didn't do it all on purpose. It seemed to come out in 'Cool' and as the gang whistle. The same three notes. (Quoted in Gussow 1990, p. 5)

Considering the nature of Bernstein's compositional methods, as discussed in the previous chapters, it seems highly improbable that Bernstein was completely unaware of the appearances and manipulations of the motif, and a leitmotif sheet in his handwriting exists for the patterns found in *West Side Story*,[6] although as this is undated it is not clear whether it was created before or after the body of the music. He was certainly aware of his process in retrospect, as proved by the previous quotation, and by a letter he wrote in reply to a question from a student asking about *West Side Story*:

> a little clue: in *West Side Story* – look for the relation among songs and dance-pieces in terms of these three notes (sort of a leitmotif). [Examples from 'Prologue', 'Maria' and 'Cool' follow.] There are many of these, if you find them! Good luck. (All this holds the work together, and makes it *one* piece instead of many different pieces.)[7]

The initial expression of this motif, as $\hat{1}$–$\sharp\hat{4}$–$\hat{5}$, can be found in several other places, including its appearance in 'Cool', as mentioned by Bernstein (see Examples 5.2a to c).

Example 5.2   Appearances of tritone-fifth motif

(a) 'Cool', b. 7
(b) 'Mambo', bb. 88–9
(c) 'Scherzo', b. 81

In addition, the phrase can be seen in 'Cha Cha' and 'Meeting Scene', both of which are based on the music of the refrain of 'Maria', and in the instrumental section between the verses of 'One Hand, One Heart'. However, this motif was not entirely new to Bernstein, as he had already used it in *Wonderful Town*, in the song

---

6   In LBC.
7   Letter dated 3 February 1969, in box 83 folder 32, LBC.

'Conversation Piece' (see Example 3.10), the tritone and its resolution specifically relating to the tension of the situation.

A second version of this motif can be found at the opening of 'Something's Coming', as pointed out by David Stearns (1985, p. 13), with the Lydian fourth approached from the tonic above, rather than from below. The song is performed by Tony, who later enthuses about 'Maria'; it appears that the expectation he expresses in 'Something's Coming' is resolved when he meets the object of his longings. These two motifs appear juxtaposed at the opening of 'Blues', with the E approached from B♭s both above and below in a unison presentation of the 'Maria' motif that turns into a whirling pattern to cover the change of scene into the Dance at the Gym. In its position between 'Something's Coming' and the first meeting of the lovers, this number can be seen as a transition between Tony's dream and its realization. In turn, the motif is undergoing a transition.

In addition to the melodic aspect of the motif, there is an element of continuity in the rhythmic presentation of the motif on the various occasions. In the majority of the above examples, the central $\sharp\hat{4}$ is shorter than the surrounding notes, and in general the $\hat{1}$ is an anacrusis, throwing the emphasis onto the dominant note.

A further variant of the phrase can be found in the 'Prologue', acting as the gang-whistle that Bernstein mentioned, the aforementioned shofar-call-derived pattern (see p. 113). Here the fifth degree of the scale has moved, changing the motif from $\hat{1}-\sharp\hat{4}-\hat{5}$ to $\hat{5}-\hat{1}-\sharp\hat{4}$. In this new version, the sharpened fourth also has a short value, and again there is an anacrusis (see Example 5.3a).

Example 5.3 'Prologue'

(a) bb. 42–3
(b) bb. 12–13

(a)

(b)

Several commentators label the gang whistle as a 'Hate' motif, and link it with the Puerto Rican gang,[8] as the notes are first heard as Bernardo enters during the 'Prologue' (at b. 41).[9] However, Block states that 'Bernstein associates his

---

[8]   Block 1997, p. 267; Gräwe 1987, p. 169; Jaensch 2003, p. 76.

[9]   This relationship may be slightly weakened by the reappearance of the motif in b. 90, when it accompanies the re-entrance of Riff and the Jets. However, the most forceful

unresolved tritone with the hate-filled Jets' (1997, p. 267), raising the question of who is whistling, the Sharks as they enter, or the Jets to draw attention to the intruders? A variation on the whistle motif can also be found in retrograde inversion, this time descending through $\hat{5}-\hat{1}-\sharp\hat{4}$ with an added note, at the beginning of the 'Prologue' (see Example 5.3b). It is interesting that this version of the motif bears a striking resemblance to the Resolution motif from the earlier *Trouble in Tahiti*, albeit with the A and the C♯ reversed (compare with Example 2.4). Both Gräwe and Jaensch call this second descending variation the 'Jet-Motiv' (1987, p. 169 and 2003, p. 76); it dominates the first 40 bars of the opening number, as the 'American' gang are shown in the streets that make up their territory. The connection between this phrase and the Jets is underlined by its inclusion in the introduction of their own 'Jet Song', and in the song itself at the lines 'You're never alone, / You're never disconnected! / You're home with your own: / When company's expected' (Bernstein 1957, p. 17). This motif had previously appeared in an earlier version of the show's opening, set with the words 'How long does it take to reach the moon-a-rooney?' and when the melody was transferred into the final version of the 'Prologue' it retained its link to the gang, despite losing its original lyric (Block 1993, p. 253).

As can be seen from the observations above, the tritone and tritone–fifth motifs feature in all of the dances during the gym scene, apart from the final 'Jump', representing the hostility of the gangs as they face up to each other in the dance floor, and also foreshadowing the melody of 'Maria' before and during the moment when Tony and Maria meet and fall for each other.

The interval between the tritone and the fifth, an ascending minor second, can also be seen as a motif in its own right, the rising semitone usually occurring over a tonic, creating a further figure that resolves from the augmented fourth to the perfect fifth; it appears in 'Something's Coming', 'Maria' and 'Under Dialogue' (see Examples 5.4a to c).

In these examples the Lydian fourth, although on the beat, has a lesser rhythmic value that again shifts the emphasis onto the fifth degree. The semitone plays a part in a further pattern in the 'Prologue', an isolated F–F♯–E phrase that reappears in the 'Rumble'. This closely resembles the beginning of the second waltz tune in 'Paris Waltz' from *Candide*, a possible further case of cross-fertilization between the shows. In turn, the ascending semitone pattern is related to the 'Somewhere' motif, a pattern heard at the climax of the song accompanying the title word, where it is transformed into a rising tone; the rhythmic pattern also becomes associated with the word 'somewhere'. The optimism of the rising tone balances out the hostility of the tritone; it appears that the tension of the gang problems is resolved into the hope of a better place. The rising tone is also utilized on several occasions in a similar context to the ascending semitone, with the same rhythmic emphasis of an appoggiatura: it appears at both the beginning and end of 'Procession and

---

presentation of the phrase (at *ff* and with the central note held over 8 beats) is at b. 134, when Bernardo and the Sharks return to the scene leading up to the final fight in the 'Prologue'.

Example 5.4   Appearances of rising semitone motif

(a) 'Something's Coming', b. 12
(b) 'Maria', b. 52
(c) 'Under Dialogue', b. 4

(a)

(b)

(c)

Nightmare', where it resembles the final figure in 'Maria', with the tone now resolving from $\hat{2}$ to $\hat{3}$, and the cadence is confirmed with a low tonic (see Examples 5.5a and b).

It is this figure that ends the whole work, the 'Procession' music reappearing as Tony's body is carried off the stage, followed by the other gang members in a solemn parade. However, at this point, the optimistic thought that this is a new beginning for the young people in undermined by the appearance of the tritone in the bass, as rather than a C being used to reinforce the cadence, an F♯ is heard (see Example 5.5c).

'Somewhere' also has a further significant phrase, the B–A rising minor seventh, followed by a descending second. The seventh can be compared to the whistle motif, which outlines a major seventh, and also resembles motifs within *Candide*. Block discusses several 'classical' sources that may have been the inspiration behind this song, and specifically this rising interval, including Tchaikovsky and Beethoven (Block 1997, p. 250). Bernstein would have been familiar with the orchestral pieces pointed out, but there is no definite indication that he based his song on them. Block also points out that the ascending minor seventh to falling minor second also reappears in 'I Have a Love', Maria's desperate plea for Anita to accept her love for Tony (1997, p. 266).

The tritone is used not only in melodic contexts, but also as a device within harmonic textures: an early example can be found in the 'Prologue', at the police whistle in b. 263, where the Jet motif is condensed into a single chord of F♯–C–E–G. In addition to being seen linearly in the opening phrase of 'Blues', it also appears later in the song, utilized as the interval between the almost parallel melodies at b. 19. In 'Promenade' the tritone features in the bass line: F–C–G♭–C,

Example 5.5   Appearances of rising tone motif

(a) 'Somewhere', b. 157
(b) 'Procession', b. 160
(c) 'Finale', bb. 26–8

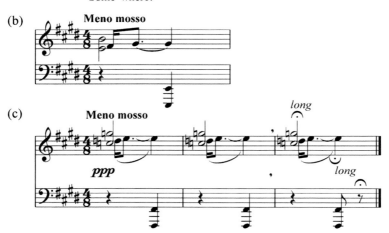

and the opening chord of 'The Rumble' is made up of C–F♯–C. In 'Gee, Officer Krupke' the first note of the vocal line for each verse is always a tritone above the bass (E♯ above B major harmony in the first verse). I have discovered that there is one further use of the tritone in *West Side Story*, within a harmonic context, and this will be discussed in the section on fugues and canons.

Despite Swain's assertion that 'it is heard in every other musical number of the play' (1990, p. 208), there are three songs that do not include any prominent use of the tritone: 'America', 'Somewhere' and 'I Feel Pretty'. The first two of these numbers were actually trunk music, the first using music that Bernstein wrote around 1940 for an unfinished ballet called *Conch Town*, the second existing from the time of *On the Town* as 'There Goes What's His Name' (Gussow 1990, p. 5); both were written before the creative process for *West Side Story* began. The absence of the tritone in 'Somewhere' could be connected to its context, and the fact that it is 'the idyllic dream of a better world' (Conrad 1992c, p. 1146), rather than being connected to the conflict. This could also be the reason that the interval does not feature in 'I Feel Pretty',[10] as despite the tragic ending of the first half, Maria and her friends are unaware of the consequences of the rumble as they pass the time in the shop at the beginning of the second act; Maria is in her own dream world about Tony, and is not thinking about reality at all.

There are few examples of Bernstein using the *Urmotiv* in *West Side Story*, perhaps due to the dominance of the tritone–fifth pattern.[11] All of the songs that contain the *Urmotiv* are again separated from the violence, and are connected with the romance or dreams of the characters: 'Somewhere', 'America' and 'Something's Coming'.

It has already been mentioned that music for the first two of these was written before the work on *West Side Story* began, but the section that contains the *Urmotiv* in 'America' was added during the creative process for the show, so 'Somewhere' is the only transplanted example of the phrase. The absence of the motif perhaps underlines the fact that the happiness that the characters feel is only fleeting, and that it pales against the tension and conflict that make up the most part of the story. This parallels the use of the *Urmotiv* in *Candide*, as mentioned in the previous chapter, in the only song that embodies a sincere emotion, 'Make Our Garden Grow'.

Dances and Rhythms

The involvement of Jerome Robbins in the creation of *West Side Story* meant that dance was always going to perform a very important and significant function in the production. The purpose of the dances in this show develops the role they played in *On the Town*. In the 1944 show, ballet was used in character and location delineation, and in the depiction of dreams through the medium of narrative dance, and it continues to fulfil this role in the 1957 musical, although with a change in mood: where the atmosphere in *On the Town* was one of happiness, excitement and anticipation, *West Side Story* is filled with hostility, hatred and antagonism. Whilst *On the Town* portrayed the dream, *West Side Story* depicts the bleak reality, and it does this from the outset. In the same way that the earlier show went against convention by beginning with a solo number, the new one again broke the rules by opening with an extended dance sequence, as 'Robbins's choreography abstracted and stylized street-wise moves and gestures to show the developing rivalry in kinetic terms … Before an intelligible sentence has had a chance to be uttered, or a single phrase of music sung, dance has conveyed the essential dramatic information' (Stempel 1992, p. 161). The jagged melodies and irregular rhythms in the 'Prologue' are comparable to the music Bernstein created

---

[10]   Conrad points out that the tritone is used as 'figuration in the interlude' of this song (1992c, p. 1146), but in this situation the descending tritone is filled with other notes ($E\flat$–D–C–A), which obscures the interval.

[11]   There are other occurrences of the pattern, but not on the scale degrees, for example, bb.242–3 of the 'Meeting Scene' ($\hat{6}$–$\hat{5}$–$\hat{3}$), and 'I Have a Love', b.93 ($\hat{7}$–$\hat{6}$–$\hat{4}$).

for *On the Waterfront*, where similar devices were used to depict the ruthlessness and violence used by the bosses to maintain control over the union members at the docks.

Within the dances Bernstein composed for *West Side Story* there is still the division between diegetic and non-diegetic music, the former consisting mainly of the 'Dance at the Gym' sequence, and the latter being subdivided into the ballet sections, and the non-narrative dances that form part of songs, such as the dances in 'America' and 'Cool'. However, the boundary between diegetic and non-diegetic, between background music and dances portraying sublimated thought or emotion, becomes blurred in the second-act 'Taunting Scene'. Here a jukebox strikes up: the music is a pre-recorded recollection of the 'Mambo' heard earlier in the first act. However, as the Jets continue to insult Anita, there is a shift, and the music instead comes from the pit orchestra, playing a distorted version of 'America' that was actually part of Bernstein's 1940 *Conch Town* ballet. As the racist insults move from verbal taunts to physical violence, the action is transformed into a grotesque dance until Anita is cornered and Baby John is dropped on her, Doc entering just in time to prevent what could have resulted in a sexual assault or rape. In this scene, the diegetic music turns to non-diegetic at the moment when the realistic portrayal of violence becomes too much for a Broadway show, and is instead transformed into dance.

Bernstein had previously employed pastiche techniques in *Wonderful Town* to evoke and maintain the feel of the 1930s, through use of characteristic and easily identifiable dance rhythms and forms. In contrast, *Candide* made no attempt to correlate location, period and music, and instead used recognizable dances and styles for parodic effect. Here in *West Side Story*, Bernstein returns to pastiche again, not to sustain a temporal frame, but to delineate between the differing cultures and origins of the two gangs.

The Latin American influence which appeared in *Wonderful Town* again comes to the fore in *West Side Story*, as a response to the Puerto Rican origins of the Shark gang; initially, Latin rhythms and dance models can be found in the 'Dance at the Gym'. In this scene, we are presented with a Paso Doble, a lively Mambo and a gentler Cha Cha. The choice of these dances demonstrates an important point about the pastiche in *West Side Story*: although the Sharks are Puerto Rican immigrants, Bernstein uses music of other Latin American countries to musically portray the gang, using general models for characterization rather than being specific. Both the Mambo and the Cha Cha have Cuban roots, but were enjoying popularity in the US during the 1950s, specifically the Mambo through the big-band arrangements of Pèrez Prado (Manuel 1988, p. 32). However, Bernstein's Paso Doble ('Promenade'), is a little unusual, as he writes it in ¢ when it would more commonly be found in compound duple time, and the music is a little staid compared with the other dances in this section. The 'Promenade' is introduced by Glad Hand as a 'get-together dance', an attempt to get the gang members to mingle with each other, rather than remain in their cliques; his old-fashioned and rather naive approach to integration is mirrored in the old-fashioned music.

One non-diegetic dance-based number accompanied by lively choreography is 'America'. The verse of this song uses Seis rhythms, a Puerto Rican form; these were juxtaposed on to music that Bernstein had originally written for *Conch Town*, but which had a much simpler accompaniment. Bernstein included the characteristic triplet rhythm of the Seis played on the guiro, and uses the guitar as an accompanying instrument, another aspect of the style (Manuel 1988, p. 39). One further traditional element, as identified by Wells, is found in the phrasing and lyrics:

> he does borrow a technique from the subcategory of the *seis de bomba* (a *bomba* being a verbal blow aimed at one of the singer's audience members). Rosalia's nostalgic reminiscences of her homeland are countered with Anita's *bombas*. Anita does not even allow Rosalia to finish her 16-bar vocal, before jumping in two measures early with her sarcastic parody of Rosalia's sincere outpouring.
>
> (Wells 2000, para. 32)

The main section of 'America' is based on the complex huapango, indicated in the score, and this music also featured in his earlier ballet. This dance is from Mexico, uses a distinctive alternating $\frac{6}{8}$ $\frac{3}{4}$ rhythm (see Example 5.6), and is performed strophically.

Example 5.6 'America' bb. 46–9

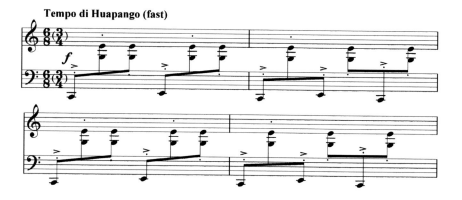

Bernstein employs the full resources of pit orchestra in this song, as well as including the Spanish guitar for the main section. There is a clear emphasis on percussion, which included the Latin American sounds of claves, guiro, maracas (used as timpani sticks), pitched drums, bongos and cowbells. It is interesting that a similar insistent hemiola effect can also be found in the 'Jet Song', where the three-crotchet rhythm of the vocal line is juxtaposed over a 'swung' accompaniment and a bass line that is in two. The effect is reversed in 'Something's Coming', with the triple time movement now in the bass, and the vocal line and accompanying chords having the feel of being in $\frac{6}{8}$. Both of these rhythmic devices create a sense of nervousness and apprehension; the Jets make their plans to challenge the Sharks, and Tony voices his aspirations and dreams. There is obviously a connection still between the gang and the ex-member Tony, as the same basic rhythmic patterns underline both numbers, but the difference in metre suggests that the distance between Tony and his old friends is growing, as he has new hopes and ideas that the solidarity and camaraderie of the Jets cannot fulfil.

Other examples of the Latin influence appear in the Quintet version of 'Tonight', where a clear beguine rhythm forms the accompaniment,[12] and 'Maria', where the underlying bass pattern suggests a rumba (see Examples 5.7a and b); although the second of these songs is sung by an 'American' character, the nationality of the object of his affection is clearly influencing his emotions at this point.

Example 5.7   Latin American accompaniment figures

(a) 'Tonight', bb. 68–9
(b) 'Maria', bb. 9–11

(a)

(b)

Both of these dances appeared in Western culture in the 1930s, coming from Martinique and Cuba respectively, the former being utilized by Cole Porter in

---

[12]   Simeone includes a quotation from Irwin Kostal, one of the orchestration team for *West Side Story*, which clearly suggests that this beguine rhythm was his idea, rather than Bernstein's (2009, p. 91).

several of his songs. The interest in Latin American music really began with 'The Peanut Vendor', a rumba that was popular in 1931 (Banfield 1998, p. 319). A final Hispanic influence can be felt in 'I Feel Pretty', an example of a cachucha (Banfield 1998, p. 103), a dance derived from the fandango, and as such more Spanish than Latin American.

In the same way that the origins of the Puerto Rican characters are portrayed musically, there are dances that are characteristically American, utilizing contemporary jazz rhythms. There is the diegetic 'Blues' which appears to be in the mould of an alley-cat or hully-gully, and which is reminiscent of the 'Ballet at the Village Vortex' from *Wonderful Town*. The 'Dance at the Gym' section also includes a fast-moving number 'Jump', the title referring to the genre of jazz that inspired the piece. This was derived from early 1940s swing, and was applied specifically to a style typified by Louis Jordan, who worked with a small group of players, the Tympany Five (Rye and Kernfeld 2002, p. 465). Jordan's instrumentation was a trumpet, alto and tenor saxes, and a rhythm section of drums, bass and piano, which is comparable with the orchestration created by Bernstein, with Irwin Kostal and Sid Ramin: two clarinets, muted trumpet, drum kit, piano and bass. The 'Jump' music itself, which is predominantly in 12-bar phrases, can also be compared with the earlier style, which was 'characterized by ... simple swing riffs (played by individual melody instruments); and blues and newly-composed popular song structures' (Rye and Kernfeld 2002, p. 465). Swing influence can also be found in 'Cool', with its offbeat accompaniment and syncopated vocal line. The 'Prologue' introduces another idea that returns throughout the show: the ⁶⁄₈ time signature and the offbeat syncopated chords; this seems unconnected to a dance form, although it does suggest a swing effect (see Example 5.8).

Example 5.8 'Prologue', bb. 1–4

It is interesting that for *Wonderful Town* and *West Side Story*, both set in Manhattan, Bernstein should begin in compound duple time. However, as can clearly be heard, the distance between 6th and 60th Streets means that these are very different sides of the city. The syncopated chord pattern continues moments later in the 'Jet Song', as the Americans describe their gang and their loyalty; the chords underline the gang's deep-felt association with the city. The phrase reappears, in ¹²⁄₈, in the 'Blues' as the tension bubbles beneath the surface when the gangs meet in the gym. The $\frac{6}{8}$ time signature returns, in 'Rumble', as the gangs fight in an underpass. The urban feel is recreated, aided by the appearance of the same distinctive chord pattern later in the piece at *ff*. The same metre is employed once more in the 'Nightmare' section of the second act ballet, as the earlier violence is reenacted.

The song 'Gee, Officer Krupke' creates its connection with American gangs in another way, by utilizing a style of song that is derived from the Broadway stage, as defined by the score, which is marked 'fast, vaudeville style'. Its $\frac{2}{4}$ march-like accompaniment separates it from both the complex Latin rhythms of the Sharks and the jazz-influenced music that represents the Jets. Instead it is in the same rumbustious manner as 'There is Nothing Like A Dame' from Rodgers and Hammerstein's *South Pacific* (1949), with solo verses and group choruses. The reason for the contrast between this piece and the rest of the music for *West Side Story* is possibly that 'Gee, Officer Krupke' was originally conceived for the Venice gambling scene in *Candide*; it initially had a lyric titled 'Where Does it Get You in the End' (Burton 1994, p. 269). The comedy element of this song led to some criticism regarding its placing in the show, as it interrupted the dramatic build-up in the second act; in Jaensch's opinion, 'the positioning of an additional cheerful number in the second act appears rather a concession to the public' (2003, p. 84). In the 1961 film version, the number was swapped with 'Cool', meaning that Riff was still alive to lead the comedy turn in the first act, and the more tense number aided the dramatic intensification towards the tragic climax. However, as pointed out in Table 5.1, there is an equivalent comic scene in the Shakespeare at this point, and it was a definite decision to leave the lighter number in the second act, as confirmed by Sondheim:

> Here is a group of kids running from a double murder, and for them to stop and do this comic number seemed to me to be out of place. I kept nudging Arthur and Jerry to reverse the two ['Gee, Officer Krupke' and 'Cool']. We didn't, and of course 'Krupke' works wonderfully in the second act, on the Shakespearean drunken-porter principle. In the middle of a melodrama, you cut in with comedy. On the other hand, when Shakespeare does it, it's an irrelevant character. For the movie, the numbers were reversed and weren't nearly as effective, in my opinion. Again, there was theatrical truth in putting 'Krupke' there, if not literal truth. (Quoted in Guernsey 1985, p. 50)

Interestingly, the treatment of the issue did not please everybody: 'The only comedy scene is staged around a sardonic song entitled "Gee Officer Krupke". Since juvenile delinquency is a painful and baffling problem, the taste of this jeering song is open to question. It takes a light view of a frightening subject' (Atkinson 1957b, p. 1).

A further rhythmic device used on several occasions is a modified foxtrot (♩ ♩ ♩). This appears distinctly American, most probably due to its derivation from the syncopated ragtime figure, and it is first employed in 'Something's Coming'.

In this song it is varied twice, once in the $\frac{3}{4}$ section to ♪♪ ⁊ ♪♩ and subsequently in the $\frac{2}{4}$ section to ♪♪ ⁊ ♪ | ♩, which more clearly resembles the foxtrot rhythm. As this song is being sung by an 'American', it seems fitting for his character, but the next appearance of the rhythm is perhaps a little more unexpected. As seen before, the Quintet version of 'Tonight' has a solid beguine rhythm. However, in its first presentation as the love duet in the 'Balcony Scene', where the first verse is sung by Maria, 'Tonight' has an ♪♪ ⁊ ♪♪♪ ⁊ ♪ accompaniment. It is conceivable that in the same way that Tony is affected subconsciously by Maria, reflected in the rumba accompaniment of 'Maria', so the American foxtrot demonstrates his effect on her in this song. This rhythm is linked to the couple, and their feelings for each other, as it is also employed in a further guise beneath the dialogue leading into the second-act ballet (here in ♪♩ ♪♪♩ ♪♪♩ ♪). This rhythm perhaps gives the clue behind one of the origins of this pattern, as it is very similar to a section from Britten's *Peter Grimes*, as the locals watch the approaching storm; there are connections both in the rhythm and the repetitive nature of the melody. Bernstein's syncopated pattern is then also utilized in various forms in the 'Transition' and 'Scherzo'. The final underlining of the rhythm's function as a leitmotif comes in 'I Have a Love', as it forms the basis for the gentle accompaniment to Maria's proclamation of her feelings (♩ ♩ ♩ | ♩ ♩ ♩). At the beginning of this song, the 'A Boy Like That' section, there is a further phrase that appears derived from Britten, as Bernstein's introduction is comparable to the music of the second Interlude from *Grimes*, both in melodic shape and in atmosphere; while Britten depicts the raging storm that has hit The Borough, in *West Side Story* it is Anita that is raging.

One song that could be considered the 'odd-one-out' in terms of rhythm is 'One Hand, One Heart'. The adagio $\frac{3}{4}$ is a perfect contrast in the midst of the dance-derived music, the effect being similar to that of 'A Quiet Girl' in *Wonderful Town*, another $\frac{3}{4}$ ballad. It was actually another song conceived for *Candide*, and was later moved into the second show. The song it exchanged places with, and which was in turn originally written for *West Side Story*, was 'Oh, Happy We', which contains echoes of the beguine rhythm in its accompaniment, despite the metre. At one point in the creative process, when it had taken its place in *Candide*, 'Oh, Happy We' had a central section which showed the couple exchanging vows with each other. This used the music for 'One Hand, One Heart' meaning that, for a while, the two songs were actually paired together. There is also an early draft of the love song where each bar begins with a crotchet rest, although its relationship with the final version is clear (see Example 5.9), and it appears that the title for this draft was 'One Word'.

The amount and nature of the dance music in *West Side Story* is significant, and is a clear result of Jerome Robbins's part in the creation of the show. This was the fourth time he had collaborated with Bernstein, the previous occasions being *Fancy Free* and *On the Town* (both 1944), and also the ballet *Facsimile* (1946). One aspect that all of these works have in common, and an element that continues in *West Side Story*, is the depiction of problematic relationships. The scenarios of the first two works have already been mentioned in Chapter 1, with the three sailors fighting

Example 5.9 'One Word', from manuscript

over two girls in the ballet, and three fleeting liaisons in the musical, with Gabey's search for Ivy. *Facsimile* focuses on three people, two men and a woman, 'who are desperately and vainly searching for real interpersonal relationships' (Bernstein 1950). It is interesting that in none of these four works do the affairs succeed or last, whether ended by logistics, as in the two ballets, or by wartime or death, as in the two shows. In the final collaboration between Bernstein and Robbins, the ballet *Dybbuk* (1974), the couple at the centre of the story is eventually brought together, but only in death. It seems that Bernstein and Robbins could not write about a happy, or normal, relationship.

Symphonic Dances

The second-act ballet contains an extended passage of continuous music, echoing the 'Dance at the Gym' section of the first act. This largely dance-based section is predominantly a dream ballet that begins as Maria confronts Tony over the killing of her brother Bernardo. Following the encounter, the scene moves into the fantasy world that the lovers sing of in the lines 'Somewhere there must be a place we can feel we're free / Somewhere there must be some place for you and for me' (Bernstein and Sondheim 1957, pp. 150–51).

There are seven clear sections in the ballet, and in a way these are comparable to the variations in Bernstein's symphony *Age of Anxiety*, where the sections are linked by development and variation of material, both melodic and rhythmic. There is a sense of organic writing, as the music appears to grow from the opening motif, and evolve symphonically through alteration and expansion; this despite the fact that the ballet went through many changes, cuts and rewritings, as described in detail by Simeone (2009, pp. 68–70). The first section, 'Under Dialogue', which is cued by the words 'Killer, killer', begins with the rising semitone motif mentioned earlier (which I have labelled 'x' in Table 5.2 and Example 5.10), and gradually builds up an F minor chord with added seventh, climaxing on a D–E♭ phrase. The ostinato rhythm at the heart of this is the previously mentioned syncopated pattern which can be found in Example 5.4c: this is rhythm 'a'. The same rhythm continues into the second section, 'Ballet Sequence', forming a bridge between the two items, and here it begins by repeating a E♮–F pattern, creating a resolving tritone over a bass B♭. The vocal melody over this consists of two descending and two ascending phrases, decorated with auxiliary notes, and would be simple harmonically, were it not for the chromatic inflections. As the singing halts, and the dream begins, the ostinato continues and a further new idea emerges, characterized by a rising tone (at b. 37 of 'Ballet Sequence'). The music becomes more rhythmically complex, as the time signature changes from $\frac{3}{2}$ to $\frac{3}{4}$, $\frac{5}{4}$ and ¢. The music builds and rises until the D–E♭ phrase is heard again, and, just as the tension seems to become unbearable, there is a 'resolution' into the next section, 'Transition to Scherzo'. The E♭ of the rising interval becomes E♮, creating the 'Somewhere' motif (a modified version of 'x' which I have labelled 'x1'), and this two-note figure becomes the new material for this section, as the counterpoint gives way to homophony. Bernstein creates this bridge passage through expansion and development of the motif. The music accelerates into the 'Scherzo', where the melody is dominated by this rising tone motif, and contrasted with new rhythmic material that utilizes a minor third, derived from a gradual expansion of the major second of the main theme.

There is a marked change of pace and mood in the next section, the song 'Somewhere', and we are introduced to the full melody of the song for the first time following the appearance of fragments of the tune in the 'Balcony Scene' and in the introduction to 'One Hand, One Heart'. The motif continues to be seen in 'Procession', the next section, in counterpoint to the melody of 'I Have a Love', another tune heard orchestrally prior to being sung.[13] This leads to a simple two-part canon for the chorus, which uses the first two bars of the 'Somewhere' melody. However, this is halted abruptly by the final section, the 'Nightmare'. Several previously heard ideas return as the dream goes sour, and the earlier killings are replayed on stage. The melody of the 'Scherzo' appears in snatches, the D–E♭–C♯ semiquaver figure from the 'Prologue', and the music from the 'Ballet Sequence' all alternate, building to a reiteration of the D–E♭ phrase and a crashing chord that signals a repeat of music from the 'Rumble'. As the fight ends in death once again, and the dream collapses, the music of 'Somewhere' returns, as a desperate plea for that place away from the warfare and killing. The ballet ends with three bars derived from the 'Procession' opening, but with the 'Somewhere' motif, and despite the horror of the nightmare, the music closes with an F major triad, a *tierce de Picardie* resolution of the F minor at the beginning of the ballet.

Looking at the relationship between the material of the sections reveals the development of the phrases and rhythms, and it is significant that both motifs x and x1 share the same rhythm, heard in the melody of the song (see also Example 5.10); the method of extension and development can be seen in Table 5.2.

---

[13]   The 'Procession' music is reminiscent of a phrase from Bernstein's music for *On the Waterfront*, which also utilizes the same rhythm, but in a descending semitone figure (two bars before fig. 44).

Table 5.2   Recurring details in the dream ballet section

	Rhythm a	Motif x	Motif x1: 'Somewhere'	
Section 1 'Killer, Killer'	♪♩♪	Semitone figure		
2 'Ballet Sequence'	♪♩♪	Semitone	Tone figure	
3 'Transition'	♪♩♪♩. (a1)		Tone	
4 'Scherzo'	♪♩♩♪ (a2)		Tone	
5 'Somewhere'			Tone	'Somewhere' melody
6 'Procession'			Tone	'Somewhere' melody
7 'Nightmare'	♪♩♩♪	Semitone	Tone	'Somewhere' melody

The melodic and rhythmic materials grow and evolve through the ballet, until the interpolation of 'Somewhere', which still maintains the sense of organicism as it includes the rising tone. It is this motif that encapsulates the whole ideal of the dream ballet, which is why the rhythm and the interval are so prominent: the vision of striving for love, hope, and a life that is free from the violence and horrors of conflict, the quintessential search for the American Dream, similar to the aspirations of the couple in *On the Waterfront*. Although also similar to the message portrayed in *Candide*, in this context it would have appeared more relevant to the audience, as it showed 1950s teenagers in New York rather than the far away locations of two hundred years ago.

In addition to the symphonic relationships between the dances, there is, of course, the symphonic nature of the whole show, the aspect that Bernstein was referring to in the letter quoted earlier when he described it as being one piece rather than many different numbers. As Gottlieb points out in his programme note for Bernstein's *Symphonic Dances from West Side Story*, the composer's first four musicals (omitting *Trouble in Tahiti*) demonstrate development in organicism: 'this is because a progressive line of stylistic integration can be traced throughout them, by virtue of an ever-advancing economy of musical means and tightening of structure from one show to the next' (Gottlieb 1964, p. 239). The number of motifs utilized, and the proportion of songs that do not use these motifs, had both decreased in this show. In *West Side Story*, the whole show is linked by the tritone motif and its various transformations, and also by rhythmic devices. As Bernstein's composition skills were developing, the results can be seen in his musical theatre works, and in his other compositions, which were also increasing in length, by

Example 5.10 Motivic and rhythmic relationships in the second-act ballet

virtue of increased integration and thematic development. Bernstein's second symphony, *Age of Anxiety*, was around ten minutes longer than *Jeremiah*, and in the four years between *Wonderful Town* and *West Side Story* he wrote several extended works: *Serenade*, *On the Waterfront* and *The Lark*. These pieces contrast with the many smaller songs and chamber works he composed in the nine years between *On The Town* and *Wonderful Town* (although this period does include the ballet *Facsimile* and the aforementioned second symphony).

Fugues and Canons

As discussed in the chapter on *Trouble in Tahiti*, Bernstein had previously employed fugal and canonic techniques, and he utilizes these methods again in *West Side Story*, but with more technical skill and confidence. There are three occasions where material is treated canonically, the first being in the 'Prologue'. In this short example, which occurs in the middle of the music underscoring the violence between the gangs, a two-bar phrase is repeated, then echoed an octave higher, and subsequently starting a further octave above, at 2½ bar intervals, over an accented off-beat bass line (bb. 192–7). On stage, the violence between the gangs is escalating, from the tripping-up of a Jet by a Shark (b. 140), up to the moment where Bernardo pierces Arab's ear (b. 242). However, this brief instance does not fully demonstrate Bernstein's use of the method. A longer example can be found in the 'Tonight Quintet', when Tony sings the melody of the earlier love-duet of the same name. When he reaches the eight-bar release of the verse, his melody is echoed at a bar's distance (and an octave higher), creating interesting contrapuntal harmonies, emphasizing the tension indicated by the preceding music and that will continue through the remainder of the song. Swain says of the canon that:

> This solution is so breathtakingly simple that it is hard to believe that the original tune was not designed for it, for it gives up none of the lyricism that the situation demands while the counterpoint intensifies the texture without extreme dissonance. (1990, p. 230)

Swain's hypothesis is vindicated by the fact that this melody initially existed within the context of the 'Quintet' before being extracted for its role in the 'Balcony Scene' (Burton 1994, p. 269); the 'reprise' at the end of first act was the original version of the song, and the duet is in fact the real reprise, but of course the audience hear them in reverse.

A similar canon occurs later, in the second act ballet sequence, in the vocal section of the number 'Procession'. In this short passage, the chorus is divided into two groups that repeat the first phrase of 'Somewhere' at a bar's distance, emphasizing the division between the two sides in the conflict.

The first example of fugal composition can be seen in the 'Prologue' (bb. 228–39). This is both longer and more developed than the earlier canon in the same number, with a more substantial subject. There is significant use of syncopation, and also chromaticism, which includes an ascending chromatic scale from D to C♯, through almost an octave. The first two bars form an introduction, prior to the entire subject being presented, and the subsequent entries occur at two-bar intervals. The counterpoint therefore includes several tritones, although none occurs linearly in the subject itself.

The positioning of the fugue is interesting, as it immediately precedes the stage action of Bernardo wounding Arab, the layering of lines reflecting the accumulating tension on-stage. Significantly, the same music is reused (from b. 232) in the 'Rumble', leading up to Tony's stabbing of Bernardo ('Rumble', bb. 84–91). There is symmetry in the violent unrest at both the opening and close of the first act, and the two brutal actions, both involving Bernardo, mirror each other. It is also interesting that the rhythm of the first two bars foreshadows the 'Mambo' rhythm ('Dance at the Gym', bb. 100–101), an occasion when the two gangs face each other in mock battle at the dance. The recurring use of the fugue in confrontational situations mirrors the form of the fugue, where one presentation of the music is 'chasing' another, and the same music is presented in conflict with itself.

The most significant piece of fugal writing in this musical, and possibly in Bernstein's output up to this point, is the fugue in 'Cool'. The instrumental dance section is framed by vocal material, and the beginning and end of the fugue are signalled by percussion: two bars swing rhythm, played on hi-hat cymbals in bb. 41–2, and 2½ bars full drum-kit solo (ad lib.) in bb. 111–13. The intervening material is based on strict fugal composition, which Bernstein would have learned during his Harvard lectures from Walter Piston, his tutor in advanced harmony and fugue (Burton 1994, p. 35). It is a four-part fugue, with a countersubject and a further rhythmic accompaniment that could be labelled an additional countersubject. The material is presented within the outlines of a *real* fugue. However, attached to the beginning of two of the phrases, and appearing twice before the final phrase, we find the $\hat{5}$–$\hat{1}$–$\sharp\hat{4}$ pattern of the 'whistle' motif, perhaps confirming that it is the Jets that are associated with the motif after all. When the ornamentation is removed, the 12-tone row of the subject can clearly be seen (see Example 5.11).

Example 5.11 12-tone row in 'Cool'

The 12 notes are divided into three groups of four, with each group sharing specific elements. Each of the three sets of notes contains two semitones and one further interval, a jump of over a fifth, and the interval between each set of notes is also a semitone. Apart from the first rising interval, the C–D♭, all other semitones descend, and the only ascending intervals are the minor seventh and sixth; Block points out that the first phrase contains the minor-seventh–semitone figure from the opening melody of 'Somewhere' (1997, p. 265). Banfield draws a comparison between the fugue subject and that used by Beethoven in his *Grosse Fuge* (1993, p. 37), although Beethoven's theme is naturally not 12-tone in nature.

In Bernstein's row the final two notes, the E–D♯, are repeated from earlier in the sequence, and bear a striking resemblance to the final intervals in the 12-tone phrase from *Trouble in Tahiti* (see Example 2.7). Here, as in the earlier work, the reason for repeated notes is 'tonal', as the final note of the phrase, the D♯, is the starting note for the subsequent answer. Over this answer, the countersubject continues in the first voice, and there is a sharp contrast between this new music and the first subject. There is extensive use of chromaticism, with an ornamented descending chromatic scale from F to A, frequent inclusion of semitones, and a 'swing' rhythm that has developed from the rhythm of the earlier vocal material (see Example 5.12).

Example 5.12 'Cool', bb. 58–61, beginning of countersubject

The opening arpeggio figure of the countersubject, the first note of which is the same as the opening note of the subject, is significant, due to its diminished nature. The diminished seventh chord partly outlined here forms an integral part of the fugue, as it governs the entries of each successive presentation of the subject: the subjects, and therefore the following countersubjects, enter on the notes of this diminished chord.

	1st voice	2nd voice	3rd voice	4th voice
Bar 43	Subject			
	Starts on *C*			
Bar 58	Countersubject	Answer		
	C	*D♯*		
Bar 70	Whistle figure	Countersubject	Subject	
	E	*D♯*	*F♯*	
Bar 82		Whistle figure	Countersubject	Answer
		G	*F♯*	*A*

The only deviation from this rule is in the second countersubject, the figure based on the 'whistle motif', which enters on E and G. Conceivably this could have continued, if Bernstein had extended the fugue, and then would have a created a second diminished seventh, with the subsequent entries beginning on B♭ and D♭. This alteration is comparable with the method utilized by Bartók in the first movement of his *Music for Strings, Percussion and Celesta*, a piece that Bernstein was certainly familiar with.[14] In this piece, Bartók manipulates fugue form in such a way that the theme entries occur on all twelve chromatic notes, in two juxtaposed circles of fifths, one ascending and the other descending (Example 5.13).

Example 5.13 Fugal entries in the first movement of Bartók's *Music for Strings, Percussion and Celeste*

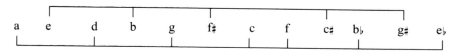

When Bernstein's music reaches b. 94, the exposition is complete, and we have one episode. The countersubject is presented in a fugue with itself, again beginning on C and D♯, this time at a distance of two crotchets. Accented chords are overlaid, rhythmically unpredictable to begin with, but settling into a hemiola pattern towards the end. At first the chords appear almost random, except that the majority contain tritones, but analysis reveals an underlying pattern. The original 12-note subject has been transformed into an accompaniment, omitting the repeated E–D♯ at the close, and is changed in character by the addition of the harmony notes. The climax of the fugue comes at b. 104, when the counterpoint gives way to homophony, and a strong syncopation that, whether intentionally or not, recreates the rhythm of 'Something's Coming'. Once the fugue is over, there is a bridge, based on the introduction to the song, which takes the music back into the vocal material. The verse is first played through by the orchestra, and both this and the following vocal verse are extended and ornamented by interruptions based on the countersubject. The same melody from the fugue returns in part in the coda.

Importantly, Bernstein's treatment of the fugue and canon in *West Side Story*, unlike in *Trouble in Tahiti*, does not involve vocal writing ('Procession' is the exception as it sets voice against voice canonically; all the other canons are instrumental, or voice set against orchestra). The technique is employed instrumentally and, certainly in the case of fugues, only in dance situations, as this is the primary medium by which the confrontations are depicted. This tension is underlined by the basis of the fugal construction on the diminished seventh chord, further evidence of the influence of the tritone on Bernstein's writing within this show.

---

[14]   He had conducted it first in September 1946 (programme in box 335, LBC), and on at least two other occasions (Burton 1994, p. 157 and p. 177).

Other contrapuntal ideas can be heard in 'Quintet', where tunes are presented separately before being juxtaposed. This way resembles 'The Venice Gavotte' in *Candide*, although here the writing is much more complex, with three lines being overlaid instead of two:[15] the gang music, which at one point includes a short canon, before ending with the two groups singing in parallel thirds; Anita's line, which is also based on the gang music, although it diverges from this at the end; and the 'Tonight' music itself, which is sung by Tony and Maria (see Example 5.14).

The music is driven by the drama here, moving imperceptibly towards the tragedy which will follow shortly, taking it almost into the realms of opera, but Bernstein manages to hold back, as Simeone describes: 'instead he has created a Broadway interpretation of a model that was the ideal fit for this critical moment in the drama' (2009, p. 106).

Candide and Cunegonde's quest for happiness is paralleled by Tony and Maria's search for a better world, although *West Side Story* presented a more relevant vision for the 1950s audiences. *West Side Story* was clearly a Broadway musical, in contrast with the previous year's operetta, with use of popular song forms in 'Somewhere' and 'Something's Coming', and with extended ballet sections that were used to further the story. Despite this, Bernstein introduced academic forms and methods, such as the fugue, and connected numbers together symphonically through the manipulation of the tritone–fifth motif. In an expansion of the technique since *Candide*, and with increased economy of means, this motif, representing the animosity of the two gangs, permeates the score to such a degree that it was only absent from three songs – numbers that relate to hopeful moments away from the violence. This organicism was also evident in the second-act ballet, with the movements linked by motivic and rhythmic development. As seen, Bernstein used pastiches of 'American' and Latin American music to delineate between the two gangs, specifically on a rhythmic level; these rhythms also suggested the subconscious effect that the lovers have on each other in 'Maria' and 'I Have a Love'. The mix of urban jazz and Latin American sounds achieved in *West Side Story* were very different from the style of music Bernstein created for his next musical theatre project: *Mass*.

---

[15]   The title 'Quintet' is perhaps misleading, as although there are five people, or groups, singing, at no point are there five completely separate parts being sung.

Example 5.14 'Tonight', bb. 134–41, vocal lines only

Chapter 6

Mass

'Kyrie Eleison'

The 14-year gap between *West Side Story* and *Mass* is the longest period between two Bernstein musical theatre works, and this suggests a definite change of direction in Bernstein's career during 1957. This gap coincided with his appointment as Music Director of the New York Philharmonic Orchestra, a post that he held from 1958 to 1969. Bernstein visited other countries and orchestras, and conducted productions of *Falstaff* (Metropolitan Opera 1963 and Vienna 1966), *Der Rosenkavalier* (Vienna 1968), and *Fidelio* (Vienna 1970). With so many commitments, including the many television appearances that he made during these years,[1] it is not surprising that compositions in this period are few in number, although they do include the substantial works of *Kaddish* (his third symphony, 1963) and *Chichester Psalms* (1965). Perhaps a point of some significance is that all the pieces that reached completion in this time were commissions, including *Mass* itself. Gone were the days of Bernstein writing works purely for the sake of the music.

On a personal level, this was a time that included moments of emotional extremes. In 1962 his third child Nina was born, in 1967 he conducted a very poignant concert in Israel in celebration of the Jewish victory in the Six Days War, and three of his books were published: *The Joy of Music* (1959), *Leonard Bernstein's Young People's Concerts for Reading and Listening* (1962) and *The Infinite Variety of Music* (1966). However, in addition to the assassination of his friend John F. Kennedy in 1963, Bernstein suffered the blows of the deaths of Dimitri Mitropoulos in 1960, Marc Blitzstein in 1964 and his father Samuel in 1969. His relationships with Blitzstein and Mitropoulos had been formed in the late 1930s, and both men had been instrumental in Bernstein's musical education and development.

The commission for *Mass* came in 1966, when Bernstein was asked to compose a dramatic piece to inaugurate the National Arts Center in Washington DC, which was now to be called the Kennedy Center. Mrs Kennedy had offered Bernstein the post of artistic director, which he declined, but he did not pass up the commission. Luckily for Bernstein, the opening of the centre was delayed from the planned date of 1969 to 1971, as he was having some difficulties in regaining his compositional frame of mind, and was lacking inspiration, as he bemoaned in a letter to Copland in 1967: 'Haven't found a work to write … : not a note on paper, not a score

---

[1]   During 1958 to 1971, Bernstein presented 51 of his Young People's Concerts, and 17 other programmes (Gottlieb 1988, pp. 71–2).

studied, a very few books read: no thoughts to speak of, no nothing [sic]' (quoted in Burton 1994, p. 366).

In true Bernstein style, he also embarked on other projects that, as was more often becoming the case, bore no fruit. There were two works based on plays by Brecht, *The Exception and the Rule* and *The Caucasian Chalk Circle*, in collaboration with Jerome Robbins and Chaim Topol, a return to his old friends Comden and Green with a musical based on Thornton Wilder's *The Skin of Our Teeth*,[2] and a film with Franco Zefferelli about St Francis. All of these fell by the wayside, but by the end of 1969, Bernstein had begun to focus on the work that would become *Mass*.

It is possible that the structure of the work crystallized in Bernstein's mind whilst in Vienna in 1970 (Burton 1994, p. 398), and in December he retreated once more to the MacDowell Colony[3] for almost two weeks to concentrate on composition (Burton 1994, p. 400). Despite this period of determined work, Bernstein was still having problems, and once again needed to find someone to collaborate with on the lyrics. A suitable person was found when Shirley Bernstein took her brother to see *Godspell* in New York on 1 June 1971, just three months before *Mass* was due to open. The work of the 22-year-old composer and lyricist Stephen Schwartz impressed Bernstein, and he proved to be the missing element of the show. In best Broadway fashion, composition continued right up until the opening on 8 September, including the writing of the main character's pivotal number within the last two weeks of rehearsals (Burton 1994, p. 405). Bernstein and Schwartz, under the direction of Gordon Davidson, moulded *Mass* into a work that received glowing reviews from the majority of the press. Perhaps the most appropriate praise came from John F. Kennedy's mother, who gave a clear seal of approval: 'It's stupendous. Jack would have loved it; it's what he was interested in: culture, art, joy and pleasure in the arts' (quoted in Burton 1994, p. 406). It was worth waiting 14 years, and more positive words came from *The New York Times* when it was performed at the Metropolitan Opera the following year: 'Mr Bernstein's score is a minor miracle of skilful mixing, mortising together folksy ballads, blues, rock, Broadway-style song and dance numbers, Lutheran chorales, plain chant and bits of 12-tone music' (Henahan 1972a, p. 34).

However, it was not received as positively by all critics; not everyone appreciated Bernstein's eclecticism. Harold Schonberg at *The New York Times* labelled the piece as 'pretentious and thin ... cheap and vulgar' (quoted in Burton 1994, p. 407), and at the same paper Clive Barnes wrote: 'Mr Bernstein is sincere but bland. He murmurs approvingly of draft evasion and ecology, and he tries rock music as eagerly as he tries to emulate the music of Carl Orff. And yet, it never seems to add up to the sum of his hopes' (1971, p. 51).

---

[2]   As will be discussed later in this chapter, music originally written for *The Skin of Our Teeth* later reappeared in *Chichester Psalms*.

[3]   Bernstein had spent time at the Colony in 1962 whilst working on his *Kaddish Symphony* (Lawson 2000).

Mass follows the structure of a Roman Catholic communion service, from the Kyrie Eleison and opening prayers through to the communion itself and the final dismissal. However, progress through the service is not straightforward. Following quadrophonic sounds of pre-recorded vocalists and percussion performing the 'Kyrie', the Celebrant appears alone on stage. A young man, he begins dressed in jeans and a shirt, holding a guitar with which he accompanies his opening 'Simple Song'. Through the subsequent songs and numbers, the people gather, and the accoutrements of religion are introduced, including robes that become increasingly elaborate as the rite proceeds; candles, a Bible, bell, censer and communion vessels are all produced at different points. However, members of the Street Chorus, who come up onto the stage through the audience, and who represent the general populace, frequently interrupt the sanctity and ceremony. They comment on the liturgy, mostly negatively, and they are particularly roused by the Preacher, whose zeal and increasingly scathing view of religion give the impression that he is a relation of Gershwin's Sportin' Life from *Porgy and Bess* (Burton 1994, p. 407). The Celebrant cannot keep control of his congregation, and in 'Agnus Dei', he struggles to be heard as he blesses the monstrance and chalice, as the stage and music gradually degenerate into disarray. The choir and chorus demand peace – an open protest against US involvement in Vietnam, thinly veiled in terms of the prayer: 'the entire ensemble rejects the Celebrant's final plea to accept the symbolic "panem" by continuing to call for "pacem"' (Sheppard 1996, p. 484). The Celebrant finally cracks, and hurls the sacraments to the ground. He then alternates between rage and distraction in his personal crisis of faith, berating the crowd and religious ritual in general until he calms and descends into the orchestra pit. During the final song, as all the singers join hands on stage, the Celebrant reappears quietly amongst the crowd, dressed as he was at the opening; he has rejected the responsibility of his religious role. The mass ends, and the people present are dismissed, as the members of the boys' choir 'fill the aisles, bringing the touch of peace to the audience' (stage note in vocal score, p. 266). Despite basing his work on the model of the sacred service, Bernstein was fully aware that the content of his theatre piece separated it from its liturgical roots: 'I have not written a Mass. I have written a theater piece about a Mass. It cannot be performed in a church. Yet it is still a deeply religious work' (quoted in Zadikov 1971, p. 42).

The visual spectacle is just as important as the music: the Choir and Street Chorus are joined on stage by the boys' choir and by dancers. Barnes described the effect thus: 'The dancing ... has just the right ritualistic power, and Mr Davidson has combined all his disparate elements ... into an animated and often even compelling stage picture' (1971, p. 51). This visual aspect reflects developments in other artistic areas of the time, as do features of the staging itself. In the realm of art-music, performances were expanding and now incorporated other sensory experiences. In John Cage's *HPSCHD*, premiered in May 1969, the audio sources were supplemented by visual stimuli: tape machines, amplifiers, loudspeakers and tapes combined with slide projectors and moving-picture projectors in an event that surrounded the audience with sounds and images. Prior to this, in *Gruppen* (1955–57) and *Carré* (1959–60), Stockhausen had begun to take the performers off the stage and place them around the audience, adding a spatial component to the music. The breaking down of this barrier between spectator and performer was also being exploited in some of the theatre groups of the time. In New York, the Living Theatre created productions that showed events in real-time, blurring the distinction between the make-believe of drama and real life, and which reduced the distance between the audience and the action on stage. Often works did not follow a definite plot, but rather presented a view of life, an idea used particularly in Jack Gelber's *The Connection* (1959) and Kenneth Brown's *The Brig* (1963), which dealt with heroin addicts, and barbarism in a US Marine prison respectively (Wardle 1993, pp. 225–6). Schiff notes a link between Bernstein's *Mass* and Peter Weiss's *Marat/Sade* (2001, p. 446), a play that Bernstein went to see in January 1966, according to his date book. In this work, the inmates of an asylum are putting on a performance about the life and death of Marat, under the direction of the Marquis de Sade. However, the boundaries between the action of the play-within-the-play and the happenings within the asylum become confused, until the scene descends into chaos, and the inmates riot.

As the lines dividing audience and artist were becoming blurred, other barriers were also being brought down. The distinction between art and the vernacular was distorted through the Pop Art movement, as everyday packaging, advertisements and cartoons were elevated to the level of 'art' by artists such as Andy Warhol and Roy Lichtenstein. In addition, the divisions that separated the different artistic movements were softened as the crossover events of Happenings reached a peak in the 1960s: theatre, poetry, art, literature, dance, music and sculpture were combined into multi-media experiences. One group that produced these large-scale creations was Fluxus, which attempted to break down the barriers between the arts, and also between life and art.

Mass takes elements of all of these concepts and combines them: the quadrophonics of Stockhausen, the multi-media spectacle of the Happenings, the elevation of the vernacular from Pop Art, and the relationship of the audience and performers from the Living Theatre. The result is an embodiment of artistic trends and ideas from the 1960s, channelled through the structure of the service of the mass into a piece that portrays the turmoil and tension of that decade, although underlined with Bernstein's perhaps naive belief that, somehow, love will find a way.

Sacred Influences

In *Mass*, we find perhaps the earliest influence yet on Bernstein's work. The origins of the Christian service lie in Jewish ceremonies, as a large number of the early converts came from Judaic traditions, and some features moved from the synagogue services into the 'new' Christian rituals, including the use of music and the role of a priest or religious leader. The rite of the early church that recalled the Last Supper developed over the centuries into the service of communion, or mass. Over time, the musical element of the ritual also expanded and acquired more significance, offering opportunities for composers to create settings for a text that was known and used by majority of Christians in the Western world. One form of the service, in particular, seems to have acquired a life for itself outside the religious setting: the mass said for the souls of the dead. The text of the Requiem was exploited by many composers who appreciated the contrasting ideas of judgement and salvation, and some of the settings are now seen as masterpieces among the output of their creators; today these interpretations are more commonly performed in concert halls than in churches. So in deciding to use the text of the Christian liturgy, Bernstein was walking a well-trodden road.

The form created by Bernstein and Schwartz can be seen in Table 6.1, which shows how it predominantly follows the liturgy. The traditions of the mass provide the basis not only for the text, but also for some of the musical forms. Bernstein utilizes a musical process that existed purely as a by-product of the mass service, the trope. The trope was a medieval addition to certain sung texts within the liturgy of the Roman Catholic communion service, the purpose of which was to 'explain or enlarge on the meaning of the official text' (Hoppin 1978, p. 145). This expansion was achieved by three principal methods:

1. adding extra musical material to existing chants, mainly by expanding melismatic phrases;
2. repeating chants with additional words; and
3. addition of both text and new music to existing chants.

Bernstein does not strictly adhere to these categories, as the methods were discarded in the sixteenth century following the Council of Trent, which prompted a return to the purity of the 'original' liturgy. In *Mass*, the tropes still fulfil the function of enlarging the meaning of the words, but, rather than presenting a sacred reflection and explanation of the writing, Bernstein and Schwartz create numbers that offer a modern, cynical consideration of the traditional Latin text. In this way, there are similarities between the function of the tropes here and the poems of Wilfrid Owen that Benjamin Britten interpolated into his 1962 *War Requiem*, composed for the consecration of a new cathedral in Coventry. Britten used the additional texts to comment and expand on the words of the Requiem mass, using the descriptions and memories of the First World War to reflect on the Catholic prayers and devotions for the dead, contrasting the English of the poems with the Latin of the ceremony.[4] In the same way, within the contemporary interpretation of the form in *Mass*, all songs that are marked as tropes are sung in English, by

[4]   The fact that Bernstein continues to use Latin for the liturgy, despite the ruling of the Second Vatican Council in 1965 that the vernacular should be used for services, is probably related to the tradition of the use of Latin in the canon of Requiems and other liturgical pieces by preceding composers.

Table 6.1   Structure of Bernstein and Schwartz's *Mass*

I. Devotions before Mass	
1. Antiphon: *Kyrie Eleison*	Soli taped voices and percussion
2. Hymn and Psalm: 'A Simple Song'	**Celebrant**
3. Responsory: *Alleluia*	Soli taped voices and percussion
II. First Introit (Rondo)	
1. Prefatory Prayers	Street chorus (SC) and boys' choir (BC)
2. Thrice-Triple Canon: *Dominus Vobiscum*	Celebrant, SC, BC
III. Second Introit	
1. *In Nomine Patris*	Taped voices
2. Prayer for the Congregation **(Chorale: 'Almighty Father')**	**Choir**
3. Epiphany	**Taped oboe**
IV. Confession	
1. *Confiteor*	Choir
2. Trope: 'I Don't Know'	First rock singer
3. Trope: 'Easy'	Blues and rock singers
V. Meditation No. 1	**Orchestra**
VI. Gloria	
1. *Gloria Tibi*	**Celebrant and BC**
2. *Gloria in Excelsis*	Choir
3. Trope: 'Half of the People'	SC, Choir
4. Trope: 'Thank You'	Soprano solo, SC
VII. Meditation No. 2	**Orchestra**
VIII. Epistle: 'The Word of the Lord'	Celebrant, Speakers, Choir
IX. Gospel–Sermon: 'God Said'	Preacher, SC
X. Credo	
1. *Credo in unum Deum*	Taped choir and percussion
2. Trope: *Non Credo*	Baritone solo and male voices
3. Trope: 'Hurry'	Mezzo-soprano solo
4. Trope: 'World Without End'	Mezzo-soprano solo
5. Trope: 'I Believe in God'	Rock singer and SC
XI. Meditation No. 3 (*De Profundis*, part 1)	**Choir**
XII. Offertory (*De Profundis*, Part 2)	Choir and BC
XIII. The Lord's Prayer	
1. Our Father	Celebrant
2. Trope: 'I Go On'	Celebrant
XIV. Sanctus	Celebrant, BC, Choir
XV. Agnus Dei	Celebrant, SC, Choir
XVI. Fraction: 'Things Get Broken'	Celebrant
XVII. Pax: Communion ('Secret Songs')	Boy soprano, Celebrant, all choirs

Items in bold type are those added to the liturgical structure by Bernstein and Schwartz.

different texts necessitating a change in the rhythm of the vocal line. [5] The process of recycling music is a natural one for a Broadway writer, where strophic forms and reprises are very common, and where time constraints often force composers to reuse material rather than create new music. In Bernstein's reiteration, however, there is a strong transformation of sound by changing the forces used: in the 'Gloria in Excelsis', it is the pit orchestra and choir who perform, but there is a sudden shift to the Street Chorus and stage band for 'Half of the People', underlining the switch from sacred and 'highbrow' to secular and the vernacular. This is the case in each of the tropes, with differing groups made up of the stage instruments accompanying the chorus and soloists. This process of contrast and distinction is similar to the technique utilized by Britten in his *War Requiem*, where the settings of the poems, sung by tenor and bass soloists, are supported by a reduced chamber orchestra, rather than by the full orchestra that plays with the full choir; a further comparison of forces can be seen in the fact that both of the works employ a boys' choir. Bernstein, Simon and Schwartz's trope points out the incompatibility between the modern 'glorious living' and the sanctity of the 'Gloria'. In response to the question 'where does that leave you, / You and your kind?' from the chorus, there is a repeat of the line 'miserere nobis, suscipe deprecationem nostram' ('have mercy on us, receive our prayer') from the choir.

This juxtaposition of sacred and secular, referred to by Bernstein as 'a subtext, simultaneously and concurrently, that consists of what might be going on in your mind or anyone else's during the Mass' (quoted in Hume 1975, p. 6), again appears derived from the work of Britten. In addition to its being found in the *War Requiem*, a further example can be seen in Act II Scene 1 of *Peter Grimes*. In this scene, a matins service occurring in the church is overlaid with action happening outside the church, with specific cross-references between the liturgy and Ellen's conversation with Peter's new apprentice. Some examples of the allusions between the two layers include the beginning of the Confession, 'we have strayed from thy ways like lost sheep', which is followed by Ellen asking John 'There's a tear in your coat. Was that done before you came?', proving that she already suspects that Peter has returned to his cruel ways, 'straying' from the correct path. Immediately after this, the congregation is heard praying 'And we have done those things which we ought not to have done', at which point Ellen notices that John's neck is sore. Prior to the liturgical responses, Ellen asks 'John, what are you trying to hide?', and the Rector sings 'O Lord, open thou our lips'. When she sees the bruise, and states that 'well, it's begun', the Gloria is heard from the congregation, with the ominous words 'as it was in the beginning, is now...'. The same proclamation is heard under Peter's later claim that 'he works for me, leave him alone, he's

[5] Although rhythmically and harmonically different, the first phrase of Bernstein's music in the 'Gloria in Excelsis' and 'Half of the People' always reminds me of the 'Laudete Dominum' section in the third movement of Stravinsky's *Symphony of Psalms* (at fig. 8); it is the repetitive chanting style of the vocal line and the similarities between the bass lines that are suggestive of the Stravinsky.

mine', suggesting that Peter has not learned from the tragedy that befell his last apprentice, and that history will repeat itself again, which, of course, is what does happen. Through most of this scene, the religious text provides a subtext for the action between Ellen, John and Peter, amplifying words that remain unsaid, and facts that the audience already know or imagine.

New Words and Music, with Reference to Previous Material

The first in this category of trope is 'I Don't Know', the first reflection derived from the text of the Confiteor. The lyrics of the trope describe the confusion of the man who accepts that he could confess his sins, but cannot see why he should when such actions and the associated emotions are false, and when he cannot maintain a righteous way of life. The music of trope and the prayer is linked by the final bar of the latter, which continues the rhythmic pulse of the piece with a dissonant chord containing the triads of C minor and A major. This pattern becomes the main accompaniment figure in the outer sections, with a slight alteration to the chord, although it still contains elements of the two juxtaposed tonalities. The men of the Street Chorus repeat the melody and words of the top female voices from the preceding piece an octave lower, creating a further link with the prayer. The C♯s and E♭s of the 'Confiteor' are changed enharmonically, and the rhythm is altered and syncopated against the duple metre, a secular jazz interpretation of the earlier sacred version. The blues influence is heavily emphasized by the presence of both minor and major thirds in the chords, and the key hovers between A major and F♯ minor. This sound is used in the outer section of what is a ternary song, with a contrasting central section. In the B section of 'I Don't Know', the key shifts to C major, and from here onto G (with Lydian fourths in both keys), and the rhythms used here appear 'rock' derived, with an emphasized regular crotchet beat, more insistent than those used in the blues sections and distinct from the compound duple metre of the opening. This contrasting music is reused later as the main melody of the 'Agnus Dei', where it is developed by harmonization in thirds.

Two of the Credo tropes, 'Non Credo' and 'World Without End', both begin in the same way – taking words and music of the line of the creed they have just interrupted, followed by an English translation of the words; the music and text are then expanded (see Examples 6.2a and b). The first trope questions Jesus' humanity,[6] particularly in the statement 'I tell you sir, you never were / A man at all. / Why? / You had the choice / When to live / When / To die, / And then / Become a god again' (Bernstein and Schwartz 1971, p. 150), while the second wonders if God is really interested in the planet and his other creations at all, or if the human race has been abandoned: 'Lord, don't you care if it all ends today? / Sometimes I'd swear that you planned it this way' (Bernstein and Schwartz 1971, p. 162). The opening music of the former example, with its overlapping descending intervals,

---

[6]   In a typical Bernstein touch, the trope which begins with the words 'And was made man' is sung by a male-only group.

Example 6.2 Transitions between 'Credo' and its tropes

(a) 'Credo in unum Deum', b. 29 and 'Non Credo', bb. 1–5
(b) 'Credo in unum Deum' (third section), b. 7 and 'World Without End', bb. 1–4

also bears a striking resemblance to sections of the first movement of the *War Requiem*, although Britten utilizes tritones, rather than fourths and fifths. After 'World Without End', the Credo continues from where it was interrupted, at the proclamation 'Et in Spiritum Sanctum', but from here to the end of the chanting, the soloists from the three tropes disrupt the creed with fragments from their own songs, gradually overlapping and increasing in intensity until the text of the Credo finally reaches its conclusion, leading into the last challenge to its statement of beliefs.

The final Credo trope also reuses the phrase that closes the preceding piece, in this case being 'Amen' at the end of the creed. This 'amen' is reiterated and leads into a number based on a variant of the creed's opening words, 'I believe in God, / But does God believe in me?'. This sentiment is developed into an assertion of the thoughts of many during the 1960s and 1970s, through to today, the search for something to believe in: 'I'll believe in twenty gods / If they'll believe in me … Is there someone out there? / If there is, then who?' (Bernstein and Schwartz 1971, pp. 168–9). When the singer makes a connection between music and faith, with each named note being sung on that pitch ascending to a tenor's high C as the tension grows, the choir is stirred into response with a phrase from their earlier chant, which the singer questions as irrelevant to his own life:

> SOLO: I believe in F sharp,
> I believe in G.
> But does it mean a thing to you
> Or should I change my key?
> How do you like A flat?
> Do you believe in C?
> CHOIR: Crucifixus etiam pro nobis sub …
> SOLO: Do you believe in anything
> That has to do with me?
>   (Bernstein and Schwartz 1971, pp. 170–71)

As the soloist and the street chorus are left in their own doubt, the Celebrant finally brings the proceedings to order by calling the people to prayer.

Both New Words and Music Added, with Few Links to Liturgy.

The second Confiteor trope, 'Easy', appears to have no musical links with its parent prayer, although it does share its sentiment with 'I Don't Know': the false nature and superficiality of confession, presented in the form of a blues number. The two tropes alternate, with different soloists each time, offering various views on the fact that 'living is easy when you're half alive' (Bernstein and Schwartz 1971, p. 90). 'Thank You', the second Gloria trope, is linked to the preceding 'Half of the People' by the repetition of a melodic figure and the connection of 'gloria' and 'glorious'. There appears to be no relationship with the 'Gloria' itself, except for the use of the same rhythm for the word 'gloria' itself ($\cdot$. $\cdot$). The female soloist reminisces of happier times when she had things to thank God for: 'There once were days so bright, / And nights when every cricket call seemed right, / And I sang Gloria, / Then I sang Gratias Deo. / I knew a glorious feeling of thank you and … / Thank you …' (Bernstein and Schwartz 1971, pp. 116–17).

'Hurry' is related to the preceding section of the Credo by only the first line, 'You said you'd come again'. This is a reference to the line 'et iterum est cum gloria' ('and come again in glory'), a concept which is questioned by the soloist in new music. The opening descending F–C interval echoes the final interval heard in the 'Credo', prior to this interruption. The opening phrase of the trope is also reminiscent of the theme Bernstein wrote for the fugue in the last movement of his *Kaddish* symphony (see Examples 6.3a and b).

The final trope, 'I Go On', opens with an ascending fifth, an echo of the 'amen' of the preceding 'Our Father', which is distinguished by being the only part of the Ordinary of the mass (the chants that remain the same through different days and seasons of the year) to be completely in English in *Mass*. This trope is also distinct from the others as it is sung by the Celebrant, rather than by members of the Street Chorus: he is beginning to seriously question his role and his own beliefs. Despite his doubts and uncertainty, he determines that he will continue: 'When my courage crumbles, / When I feel confused and frail, / When my spirit falters on decaying

Example 6.3 Comparison of 'Hurry' and *Kaddish*

(a) 'Hurry', bb. 1–3
(b) *Kaddish*, Finale, Fuga, bb. 1–3

(a)

(b)

altars / And my illusions fail, / I go on right then, / I go on again' (Bernstein and Schwartz 1971, p. 192). The continuation here appears unconnected to the preceding prayer, either musically or textually, instead being the manifestation of the Celebrant's thoughts at this point in the ritual. The last phrase, however, is a repetition of material from the hymn and psalm from the beginning of *Mass*, a reiteration of the 'Laude' cadenza from 'Simple Song'.

In addition to the items denoted as tropes in the show's listing, the ending of the 'Agnus Dei' may be seen as a further example of this genre; an expansion of the liturgy which it follows. Phrases are repeated until the words 'Dona nobis pacem' ('Grant us peace') are formed into an accompaniment for soloists who sing and later extemporize over the top of this recurring phrase. The music becomes a 'jam session', containing both vocal and instrumental improvisations, while from b. 219 'the Choir may sing increasingly loudly and unrestrainedly' (score note, Bernstein and Schwartz 1971, p. 229). It is in this section that Bernstein sets out his anti-war sentiments most clearly, as although the singers appear to be protesting to God for peace, the message would have been heard clearly in a Washington that was still the venue for anti-Vietnam demonstrations. Lyrics such as 'Give us peace now and we don't mean later', and 'We're fed up with your heavenly silence, / And we only get action with violence, / So if we can't have the world we desire, / Lord, we'll have to set this one on fire!' (Bernstein and Schwartz 1971, pp. 225 and 228–9) were hardly ambiguous in 1971.

Beethoven and Rock Music

In addition to the influence of Britten on this work, the shadow of Beethoven can also be clearly heard, beginning with the just discussed 'Agnus Dei'. Traditionally, this movement is gentler, as it is a prayer for forgiveness and peace. However, Bernstein was not the first to break this tradition, and his inspiration may have come from the Beethoven *Missa Solemnis*, where the end of the movement is disrupted by 'the unequivocally warlike music of blaring trumpets, and the reactions of panic-stricken terror from the solo singers – a superbly dramatic situation' (Werner-Jenson 1979, p. 7). The outside world has become involved in the sacred liturgy, and at this point Beethoven is presenting a small example of what Bernstein is doing throughout the whole of his work: breaking down the distinction between the holy and the worldly (Werner-Jenson 1979, p. 7). There is a further parallel between the two pieces in the structure of the 'Credo' in each: the places in the text of the creed where Bernstein 'interrupts' the liturgy to insert three of his tropes mirror moments in Beethoven's setting where the tempo and style of the music change – at 'et homo factus est', after 'regni non erit finis', and at the 'Amen'.

There are significant connections between Bernstein's *Mass* and another of Beethoven's works: his Symphony No. 9; with which Bernstein was very familiar, having conducted two performances in 1970, with the Boston Symphony Orchestra and the Vienna Philharmonic, both in their respective home cities (Burton 1994, p. 395). The same piece had also been the subject of one of Bernstein's television programmes in 1958, as part of the 'Lincoln Presents' series, and he went on to win a Grammy in 1980 for a recording of this piece (Gottlieb 1988, p. 67). The Beethoven symphony would, of course, go on to provide a pivotal moment both in musical and political history when Bernstein conducted it in 1989, to celebrate the bringing down of the Berlin Wall; the changing of the word 'Freude' (joy) to 'Freiheit' (freedom) underlined the significance of the event. The influence can also be seen in the second 'Meditation', an orchestral interlude added by Bernstein between the trope 'Thank You' and the Epistle. The 'Meditation' has the subtitle 'on a sequence by Beethoven',[7] and this sequence formed the basis for a set of variations. At first the theme is presented with a very disjointed rhythm, although in the same key as the Beethoven. It is interesting that Bernstein should choose this phrase, which occurs in the Finale of the Ninth Symphony (bb. 730–45), as his theme, as it contains all 12 notes of the chromatic scale, with three being repeated. The intervals between consecutive notes are semitones, tritones or sixths, and so in isolation this music sounds more like Bernstein than Beethoven. Following the initial presentation in *Mass*, Bernstein then employed the theme in a rhythm that is very similar to that used by Beethoven originally, and added a chromatic melody over the top, using his characteristic semitone intervals (see Example 6.4).

In subsequent variations, the theme is treated in a range of ways: being placed vertically in chords (var. 2), being spread in arpeggio figures (var. 4), and being played rapidly in quaver triplets (var. 3). In the last of these, Bernstein quotes a further phrase from the Ninth Symphony: placed contrapuntally against the triplets we hear the first six notes of the 'Ode to Joy'.

---

[7]   This subtitle is not in the score, but can be found on the CD listings for *Mass*, and also in a reference to 'Meditation II' in Bernstein's book *Findings* (1982, p. 370).

Example 6.4   Sketch of chromatic melody used in 'Meditation No. 2', bb. 13–19

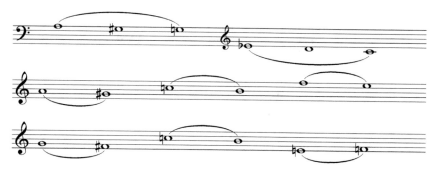

   The use of Beethoven's music in the 'Meditation No. 2' is interesting, and also appropriate. The words that accompany Beethoven's sequence in the symphony begin 'Ihr stürzt nieder, Millionen' ('You fall down, O millions'), and the words sung at the end of Bernstein's preceding number, 'Thank You', quote the opening of the previous trope – 'Half the people are drowned and the other half are swimming in the wrong direction', surely a similar indication of a fall from grace.
   A final reference to Beethoven's work comes at the start the coda of Bernstein's 'Meditation II', with the appearance of the chords that accompany the words 'Brüder' in the 'Ode to Joy'. In a 1970 letter to Franz Endler, music critic of Vienna's *Die Neue Freie Presse*, shortly after the Boston and Vienna performances, Bernstein talked of Beethoven's childlike belief, and of the need to share in that faith in order to play and fully understand the work:

> [The Finale] is simply unplayable unless we go all the way with him, in total, prepubescent faith, in that certainty of immortality that only children (and geniuses) really possess – to go all the way with him as he cries out 'Brüder!', 'Tochter!', 'Freude!', 'Millionen!', 'Gott!' But especially 'Brüder!' That above all is his child-inspired cry. (Bernstein 1982, p. 298)

It is clear that Bernstein placed a great deal of importance upon these words, and thus upon the chords that accompany them, and it is therefore significant that the next words heard in *Mass*, which are taken from one of St Paul's letters in the Bible, should be 'Dear Brothers'.[8]
   Beethoven's '12-tone' sequence is heard again in 'Fraction', as the Celebrant finally loses control and smashes the chalice and monstrance. In the service of the mass, the Fraction is the time when the bread is broken before communion, but, in Bernstein's adaptation, it is the Celebrant who breaks, crumbling under the pressure of the religious trappings and the expectations of his congregation. Again the rhythm is disjointed, reflecting the disorderly thoughts inside the Celebrant's head

---

[8]   The same connection is noted by Hume (1975, p. 12).

as he has the musical equivalent of a breakdown. Following a six-bar introduction, which reiterates the final 'pacem' from the preceding 'Agnus Dei', and during which the communion vessels are thrown to the floor, the Celebrant begins his disorganized reflection on the situation. The first eight bars use the original version of the sequence in both vocal line and accompaniment, but in fragments, some of which are repeated before the row moves on. In subsequent phrases, bb. 15–31, the vocal line moves away from the sequence, but the orchestra still uses cells from the Beethoven phrase, although here Bernstein used transpositions of the sequence, beginning on E♭, E, D and A, in conjunction with the original version of the row (see Example 6.5).[9]

The sequence is used again later in 'Fraction', in bb. 110–17 and bb. 310–14, and in both of these sections it is only the untransposed row that is utilized, notes 1–12 in the first instance, and notes 9–16 in the second. In 'Fraction', we also hear fragments of other songs from *Mass*, in a scene reminiscent of Britten's portrayal of the breakdown of the eponymous fisherman in *Peter Grimes*, a further example of the opera's influence on Bernstein's work. There is no set order to the pieces that are presented, although Bernstein links the sections in a word game reminiscent of the 'trance' section in 'Swing' from *Wonderful Town*, as seen in the lyrics in this continuous section from bar 249:

Let there be and there was…	from 'God Said'
God said: Let there	
Be – atam Mariam semper Virginem,	'Confiteor'
Beatam miss the Gloria,	'Thank You'
I don't sing	
Gratias agimus tibi propter magnam	'Gloria in Exelsis'
Gloriam tuamen	
Amen. Amen	'I Believe in God'
I'm in a hurry	'Hurry'

Through the rest of the piece there are other quotations, including phrases from 'Simple Song', 'Gloria Tibi' and 'I Don't Know'. It appears that the evening's proceedings are all crowding into the Celebrant's mind, as his faith in the religious ritual is broken.

The Beethoven sequence and its derived row in 'Meditation 2' are not the only examples of 12-tone music in *Mass*. The first piece of the Credo section, 'Credo in unum Deum', is also based on a phrase that employs all 12 chromatic pitches (see Example 6.6). One note is restated within the row, but this is the only exception in the series. Although no transpositions of the row are used, it is presented in inversion as well as in its prime version. When set to the words, notes within the

---

In this example, P denotes the original version of the phrase, T3 a transposition up three semitones, T7 a transposition up seven semitones, and so on. The numbers in the brackets indicate the position of the notes within the row.

Example 6.5 'Fraction', bb. 20–30

Example 6.6 'Credo in unum Deum', tone row

row are repeated to facilitate the differing numbers of syllables within the lines of the creed, but it is always the same notes that are reiterated: the first, sixth and last (C, A♭ and F in prime; C, E and G in the inversion). The lines of the text do not always correspond with the beginnings of the rows, and so there is some overlap of musical phrases with textual phrases. This in part connects with the tropes, which interrupt the creed at various places to comment on the text, beginning with different intervals as they echo the music they have just disrupted. When the 'Credo' continues between the two tropes 'Hurry' and 'World Without End', we hear both the prime and inversion forms of the row together in counterpoint. This creates some diatonic moments, as the repeated notes that occur together are C against C, E against A♭ (major third), and C against G (perfect fifth). As already discussed, over the top of the final section of 'Credo', the soloists from the tropes sing fragments of their songs, and at this point the setting of the creed ends with presentations of the prime and the inversion consecutively, ending the piece on what could be seen as a dominant repeated G.

There is one further element in *Mass* that can be traced back to both the *War Requiem* and the *Missa Solemnis*. In the Beethoven work, there are several moments that are very testing for the performers, particularly the sopranos of the chorus, as the composer 'takes the human voice to its utmost limits' (Werner-Jensen 1979, p. 4), both in terms of range, and in complexity of vocal line. The effect of these passages, especially in the Gloria and the Credo, is that the music is trying to break free of its human confines and attain a sense of spirituality and ecstasy. It is comparable with the phenomenon of speaking in tongues, glossolalia, where mortal speech is displaced by divine utterings. Britten achieves a similar effect at the opening of his Sanctus, where the text is declaimed at a speed left to the discretion of the individual performers, in 'an extraordinary passage of unsynchronised chanting' (Cooke 1996, p. 70). Whereas Britten dictated the notes but not the rhythm, Bernstein asked the reverse in a section in his 'Offertory', by prescribing the rhythms, but allowing some freedom in the pitches used. The use of such a device is fitting within these three works, as they all attempt to portray part of the mystery of the religious ritual, and the mystical nature of the sacred experience.

One review of *Mass* mentioned the presence of the styles of Orff and Stravinsky (quoted in Secrest 1995, p. 330), and certainly there are moments of textural writing that reflect the sounds of these composers – the lines moving in thirds in 'Sanctus', and the bi-tonal rhythmic chords of 'Confiteor' respectively – but an echo of Mahler went unnoticed.[10] There are similarities between the Chorale in *Mass* (the 'Prayer for the Congregation: Almighty Father'), and a part of the final movement of Mahler's Symphony No. 2, 'Resurrection', a work Bernstein had conducted in the memorial concert following Kennedy's assassination in

---

[10]   The presence of Mahler's influence is noted by Sheppard (1996, p. 477), although he does not go on to detail where this influence can be heard in Bernstein's score. In *The New York Times*, Henahan declared that in this piece, 'Bernstein has tried to write a Mahler opera, a personal passion play and a morality drama for our time' (1972b, p. D9).

1963; it is fitting then that an echo of the symphony should appear in the work written for the Arts Center that would bear the president's name. Both pieces of music are begun by voices singing a cappella, with homophonic vocal writing, and they both start with an auxiliary note figure (Bernstein: $\hat{3}$–$\hat{4}$–$\hat{3}$, Mahler: $\hat{5}$–$\hat{6}$–$\hat{5}$) (see Example 6.7).

Example 6.7 'Chorale; Almighty Father', bb. 1–4

Bernstein's chorale reuses the melody from the preceding 'In Nomine Patris', changed rhythmically, in the same way in which he created his chorale in *Candide* by altering and reharmonizing the verse from 'Best of All Possible Worlds'. In *Mass*, the chorale reappears on two more occasions, the first in a further rhythmically altered version in the second Offertory 'De Profundis, part 2', and then once more in its simple choral version at the close of 'Secret Songs' to end the piece.

The 'Prefatory Prayers' begin with a march, which has chromatic harmony that removes it slightly from the realm of Sousa, perhaps the model for American marches. The main reason for this can be found in the bass line which, rather than stating the tonic and dominant in its home key of G major, moves for the majority of the time between the tonic and the flattened sixth, E♭ (see Example 6.8). This pattern echoes Prokofiev's march from *For the Love of Three Oranges*, which has an A♭–E♮ bass line under the main melody in A♭ major. However, in Prokofiev's case, the E♮ is the tonic of the chord formed above, creating an A♭– E[7] progression that distorts the usual tonic–dominant relationship by a semitone. In *Mass*, the E♭ in the bass is not the tonic, but the seventh of the chord above, which appears in third inversion, generating a progression that moves from the tonic chord of G to a seventh chord on the flattened seventh of F♮. The same harmonic

Example 6.8 'Prefatory Prayers', bb. 4–5

progression is used in the central contrasting section of 'Easy' under the relaxed blues melody. This use of the $\flat$VII chord can also be seen in Lloyd Webber's *Jesus Christ Superstar* of two years earlier,[11] in the song 'Superstar', but here, as in other rock songs of the time, including various numbers by The Beatles, it is within the context of a double plagal cadence: B$\flat$–F–C.

There is a further version of this pattern, where the descending interval is inverted to become an ascending minor third, changing the progression to I–$\flat$III$^{(7)}$. This bass figure occurs in the final blues-based section of the 'Agnus Dei', with the slight alteration that the tonic chord contains both major and minor thirds, creating an ambiguous chord with a jazz sound, the same sound that can be seen in the accompaniment of 'I Don't Know', and that also represented the urban feel of New York at the opening of *West Side Story*. The A/A minor–C^7 progression in 'Agnus Dei' provides the opportunity for flattened thirds and sevenths within the melody, underlining the blues sound that Bernstein clearly wishes to exploit at this point in the score. This section contains a repeated refrain that at first appears to be conforming to a 12-bar blues structure, but which is actually cut short into 10 bars, with an interesting harmonic structure within these bars. We see again the use of the flattened seventh chord, but once more Bernstein does not use it within a plagal cadence, leading instead onto an ambiguous dominant chord, ready for a perfect cadence into the repeat of the music. In 'Gloria in Excelsis', where the same bass line is used in the introduction and opening vocal phrase, the chord formed on the flattened third is a minor triad, leading to an E–G pattern.

In 1966, in the introduction to his book *The Infinite Variety of Music*, Bernstein wrote that 'pop music seems to be the only area where there is to be found unabashed vitality, the fun of invention, the feeling of fresh air' (p. 10). Despite this sentiment, and the fact that his collaborator Stephen Schwartz had just written *Godspell*, a musical incorporating many contemporary sounds, *Mass* contains little music that is influenced by chart music of the late 1960s, a fact noticed by Hume: 'There is a group of dancers, two rock bands, though there is not a note of rock music in the score' (1975, p. 6). Instead, the popular sounds utilized, mainly in the tropes and the music of the Street Chorus, are those of blues, soul and jazz; these genres are heard clearly in 'I Don't Know', 'Easy', 'World Without End' and the end of 'Agnus Dei'. There is also an echo of the popular vocal group the Swingle Singers in the syncopation and layered writing of 'Alleluia' (Schiff 2001, p. 446). The very appropriate gospel sound of the Gospel-Sermon number, 'God Said', with its call-and-response structure closely resembling Schwartz's 'Light of the World', appears more indebted to old spiritual traditions than to the Jackson Five, one of the top-selling bands of 1970. The dance section of this song is derived from

---

[11]   It was the album of the music that was released in 1969. The stage version of *Jesus Christ Superstar* actually appeared on Broadway in October 1971, after *Mass* had been produced. It is interesting that, while working on *Mass*, Bernstein auditioned Murray Head, who had sung the part of Judas on the album, presumably for the role of the Celebrant (27 July 1971, in Bernstein's date book, box 324, LBC). The part eventually went to Alan Titus.

Thirds and Fifths

In *Mass*, as had been the case in his previous musical theatre works, Bernstein turned once more to motifs to create a sense of continuity throughout the work. However, this time there is little manipulation of the figures when compared with some of his earlier works, as they are nearly always found in their original forms. In addition to the *Urmotiv*, there are two principal motifs employed in *Mass*, and either one or the other, and on some occasions both, can be found in all but three of the items in the work. The first of these figures is the three-note cell that opens the work, heard beneath the taped soprano solo in 'Kyrie Eleison' (see Example 6.9); Gottlieb states that Bernstein called this the 'Holy Spirit' motif (2005, p. 6). This ascending minor third to descending major second phrase bears a resemblance to the three-note figure seen in *Trouble in Tahiti*, and in particular to the final transformation of this figure at the very end of the opera, but in the majority of appearances in *Mass* the cell begins with the minor third, as opposed to the major third seen in the earlier work.

In 'Kyrie Eleison', the motif is heard four times in the soprano line, and eight times in the tuned percussion accompaniment, nine of these being at the pitches B–D–C, an implied $\hat{7}\hat{2}\hat{1}$ pattern within what seems to be the key of C major. Of the remaining three occurrences, two are D–F–E♭ ($\hat{2}\hat{4}♭\hat{3}$), and the last is G–B♭–A ($\hat{5}♭\hat{7}\hat{6}$), both of which use 'blue' notes.

The harmonic context of the motif in *Mass* is not constant, some of the examples being tonally ambiguous at that point in the music. For of the eleven movements that contain the motif, usually at the beginning or end of a phrase, the degrees of the scale employed can be seen in Example 6.9.

Mostly the motif involves patterns that end on the dominant, with five of these instances having slight variations in the preceding intervals (major thirds in three cases, and minor seconds in two) to accommodate this. Gradenwitz (1987, p. 215) considers that this cell also forms the basis for the figure from which 'Meditation No. 1' is derived: E♭–D–C. However, this is very unlikely, as the music that formed the basis for the meditation was actually written in 1970, as an 'anniversary' piece for Helen Coates.[17] It is true that this phrase also outlines a minor third, but there the links between the two end, especially taking into account the harmonic context of the linear descending third: $\hat{3}\hat{2}\hat{1}$. There is, however, a phrase that uses notes that can be treated as a variation of the motif, within the Psalm section of the Celebrant's opening song 'A Simple Song'. Here the melody of the first bar can be seen to be a 'stretching' of the motif, with the descending second being displaced by an octave to create a leap of a seventh (see Examples 6.10a and b).[18]

---

[17]   Published as number seven in *Thirteen Anniversaries*, and dated 17 July 1970.

[18]   I first explored the use of the three-note motif in my PhD in 2003, citing the examples given here. Gottlieb has also investigated how Bernstein employs the notes in *Mass* in his 2005 article 'The Little Motive That Could'. He considers other instances

Example 6.9   Uses of the 'Holy Spirit' motif within *Mass*, showing scale degrees

Not included in this table are examples that occur when music is repeated in other items,
for example, when the 'Epiphany' is reused at the beginning of 'Secret Songs'.

Example 6.11 *concluded*

The movement which stands alone, without any motifs, is 'Meditation No.2'. The exclusion of this item is a result of its basis on external material, the Beethoven sequence. However, its place within the structure of *Mass*, and the organic development that links the pieces within the show, is preserved in the references to Beethoven's Ninth Symphony, and specifically in the use of the 'Brüder' chords.

It is particularly interesting that *Mass* is unified by these three motifs as a number of the songs existed prior to the theatre piece being written; those already mentioned include 'Allelulia' ('Warm Up'), 'Meditation I' (number seven in 'Thirteen Anniversaries'), and sections of 'God Said' and 'Prefatory Prayers' (*Shivaree*). There are several other items that were imported into Bernstein's new work, including the music of the 'Sanctus', which was another piece originally composed for Helen Coates, 'A Springate Souvenir', written in celebration of her 70th birthday, denoted on the manuscript as 'on the Biblical birthday'.[20] The Celebrant's opening song was first created for another aborted Bernstein project: the collaboration with Zeffirelli on a film about St Francis. In Burton's words: '"A Simple Song" was to have been to have St Francis's "Credo" before it became the Celebrant's hymn' (1994, p. 408). One final interpolation was 'Secret Songs', the melody of which Burton describes as having been written as a thank you for Susann Baumgärtel, who was the wife of Bernstein's Austrian assistant, in June 1970. It seems that this music was recycled even before appearing in *Mass*, as a further manuscript copy of the melody exists dated 14 November 1970, where the piece is called 'Aaron's Canon' (14 November being Copland's birthday).[21]

In light of the variety of sources for the music in *Mass*, and the time scale over which the pieces were composed (up to two years before the theatre piece), it should be remarkable that Bernstein still demonstrated his characteristic organicism, but as such use of trunk music has been documented for his earlier musicals, it appears that once again he successfully integrated 'old' music with the newer material created specifically for the piece at hand.

Other Religious Works

Mass marked a significant point in Bernstein's compositional output, as this was the last major liturgically based work that he produced. His *Missa Brevis* of 1988 includes texts from the mass, but reused music he had written in 1955 for Hellman's adaptation of *The Lark*. The only new work with specific religious origins after *Mass* was the ballet *Dybbuk* (1974), a further collaboration with Jerome Robbins. This does include text from the Jewish synagogue services, but within the context of the Ukrainian folk-story of the ghost that possesses a living person, based on a 1920s play of the same name by S. Ansky (Burton 1994, p. 422); Robbins and Bernstein had originally planned this ballet shortly after finishing *Fancy Free* (Robbins on Burton 1996/7).

Bernstein's earlier sacred works, not surprisingly, reflect his own Jewish faith, even *Chichester Psalms*, which despite being commissioned for an English

---

[20]   Manuscript in LBC.
[21]   Manuscript in LBC.

cathedral has the psalm texts sung in Hebrew. Similarly, in *Mass*, the 'Sanctus' contains the words of the blessing first in Latin, then English, then Hebrew.[22] His previous religious works included his first and third symphonies, *Jeremiah* and *Kaddish*, and the choral pieces *Hashkiveinu* and *Yigdal*. These pieces employ a range of sacred texts, as shown in Table 6.2.

Table 6.2   Sacred texts employed by Bernstein in his compositions

1942	*Jeremiah* Symphony	Bible: Lamentations of Jeremiah 1:1–3, 8; 4:14–15; 5:20–21
1945	*Hashkiveinu*	Talmud: Friday Evening Service
1950	*Yigdal*	Sabbath Evening Service
1963	*Kaddish*	Symphony Synagogue Services
1965	*Chichester Psalms*	Bible: Psalms 2:1–4; 23; 100; 108: 2; 131; 133:1

In his article 'Symbols of Faith in the Music of Leonard Bernstein', Gottlieb identifies a three-note cell in the first theme of *Jeremiah* that has clear connections with part of a prayer used at Rosh Hashanah (see Example 6.12a); he later calls it Bernstein's 'Faith Motive' (2004, pp. 182–3); this motif forms a clear musical connection between the pieces named:

This motif also reappeared as the last music sung by the soprano solo in the final movement of the symphony, meaning that it both opens and closes the work. Gottlieb then goes on to demonstrate the presence of this cell in *Kaddish*, in the fugue subject mentioned earlier in this chapter (see Example 6.3b). In *Chichester Psalms* the motif once again has a structural function, as it can be seen in the opening and closing moments of the work. In these appearances it has developed, and the second is inverted, although the figure can be seen in its original guise in the 11th bar of the first movement (see Examples 6.12b and 6.15). Gottlieb points out the use of the cell in *Mass*, in a further variation in the final song (see Example 6.11 'Pax'). In the interest of symmetry, it also appears in the first sung number of the same work, in 'A Simple Song', an example omitted by Gottlieb (see Example 6.12c). To complete the link between Bernstein's sacred works, the motif can be found in *Hashkiveinu*, again in a slightly altered version, appearing significantly

---

[22]   This was seen as a weakness by one particular critic, who attacked the *Mass* for its diminishing of the sanctity and holiness of religion by bringing it down to the 'everyday'. In his mind, 'by dispensing with the name of Jesus and the sign of the cross in this text created specifically to commemorate his crucifixion, the work stands virtually on its head; the insertion of the word "kadosh", which appears absolutely without any logical motivation, only reveals the dilemma of the composer' (Berlinski 1972, p. 7). Personally, I see no problem with including a Hebrew translation of the Sanctus, especially as the origins of the prayer are in book of Isaiah (6:3) which, of course, would have been read and spoken in Hebrew long before being translated into Latin.

Example 6.12 Bernstein's 'Faith Motif'

(a) Cadence figure from Rosh Hashanah liturgy
(b) *Chichester Psalms*, movement 1, bb. 11–12
(c) 'A Simple Song', b. 30
(d) *Hashkiveinu*, bb. 57–8
(e) *Yigdal*, bb. 1–2

in the cantor's part, and also in *Yigdal* (Example 6.12e).[23] Bernstein is not alone in being influenced by this figure, as it can also be found in the 'Ballad of the Cities' in Blitzstein's *Airborne Symphony* of 1946. This movement commemorates the cities across Europe that were destroyed during the bombing raids of the Second World War, and Bernstein had conducted the world première of the symphony in 1946.

It is only right that any consideration of Bernstein's musical theatre works should include an analysis of *Chichester Psalms*, as the piece has its origins very firmly in the theatre.[24] During his 1964 sabbatical from the New York Philharmonic, Bernstein received a commission from the Three Choirs Festival in England, to

---

[23] Gottlieb also observes that the cell is seen in retrograde in *Dybbuk*, completing the connection between the cell and the works.

[24] Sections of this analysis appeared in programme notes that I wrote for the City of Birmingham Symphony Orchestra, when they performed the *Chichester Psalms* in July 2004 and February 2005.

compose a piece for choir and orchestra to be performed in Chichester Cathedral in 1965. The Dean of the Cathedral, Dr Walter Hussey, included the request that 'I think many of us would be very delighted if there was a hint of *West Side Story* about the music' (quoted in Burton 1994, p. 348), a request that was certainly fulfilled. (The work was actually premièred in the US a few weeks before being performed in Chichester, the American performance being presented by a mixed choir, as opposed to the boys and men who sang in the British performance.) *Chichester Psalms* is divided into three movements, although employing text from six different psalms, mirroring the structure of Stravinsky's 1930 *Symphony of Psalms*. Unusually for a piece for a British place of worship, Bernstein set the words in the original Hebrew, rather than Latin or English. The first movement begins with a joyful exclamation of the first melodic idea, which is transformed at the beginning of the subsequent dance-like section. This music is in $\frac{7}{4}$, and is perhaps reminiscent of the 'Old Joe' round in *Peter Grimes* (see Example 6.13).

Example 6.13 *Chichester Psalms*, movement 1, bb. 14–16

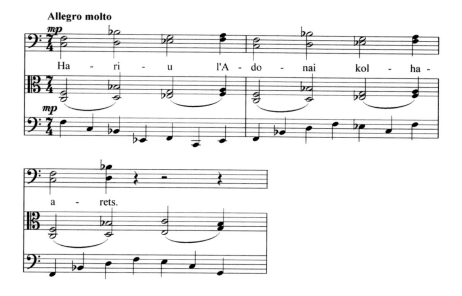

This melody was originally composed for *The Skin of Our Teeth*, with words by Comden and Green, under the title 'Look, Here Comes the Sun'. The melodic material moves between voice parts, with the ends of the lines overlapping, until a *fff* climax is reached at 'Bo-u sh'arav b'todah, Hatseirotav bit'hilah' (Enter into His gates with thanksgiving, And into His courts with praise). The dance aspect of the music is emphasized by the use of bongos in the orchestra which, incidentally, contains no woodwind, but consists of strings, three trumpets, three trombones, two harps, timpani, and the usual Bernstein-esque battery of percussion instruments, to be played by five players.

The second movement, a setting of the 23rd Psalm, begins with a lyrical solo supported by harps, another import from the earlier musical, a number titled 'Spring Will Come Again'. Despite the disjunct nature of the opening of the melody, there is a lyrical simplicity to Bernstein's writing here, emphasized by the allocating of the solo to a boy or a counter-tenor, the elegance and delicacy of the tune being matched by the purity of the voice (see Example 6.14).[25]

Example 6.14 *Chichester Psalms*, movement 2, bb. 3–7

The soloist is echoed by the women, but the tranquillity is disrupted by the men, who interject with a violent canon. This is Hussey's longed-for *West Side Story* moment. The music that Bernstein uses for the words 'Lamah rag'shu goyim' (Why do the nations rage?) appeared originally in a number for the Jets called 'Mix!', which was cut prior to the Broadway opening . I wonder how many choral societies and choirs have performed this work without realizing the violent and quite racist nature of the initial lyrics for this section, which included reference to 'little brown bums', 'we can cut them up', and the line 'Ev'ry brown little greasy son of a Puerto Rican, / Gets a kisser full of bricks'?[26] Fortunately, in *Chichester Psalms*, the outburst is calmed by the intervention of the women's lyrical music, and gradually the peacefulness returns, although there is still a hint of the unrest beneath as the movement ends, underlined by a rebellious *f* bass drum solo at the end, marked 'chiaro' (clear).

The Finale begins with an extended orchestral passage (echoing Stravinsky's orchestral introduction to the second movement of his *Symphony of Psalms* perhaps?), based on the work's opening melodic idea, before the chorus enters with a graceful and flowing melody in $^{10}_{4}$, another rescued item from *The Skin of Our Teeth*: 'We Never Took the Time'. The music from the very opening of the

---

[25]   At the beginning of his score, Bernstein stipulates that 'the long male-alto solo in the second movement must not be sung by a woman'.

[26]   Lyrics on a manuscript in LBC.

piece now returns to bring it to a close, as the motif is used as a basis for an a cappella section, which I think is some of the most beautiful music Bernstein ever wrote; this too was salvaged from the Wilder project. The choir sings 'Hineh mah tov, / unah nayim, / Shevet ahim / Gam yahad' (Behold how good, / And how pleasant it is, / For brethren to dwell / Together in unity) in hushed tones, before resolving onto octave Gs while a solo muted trumpet and harp (playing harmonics) play the opening five-note phrase once more over the voices, the one difference being an alteration of the last note from the expected C to the tonic G, concluding the piece on *ppp* unison octaves, a pure sound for a perfect ending (see Example 6.15).

Example 6.15 *Chichester Psalms*, movement 3, bb. 63–5

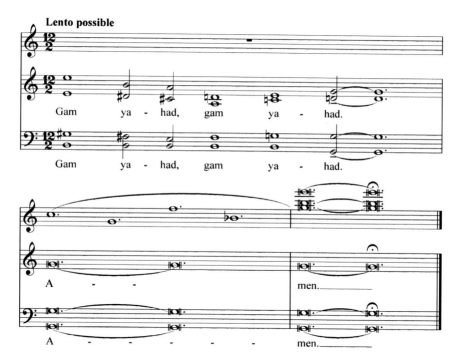

Bernstein appears to have been attracted not only by the spiritual but also by the theatrical aspect of religion: the elements of ritual and spectacle, use of gestures and movements, and the central role of the rabbi, cantor or priest. Churches and synagogues have separation of officiate and congregation, and raised areas for speaking and teaching, both of which reflect similar concepts in theatre design. The exploitation of these architectural factors can clearly be seen in the service of the mass, with the priest set apart from the people, reciting the liturgy from the 'stage' of the sanctuary and altar, from where he re-enacts the Last Supper in the prescribed actions of the Eucharist. The ritual is observed by the people who, although they have the opportunity to approach the sanctuary, are kept from entering the holy place. The choir form the connection between the elite figure of the priest and the congregation, but are *of* the people, and echo their feelings and views.

The position of religious leader is one that Bernstein empathized with, perhaps in part due to the parallels between priest and conductor. This empathy is affirmed through the presence of a solo voice or protagonist, a thread common in the symphonies, and which continues in *Mass*. This last work can be seen as 'a logical sequence to his three symphonies … Each of these is concerned with the crisis of faith in our own times' (Hume 1988, p. 57). Bernstein himself talked of this thread of belief through his works: 'The work I have been writing all my life is about the struggle that is born of the crisis of our century, a crisis of faith. Even way back, when I wrote *Jeremiah*, I was wrestling with that problem' (quoted in Hume 1988, p. 58).

The role of the protagonist develops through the symphonies, starting with the mezzo-soprano solo in the third movement of *Jeremiah*. The words from the book of Jeremiah describe the despair of the people as they suffer, believing themselves to be forsaken by God, perhaps an apt cry for Bernstein as the Second World War was raging when the symphony was written. In *The Age of Anxiety*, it is a wordless commentary that takes us through the action of Auden's poem, as Bernstein's voice is transferred to the piano solo, his own instrument. The musings, discussions and dreams of Auden's four characters, as they struggle with their own loss of faith, are reflected in the music, as they mourn for 'our lost dad, / Our colossal father' (Auden 1968, p. 331).[27] Again, the shadow of war falls over the work, as the poem had been written between 1946 and 1947, and two of the characters were in the Forces during the conflicts. The *Kaddish* symphony sees the further growth of the solo, which becomes a narrating voice. The speaker converses and argues with God, a Jewish trait,[28] in an increasingly confrontational manner. This one-way tirade can appear peculiar and irreverent to a non-Jew, but Bernstein explained and defended himself: 'I intend no sacrilege. The argument with God has its origin in love; this is the great conflict in man's soul' (Burton 1994, p. 340). In *Mass*, the protagonist now takes on the function of leader and priest, although the crisis continues until resolved by the acceptance of love as a solution. As with his previous principals, the lead character represents part of Bernstein himself: 'the Celebrant is an extension of my thought' (quoted in Burton 1994, p. 408). In an interview given between composing *Mass* and completing *Dybbuk*, Bernstein said, 'I'm turning out to be more and more a religious man (in my own special way, anyhow) and I suppose I'll go on battling with my faith' (Ramey n.d.). Despite this sentiment, it is interesting that *Mass* was the last work with both a religious basis

---

[27]   Interestingly, there is the suggestion that one of the four characters, Rosetta, is Jewish, as she says 'Your Jesus wept' (Auden 1968, p. 345), and her final phrase is a Jewish prayer 'Sh'ma' Yisra'el. 'adonai 'elohenu, 'adonai 'echad' (p. 347).

[28]   This can be also be seen in some of Teyve's dialogues in *Fiddler on the Roof*, and throughout the biblical book of *Job*.

and a protagonist. Perhaps facing the crisis of faith through the role of a priest and finding resolution ended Bernstein's need to continue his quest through his music:

> The faith or peace that is found at the end of *Jeremiah* is really more a kind of comfort, not a solution. Comfort is one way of achieving peace, but it does not achieve the sense of a new beginning, as does the end of *Age of Anxiety* or *Mass*. (Quoted in Hume 1988, p. 58)

In *Mass*, Bernstein embraced both old and new traditions, with a variety of influences ranging from Beethoven, through Britten, to contemporary pop music; medieval liturgical structures and methods are blended with popular song forms and sounds, an eclecticism that did not please everyone. The popular music is referential, and is used to embody the convictions of the Street Chorus, who are representative of the general populace. The number of motifs utilized has increased, perhaps suggesting that Bernstein was moving away from the symphonic unity he sought in *West Side Story*. However, there is the sense that, rather than forming part of his series of musical theatre works, *Mass* is the resolution to Bernstein's sequence of symphonies, each with their own crisis of faith. There is also a political angle in this piece, more overt than the references to the McCarthy era in *Candide*, and this aspect would also go on to play a part in Bernstein's next show.

black American family. The episodic nature of the plot, spanning over 100 years in ten scenes, mirrored the plan Lerner had used in his earlier work *Love Life* (1948), which he had written with Kurt Weill. This told the story of the Cooper family, Sam and Susan, who remained the same as the world changed around them, from the American Revolution through the years to the Great Depression and beyond.[5] As this show had not been a success, perhaps Lerner should not have attempted to repeat the experiment with time. In *1600 Pennsylvania Avenue*, the White House itself remains constant, or at least the notion of the House as a representation of American ideals, while the occupants and American society change around it. The subtitle of the show, 'The Problems of Housekeeping', refers not only to the domestic chores of the servants, but to the difficulties of keeping the house despite the efforts of various groups to destroy or undermine this symbol of the nation. The passage of time would be shown by depicting various events in history, from the Civil War, the Proclamation of Emancipation through the impeachment of Andrew Johnson to the end of the nineteenth century, 'ideas which are particularly related to the White House kitchen help' (Oberdorfer 1974, p. 1). It sounded like a promising idea, but the concept was not easily transferred onto the stage, especially when the historical events were portrayed almost abstractly as a play-within-a-play, with the same actor playing all the presidents, and the same actress all of the respective wives; a similar trick was used in for the servants, with the same three people playing members of the different generations of the Simmons family. The confusion this leads to is actually brought up in the show itself, at the beginning of Act 2, in a dialogue between Luddy (the young boy) and Seena, as she tries to explain that he isn't going to marry his mother: 'Just remember, I'm always your momma when you're a little boy and I'm always your wife when you grow up' ('gypsy' run-through script, p. 61).

Bernstein was willing to make changes when needed, but Lerner was not only having problems being in awe of Bernstein, but was also struggling with his use of amphetamines, which affected his ability to work (Lees 1991, p. 278). When Coca-Cola stepped in to finance the show in 1975 (Lerner was friends with an executive there), *1600 Pennsylvania Avenue* became part of the planned Bicentennial celebrations. But the problems with the span of the show, and the heavy nature of Lerner's book, became more and more evident, so much so that at the initial tryouts in Philadelphia there was a well-documented case of a customer who kicked in the glass of the box-office when refused a refund (Citron 1995, p. 364). A change on the production team led to Gilbert Moses and George Faison replacing Frank Corsaro and Donald McKayle, neither of whom felt they could continue with the show. Significantly, both the new men were black, and they set about changing many aspects of *1600*, particularly those involving the black

---

[5]   Wilder's play *The Skin of Our Teeth* (1942) utilizes a similar structure, as the Antrobus family exist consecutively in a New Jersey suburb and through an Ice Age, the Great Flood and the Napoleonic Wars; as previously mentioned, Bernstein had worked on a musical version of the show in 1964, although the project did not reach fruition.

servants. Other aspects that were changed included a reduction of the play-within-a-play concept, and the deletion of scenes where the characters dropped out of their roles for discussions of the issues (Mandelbaum 1991, p. 326). Unfortunately, this further fragmented an already patchy work, and by the New York opening on 4 May 1976 the musical had been dramatically changed from its original concept, and obviously not that much for the better; *1600 Pennsylvania Avenue* lasted only seven performances. Clive Barnes, of *The New York Times*, asked 'if this is meant as a Bicentennial offering ... maybe we should wait for the Tricentennial'. He said the show was 'as equally patronizing to women as blacks', and that the 'theme of race relations ... works most terribly'. Barnes did save a good word or two for Bernstein: 'Mr Bernstein's contribution is more distinguished' (1976, p. 48). Bernstein was heartbroken by this failure: 'I'm shattered by the whole thing. The score was completely fragmented, not at all as I wrote it' (quoted in Citron 1995, p. 365). In a concise description of the show's failings, Mandelbaum outlined the basic problems behind the work:

> *1600* began with a practically impossible concept. By definition episodic, the show moved swiftly from one president to the next, and there was no way of developing a story or doing more than sketching in a personality or character trait for each tenant. It was a show about a house, about democracy itself, rather than about people, and it is questionable if this idea could ever have been brought off successfully. (1991, p. 326)

Over a decade after the dust had cleared, Erik Haagensen returned to the show, and through a great deal of research he drew together material that reflected the show as it had been seen in the 'gypsy' run-through, before a note or a scene had been cut. This version was then performed by students of the Indiana University Opera group in 1992, firstly in a workshop at the university, then at the Kennedy Centre (Haagensen 1992, p. 32). The score alone was subsequently salvaged in 1997 in a concert performance of the historical scenes of the show in a version called *A White House Cantata*, performed at the Barbican Centre in London on 8 July; the concert was narrated by Bernstein's son Alexander in an unannounced appearance. This version has since been released on CD by Deutsche Grammophon, and together with the score, which can be hired from Boosey and Hawkes, provides the only official record of the show's music.[6] However, some of the numbers in *A White House Cantata* did not appear in the version that was presented on Broadway ('Time' and 'The Grand Old Party'), while others that were on the stage did not reappear in the 1997 version ('Rehearse!', 'Auctions', 'The

---

[6]   Manuscripts of the numbers that were cut from the original show, both at the run-through stage and prior to the Broadway première, together with songs that never made it into the stage version and programmes for the tryouts, previews and the opening night, can be found in the LBC.

Ball' and 'Forty Acres and a Mule').[7] As Harmon points out: 'Leonard Bernstein composed more music for *1600 Pennsylvania Avenue* than for any other of his works for the theatre. There were numerous revisions in the course of the first few performances. Whole new scenes were written, discarded, replaced by others' (Harmon 1997b, p. 7). This creates some problems when considering what music belongs in the show and which pieces should be studied, so for this book I have relied on the materials that are available, and concentrated on the score of the 1997 cantata version, with mentions of other numbers if manuscripts were accessible in the Library of Congress.

A major issue with the show lay in the fact that not only was the story patronizing towards blacks and women, but that also the episodes chosen for the story were critical of the American people themselves, a detail that the US public found difficult to associate with. The black slaves are presented, for the most part, quite sympathetically, and slavery is quite rightly condemned as a wrong perpetrated by the whites. This was not 'feelgood' entertainment, and as a supposed celebratory piece about two hundred years of independence 'it was a strange bicentennial tribute, one sharply critical of many White House residents' (Mandelbaum 1991, p. 324); people were not happy seeing their historical figures vilified. Taking these points into consideration, it would have seemed reasonable that, once the text and plot were removed, the material would stand a chance of being successful, but this was not the case. The staging of *The White House Cantata* received a lukewarm reception from the British press following the world première of the new version: 'the work is dire' (Norris 1997, p. 29); 'Despite massive forces on stage and the almost demonic conducting of Kent Nagano, revamped Bernstein still carries the flavour of heated-up turkey pie' (Higgins 1997, p. 37). Purging the intervening text removed one of the only linking elements, leaving barely connected episodes that leapt through history at an alarming rate. Never one to let good music be rejected or remain unplayed, Bernstein himself rescued some of the pieces from the doomed show, as music from songs was transplanted into his later works *Songfest* and *Slava!* (both 1977), and his final opera *A Quiet Place* (1983).

Given the problems, and the failure of the show, it might seem curious to spend so much time and effort considering and analysing the music left behind. However, on a personal note, I was present at the première of *A White House Cantata* in 1997, and was struck by the vitality and beauty of the music that Bernstein had created for the piece. As already mentioned, he wrote a substantial amount of songs for the show, and, as I hope to demonstrate, he certainly did not skimp on the

---

[7]   Haagensen's 1992 version had incorporated other numbers, including 'Philadelphia', 'The Nation That Wasn't There' and 'American Dreaming'. Matters are confused further by the fact that some numbers changed titles during the process, so that 'Rehearse!' was also called 'Rehearsing', 'To Make Us Proud' became 'I Love This Land', returning to a simplified 'Proud', and the two sections of 'The Monroviad' are sometimes called 'The Little White Lie' and 'The Mark of a Man', the two songs which are joined together in this scene. For a sense of continuity, I will use the titles from *A White House Cantata*.

intellectual or creative energy he put into the work. I feel that this music deserves as much attention as his contributions to his other musical theatre pieces, if not more, as it is largely unknown in his repertoire.

The historical scenes of *1600 Pennsylvania Avenue* and the musical numbers, as performed in *A White House Cantata*, are as follows:

'Prelude'

1789–97: President George Washington

Washington and Congress choose a location for a capital city, with confrontation between the Northern and Southern delegates.

'Ten Square Miles by the Potomac River'

1797–1801: President John Adams

Little Lud escapes from slavery and helps Abigail Adams find the unfinished White House.

'If I Was a Dove'

'Welcome Home, Miz Adams'

'Take Care of This House'

1801–09: President Thomas Jefferson

Thomas Jefferson entertains, complete with the Marine Band and exotic food from his foreign travels.

'The President Jefferson Sunday Luncheon March'

1809–17: President James Madison

Grown-up Lud admires Thomaseena, another young servant who is possibly the child of Thomas Jefferson.

'Seena'

The British dine at the White House in the midst of the War of 1812, before attempting to burn down Washington.

'Sonatina'

1817–25: President James Monroe

Lud and Seena have both grown up and are married by Reverend Bushrod.

'Lud's Wedding'

Upstairs, James Monroe has decided to send all the blacks, including the servants, to Liberia. His wife disagrees.

'The Monroviad'

For Lud and Seena and for all blacks the streets of Washington have become dangerous, and they risk being snatched and deported.

'This Time'

1857–61: President James Buchanan

James Buchanan puzzles about averting a civil war, preferring to ignore the problem while concentrating on more important things, such as a party.

'We Must Have a Ball'

INTERVAL (THE CIVIL WAR)

1865–69: President Andrew Johnson

    Eliza Johnson arrives at the White House,

        'Welcome Home, Miz Johnson'

    while downstairs, the servants celebrate their future as free people.

        'Bright and Black'

1869–81: Presidents Ulysses S. Grant and Rutherford B. Hayes

    At the Inauguration, Julia Grant and Lucy Hayes reflect on their husbands and on one another.

        'Duet for One'

1881–85: President Chester Alan Arthur

    Chester Alan Arthur entertains Mr Rockefeller and Mr Vanderbilt with a minstrel show, as business tries to control the decisions at the White House.

        The Money-Lovin' Minstrel Show:

            'Minstrel Parade'

            'Pity the Poor'

            'The Grand Old Party'

            'Red, White and Blues'

1901–09: President Theodore Roosevelt

    Theodore Roosevelt brings new dedication to a new century.

        'To Make Us Proud'

            (adapted from programme for *A White House Cantata* 1997)

A show that moves through a period of over 100 years offers the opportunity for the use of the device of narrative pastiche, as a medium for indicating the passage of time, as opposed to the static pastiche of *Wonderful Town* and *West Side Story*.[8] This technique was employed by Kern in *Show Boat* (1927), the first musical work to tackle such a large-scale historical plot, and a great deal of skill was needed to traverse the 50 years between the opening, set in the 1880s, and the end, by which point time had advanced to the present day of the 1920s. The time of the opening scene is established by the use of pastiche songs, mainly based on the Black American styles prevalent at the time: 'Misr'y's Comin' Aroun'', a spiritual; 'C'mon Folks!', a cakewalk; and 'Gallavantin' Around' and 'Can't Help Lovin' Dat Man', both coon songs (Morddern 1983, p. 106). The last of these songs acts as a time marker, as when it is heard subsequently in Act 2, which is set in 1904, its style is altered and 'ragged'. It is brought up-to-date by modifying the rhythm to conform to the 'contemporary' popularity of ragtime. A similar transformation happens to 'Cotton Blossom', where the rhythm of the song is also changed from the first hearing (the 1880s), and the second (1927). A further time marker comes in the shape of Charles K. Harris's 'After the Ball', which is introduced at the Trocadero Music Hall in Act 2 (1904), as an 'old favourite'. As this song was first

---

[8]   The following discussion on *Show Boat* was originally published in *British Postgraduate Musicology*, vol. 2, 1998.

published in 1892, in Kern's setting it would have been 12 years old, and, as it had been a very successful and popular song, would in all likelihood still have been performed in such circumstances. The dances used in *Show Boat* also indicate the passing years, with the shuffle and buck and wing of the 1880s giving way to the jive (1893). The differences in the music that denote the different years were noticeable to some of the theatregoers of the time:

> Here [Kern] has blended the Negro spirituals of the Southland with the jazz of today. What is even more noteworthy, he has caught the subtle distinction that exists between jazz and the ragtime of twenty or twenty-five years ago, and several of his numbers of the last category are amazingly characteristic of the early years of the present century. (Waters 1927)

Given that Bernstein was presenting double the time span that Kern and Hammerstein had engaged with, he could have utilized accurate examples of American music to depict the passing of time, but, as with his earlier shows, Bernstein's concern was not to be completely precise, but to create music that was fitting and entertaining. In this way, he employed styles and genres that were appropriate for the characters being portrayed, but the temporal settings are not always exact, although Bernstein's examples of black American music do broadly reflect the developing genre through the period shown. This cannot be seen as a criticism, as historically accuracy is almost never the remit of musical theatre, and as Lerner made no effort to be linguistically correct for the period, there is no reason why strict narrative pastiche methods should have been used.

Bernstein's approach was different to that that taken by the creative team in Lerner's earlier epic story, *Love Life*, which despite spanning over 100 years does not employ pastiche. Instead there is a vaudeville feel to the show, with a reappearing male chorus that comments on the proceedings in the manner of a minstrel show. In addition, the composer did not always help the situation, as demonstrated in the early love song: 'Weill's gorgeous melody is one of the best and most up-to-date show tunes that 1948 offered, while the characters are supposed to be set in Colonial New England' (Citron 1995, p. 203).

Some of the scenes in *1600* depict real proceedings, such as the British invasion and the inauguration of President Hayes, though not necessarily with complete historical accuracy. This portrayal of actual events through musical means is called 'documentary vaudeville' by Sondheim (Banfield 1993, p. 256). It is a technique Sondheim used in both *Pacific Overtures*, another show that Bernstein had watched in 1976, prior to the opening of *1600*,[9] and Sondheim's own musical relating to the American Presidents, although this time describing attempts on their lives, both successful and unsuccessful, in *Assassins* (1991).

---

9   On 10 January 1976, according to his date book (box 325, LBC).

Characterization: Upstairs and Downstairs

In the same way that the two gangs in *West Side Story* are defined by their differing musical styles, so are the two main groups in *1600 Pennsylvania Avenue*. There are clear differences between the material written for those 'upstairs' in the house, and for those 'downstairs'. The music of the servants, particularly in the chorus numbers, is based on black American genres. The first time we see and hear the staff they are welcoming Mrs Adams to the not quite completed President's Mansion with homophonic a cappella singing, reminiscent of hymn singing. The syllabic and declamatory setting would have been familiar to the servants as they would have learned hymns and spirituals from their white employers and owners. However, arrangements of spirituals only began to be written following the Emancipation, as groups such as the Fisk Jubilee Singers included the traditional black forms in their concert repertoire (Oliver 1986, p. 193). At the time when 'Welcome Home, Miz Adams' is set, such part-singing was unknown, with songs only being performed in a monophonic texture. Bernstein adapts this genre to his own means, and he expands the harmonic language, as the piece appears to begin in G♭, before moving to the 'real' tonic of B♭. There is a touch of the blues influence when the opening note of D♭ returns in a fermata chord in b.6, the note appearing here as a flattened thirteenth within a dominant seventh chord (see Example 7.1). There is some correlation between the music here and the eight-voice a cappella writing at the end of *Candide*, and in addition Bernstein may have been inspired by the vocal textures of the black chorus in Scott Joplin's 1911 opera *Treemonisha*, which Bernstein had gone to watch on 30 October 1975.[10] In his work, Joplin wrote for up to six parts, although his harmony is less adventurous, and follows simpler progressions.

A further temporal anachronism can be found in the song celebrating Lud and Seena's wedding. This is set to a lively calypso rhythm that could not possibly have reached Washington by the date of this scene (1817–25), although it clearly demonstrates one aspect of the emerging and developing black music, which was beginning to move away from the religious and white-derived origins. The style originated mainly in Trinidad, as a development of a West African working song brought by slaves to the plantations of the West Indies. Although it is true that thousands of slaves migrated to the Mississippi area in the first decade of the nineteenth century (Chase 1966, p. 303), it is highly unlikely that the music could have moved so far north in such a short space of time. The first examples of the calypso being incorporated into American music can be found in the compositions of Louis Moreau Gottschalk,[11] and, as he was only born in 1829, this is unlikely to be a source for Bernstein's song. There are elements of cakewalk in some phrases, but the dance section, which has changing time signatures, is reminiscent of Bernstein's *Jeremiah* symphony with its Jewish overtones, rather than a black

---

[10] According to his date book (ibid.).

[11] Many thanks to John Graziano for clarifying this fact for me.

Example 7.1 'Welcome Home, Miz Adams', bb. 1–7

Example 7.2 'Lud's Wedding', bb. 135–8

American dance (see Example 7.2). Despite this, the calypso is the ideal genre with which to capture the festive mood of the celebration taking place, and still underlines the slave roots of those enjoying the wedding.

'Bright and Black', a chorus number led by Henry, Lud, his son Little Lud, and Seena, is sung following the Civil War (represented by the interval), in celebration of the Emancipation of the slaves. It is in two clear sections, although both are based on the same music. The first section is a funeral march, sardonically lamenting the passing of 'Uncle Tom', the archetypal black slave. It begins with a solo bass (Henry), who is gradually joined by more members of the chorus. In between his vocal phrases, there are spoken lines, in a quasi-call-and-response form. In the B section of the segment of the song, the responses are sung, with an emphasis on minor thirds within the melodies. These phrases are reminiscent of figures from the funeral march in Gershwin's *Porgy and Bess*, 'Gone, Gone, Gone'. When the music accelerates into the second half of the number a clearer link with the earlier opera can be found. The same tune is now presented in a major key, with a crotchet-based accompaniment, and a banjo added to the instrumentation. A comparison of melodic lines shows the relationship between the first phrase of Bernstein's banjo song, and that of Gershwin's work, 'I Got Plenty o' Nuttin', including the interesting point that both phrases end with a syncopated rhythm. The music for this section can be seen in various sketches in the Bernstein Collection, under a variety of titles. The most interesting of these is an undated sketch labelled 'It's the Jews'; this title corresponds to a note in a copy of *Romeo and Juliet* in the Collection: '(song on racism) ("It's the Jews")'.[12] A song that began as descriptive of the minority in the original version of *West Side Story* eventually ended up relating to a different minority in *1600*.

Both 'Bright and Black' and 'I Got Plenty o' Nuttin'' are contained within an A–A–B–A–coda structure, although 'Bright and Black' is then expanded with a repetition of the music, with the first three sections becoming a dance break in the new key of E♭ (a mediant modulation from the key of G, and also the relative major of the opening key of C minor). The coda contains a Bernstein touch, as syncopation is used to increase the sense of excitement in the song, and a three-against-four cross-rhythm is created, similar to phrases seen earlier in *Candide*.

Lud's solo song, 'Seena', also reflects the influence of the blues, not so much in the structure of the piece, which is set in eight-bar rather than 12-bar phrases in an A–A–B–A structure, but in the melody. The fifth of the scale appears both as an A♮ and an A♭, although Bernstein uses the flattened fifth only twice, both of these occurring in descending patterns. This is an expected use of such a blue note by Bernstein, as he pointed out the normal positioning of the variable notes in the blue or Negro scale in his Bachelor's thesis, many years before writing *1600*: 'The three flattened degrees of the scale [3rd, 5th and 7th] are used almost exclusively in descending figures' (Bernstein 1976, p. 53). More unexpected are the flattened ninth and sharpened sixth, both of which appear in the same bar (b. 8) (see Example 7.3).

The scene when Lud is singing this song is dated somewhere between 1809 and 1812, during the tenure of James Madison, and before the British invasion. This is a very early date for a blues number, as the genre only began to gain popularity towards the end of the nineteenth century; it is a further example of Bernstein manipulating the idea of narrative pastiche, but maintaining the overall progression of black music within the timeframe.

The remaining songs for the black characters, 'If I Was a Dove' and 'This Time', do not fit into recognizable genres. The first, which carries on directly from '10 Square Miles' and introduces the character of Lud Simmons, is in $\frac{9}{8}$, suggesting a pastoral feel, and has no real parallel in traditional black forms. The harmony is unstable, reflecting the melody line, which alternates F♯s and F♮s in the

---

[12]   Box 73, folder 10, LBC.

Example 7.3 'Seena', bb. 5–12

first two bars. The harmony in the opening bars is ambiguous, as the first chord could be D major or B minor, creating either a I–IV⁷ or I–VI⁷ pattern; the overall tonality of the song appears to be B minor, with a Phrygian tinge. In whichever case, the G⁷ chord is used to take the music into C major, where we have the added chromaticism of the flattened seventh, B♭. The key shifts rather than modulates back into B for the final cadence. The rhythm of the melody is quite free, with little repetition, and it follows the rhythm of the text. The form of the song is very simple, relating to the fact that Lud is a child at this point, and comprises two verses of nine bars each, and a seven-bar coda based on the same material.

'This Time' is a duet for Lud and Seena during the time of President Monroe. This did not appear in the Broadway production, but in the 'gypsy' version and in *A White House Canata* the preceding scene shows a slave auction in Washington, and a discussion between the Monroes about the proposed relocation of black slaves to the African country of Liberia. Seena is scared of losing Lud as he journeys to the White House every day, and the introduction to this song demonstrates this anxiety, with a figure reminiscent of the opening of 'A Boy Like That' from *West Side Story*. The first section of the song, which is in ¾, has similarities to 'My Man's Gone Now' from *Porgy and Bess*; the two songs share the same key, and a syncopated accompaniment. Unlike Gershwin's song, 'This Time' does not have balanced eight-bar phrases, emphasizing the uneasiness and tension. The first phrase is seven bars long, and is also faster, with more of a jazz-waltz feel. When the time signature changes to ¢ (with occasional ¾ bars) for the second section, there is the familiar ♪♩ ♪♪. ♪ rhythm that can be found in the ballet in Act II of *West Side Story*. There is a third section, beginning at b. 91, where the melody line is comparable with that of 'I Go On' from *Mass*, with a turn figure and descending fifth (the turn is inverted in the earlier song, while the fifth is diminished in the *1600* number) (see Example 7.4).

This section is calm in comparison with the previous two parts of the song, the more peaceful feeling emphasized by a nearly constant crotchet pulse in the accompaniment, which contrasts the driving rhythms and syncopation from

Example 7.4 'This Time', bb. 92–5

Sud - den - ly a pro - mise land____ blos - som in - to view. God reach out a

help - in' hand____ like he used to do.

before. The time signature changes between $\frac{5}{4}$ and $\frac{7}{4}$, with bars in $\frac{9}{4}$ and $\frac{6}{4}$, creating a slightly unbalanced impression that underlines the 'in a dream' indication on the score. At the end of the song, Seena's protestations and pleadings with her husband prove ineffective, as Lud is drawn back to the memory of the promise he made to Mrs Adams when he was a boy, and we hear the replies he made to her in a reprise of 'Take Care of This House'.

In a similar manner, the music for the characters of the President and the First Lady also utilize appropriate genres. Specifically, the two songs featuring the President in a public situation, '10 Square Miles' and 'The President Jefferson Luncheon Party March', are both based on the march rhythm suggested by the title of the latter. It is hardly surprising that music associated with President Washington should be in a march style. The military feel created by the genre underlines the fact that he had been Commander of the Continental Army throughout the Revolutionary War, the conflict that had led to the establishment of the United States as a free nation in 1783. The earliest march connected with the position of the President was published in 1795: 'The President's March' by Philip Phile; three years later this tune acquired lyrics and became 'Hail Columbia' (Kirk 1986, p. 13). The section of '10 Square Miles' that is based on march rhythms, however, has a twist in the harmony, as the bass line chromatically shifts from a tonic–dominant pattern in C major to the same degrees on the flattened supertonic chord of D♭; this is comparable with the 'twist' in the march in *Mass*, mentioned in the previous chapter. This harmony is also reflected in the first two bars of the melody and inner accompaniment, although the bass now remains in the tonic key (see Example 7.5).

The opening four crotchets of the tune emphasize the solid and striding sound of the music following a triplet figure in the introduction. The oom-pah accompaniment is present for the majority of this section of the song, but there are four bars where there is a change in rhythm. These occur when Washington is talking of the contrast between the northern and southern elements of his proposed city. There is a shift to a ♩. ♪♩ ♩ pattern in the bass, with a syncopated rhythm over this, and quite large leaps in the melody. The exotic image of the South has influenced the President, resulting in a rumba-style phrase that is a little before its time, but which is very evocative of the contrast between the north and south of the country.

Example 7.5 'Ten Square Miles', bb. 63–6 (bass line and melody only)

The second march, 'The President Jefferson Sunday Luncheon March', has its musical origins clearly defined in the first few lines of the lyric, where the Marine Band are introduced. America had first been entertained by military bands visiting from Britain before the American Revolution, and during the War US regiments had begun to form their own ensembles (Cipolla and Camus 2001, p. 563). The band associated with the US Marine Corps was officially formed in 1798, but it was only in 1801 that they began to perform at social functions (Kirk 1986, p. 9). Jefferson held such receptions only twice a year: New Year's Day and Fourth of July, beginning on 4 July 1801 (Kirk 1986, p. 28). The Marine Band were certainly present at these events, and played fitting music, as noted by a guest in 1801:

> Martial music soon announced the approach of the marine corps of Captain Burrows who in due military form saluted the President, accompanied by the President's march [probably 'Hail Columbia'] played by an excellent band attached to the corps. After undergoing various military evolutions, the company retired to the dining room, and the band from an adjacent room played a succession of fine patriotic airs. (Quoted in Kirk 1986, p. 28, brackets by Kirk)

In his march, however, Bernstein again has a surprise in store, this time a rhythmic twist in the bridge section before verse three. The oom-pah accompaniment is disturbed by cross-rhythms, appearing at first to become a waltz figure, but changing again, forcing the beat to feel as though it has 'skipped'; the ¢ and $\frac{3}{4}$ bars add up to Bernstein's familiar seven-beat metre. The peculiar feel of this phrasing continues into the next verse (see Example 7.6).

Patricia Routledge, who played the First Ladies in the show, recognized the faltering nature of the music, although not the exact metre:

['The President Jefferson Sunday Luncheon March'] was a march in $\frac{5}{4}$ time, and there was a great discussion going on as to how you do a march in $\frac{5}{4}$ time, and I said 'That's all right, you do right, left, right, left, and a limp, really.' That's the way you fit it in, I suppose. (On Burton 1996/7)

Example 7.6 'The President Jefferson Sunday Luncheon March', bb. 113–18 (accompaniment only)

The sound of the Marine Band and the idea of American marches are both inseparable from J. P. Sousa, who was appointed leader of the Marine Band in 1880, and wrote many of his best-known marches in the 20 years following this. However, the Jefferson scene is set some 80 years before this, meaning that although the figure of Sousa appears to be present, it is again a little premature for such a reference.

In contrast to these marches, the private side of the President, in his various incarnations, is portrayed for the most part by less military-sounding music. The first occasion we see the President in a more intimate situation is in 'The Monroviad'. The opening words of James Monroe are tentative, as he enquires of his wife Eliza whether she is awake. His following phrases are fragmented and rhythmically varied in a recitative style as he describes his insecurities. There are touches of a pompous military sound as he gains confidence in his thoughts and decisions, but these are followed by short phrases, as self-doubt returns. The main contrast comes in the last section of the song, 'The Mark of a Man', where the gentle rocking feeling of the $\frac{9}{8}$ time signature is a marked difference from the strident $\frac{4}{4}$ of the marches. There is a more detailed analysis of this piece later in this chapter.

James Buchanan's 'We Must Have a Ball' appears to begin in private, as the President rants about the supposed threat of secession, and suggests that the best thing to do is ignore the problem and have a party instead. The *valse élégante* used to support these ideas underlines the frivolous concept of such an idea, but the hemiola in the introduction, which also recurs throughout the song, hints at instability in the situation, and the feeling that things could quite easily come unstuck. Waltzes had been established in Washington society in the 1820s, and the First Lady of the time had been the subject of a dedication of such a piece around 1811: 'Mrs Madison's Waltz' (Kirk 1986, p. 36). The employment of the dance-based style at this point in *1600* was so that a transition could be made into the scene of the ball itself. There was originally a suite of dances included in this number, played as the ball progressed, containing a Schottische, Polonaise, Polka, Hornpipe-Quadrille and Ländler (Harmon 1997a). What is perhaps most startling about this scene is that it reflects a real event; Buchanan did indeed host a gala event for the Prince of Wales in October 1860 (Kirk 1986, p. 74), just two months before South Carolina seceded. By April the following year, Civil War had begun, but by that point Buchanan had been replaced by the rather more pragmatic and realistic Abraham Lincoln (Jenkins 1997, p. 135).

In this show, the First Ladies appear generally more moderate and calm than their husbands. The first wife we meet is Mrs Adams, in 'Take Care of This House'. This song begins with a reiteration of the march music from '10 Square Miles', altered into $\frac{3}{4}$ time as she berates the house that has been built for their accommodation, and, after a bridge section, the main verse begins. The compound triple time, with occasional changes from $\frac{9}{8}$ into $\frac{6}{8}$, creates a gentle feel, similar to the mood of the earlier 'If I Was a Dove'; the connection between the two songs is Little Lud, as singer of the first, and listener to, and later participant in, the second. The compound time link continues with Eliza Munroe's contribution in 'The Monroviad', as her lullaby interjection, an attempt to placate her husband, moves the music from changing simple time signatures to $\frac{9}{8}$. However, the last song featuring the First Lady is far less genteel and ladylike. The 'Duet for One' presents two of the wives at an Inauguration, and contrasts the differing characters of the two women. The outgoing First Lady, Julia Grant, is portrayed by jig-like music reflecting her Southern origins, with parallel fifths creating drone sounds in the bass, and repeated melodic figures. This contrasts sharply with Lucy Hayes's *Valse Lente*, a more sophisticated and stylish sounding section (see Examples 7.7a and b).

In real life, Lucy Hayes was a very refined and civilized woman, and this influence was exerted over the household: 'The Hayes entertained with elegance, grace and conservatism (no liquor was served at the White House during their term)' (Kirk 1986, p. 114). The waltz melody dominates the end of the piece, as Lucy revels in her new role, but there is a reminder of her predecessor in the coda, as under the 'Hail Hayes' chords, the Southern music is juxtaposed in $\frac{3}{4}$.

In is notable that in the portrayal of the American characters within *1600* the influence of one significant composer is conspicuous by its absence: that of Stephen Foster. Foster wrote copious songs that have passed into American musical tradition, such as 'Camptown Races', 'Old Folks at Home', 'Beautiful Dreamer' and 'I Dream of Jeannie With the Light Brown Hair'. However, it must be remembered that his most prolific writing came between 1846 and 1864

Example 7.7   Contrasting themes in 'Duet for One'

(a) 'Duet for One', bb. 161–4
(b) 'Duet For One', bb. 175–81

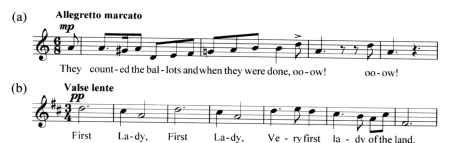

(Earhart and Brige 1953, p. 6), and this time is shown in *1600* by 'We Must Have a Ball', and the Civil War, which is represented by the interval.

Characterization: The Others

Of course, the characters in *1600 Pennsylvania Avenue* are not limited to the inhabitants and employees of the Presidential Mansion. In the first half, there are also the British, who invaded Washington during the War of 1812. For a large part of their number, 'Sonatina', the officers do not sing, but speak in rhythm, a technique previously employed by Gershwin in the recitative sections of *Porgy and Bess*. This marks them as distinct from the Americans. However, as the number progresses, they do begin to sing, starting with Admiral Cockburn, as he rouses his men to sing 'To Anacreon in Heaven' (c.1780; Sonneck Society 1976). This song is particularly apt, as although it began life as a British drinking song, also called the 'The Anacreontick Song', it was appropriated by the Americans in 1798 with new lyrics as 'Adams and Liberty', although its best-known rendering originated in 1812 with words by Francis Scott Key, as 'The Star Spangled Banner'. Cockburn is thus quite correct in his observation that 'our fav'rite drinking song which lately, I am told, / These Yanks have plagiarised'. The a cappella setting that Bernstein uses at this point is not actually of his own creation, but is instead a genuine arrangement of the song from 1780;[13] a more detailed analysis of 'Sonatina' can be found later in this chapter.

---

[13]   A copy of the manuscript is in the Bernstein Collection, with a handwritten note on the bottom: 'marginal notes – points where 1780 ms differs from 1785 ms in lyrics'; on this manuscript it is titled 'The Anacreontick Song'. On the programme for the opening night of *1600 Pennsylvania Avenue*, the source of the arrangement is dated erroneously as 'an authentic harmonization of "To Anacreon in Heav'n" (1740) later known as "The Star

The minstrel show in the second half represents 'the buying of the presidency by the robber baron industrialists in the late 1800s' (Haagenson 1992, p. 26). The four songs are presented in the form of 'The Money-Lovin' Minstrel Show', using forms and genres found in minstrelsy, certainly appropriate for this scene in the 1880s, and by persons from outside the White House. It begins with 'Minstrel Parade', which is in a ragtime style: there are characteristic sections where melody and bass are in octaves, and echoes of an oom-pah bass line; there is also chromaticism and use of blue notes. The device of the parade itself was used by minstrel companies to advertise that evening's performances in a town, and would feature marches and other tunes (Southern 1997, p. 235). In between the songs of this scene, there is comic banter between the two 'end men'[14] of the supposed company, Mr Simoleon and Mr Greenback, and the character of Uncle Sam, in the style of the comedy of the minstrel shows. The minstrel-show device had already been utilized in *Love Life*, and in *Pacific Overtures*; both of these shows also include references to economic change, and the power of money, in the songs 'Economics' and 'Next' respectively. The second song begins as a lament, a 'slow, sentimental waltz' (score note), as the Shekel Brothers (a reference to Jewish money-lenders?) sing of how they 'Pity the Poor', in parallel thirds for most of this section. However, the final five bars of this very short song revert to a ragtime $\frac{2}{4}$ and syncopated melody as they reveal that the poor are poor ''coz dey's dumb'.

The next number, 'The Grand Old Party', begins with an introduction and vamp very similar to that of 'Gee, Officer Krupke!'. The march feel of this song, a two-step, is disrupted by occasional $\frac{3}{4}$ bars, suggesting an instability in the concept of the 'grand old party', underlined by lyrics referring to bribery and corruption.

The final song is performed by a female impersonator, in a style suggested by the title: 'Red, White and Blues', a play on 'Red, White and Blue', another title for the patriotic song 'Columbia Gem of the Ocean', and also an alternate name for the US flag. The song contains Bernstein's characteristic blues touches: chromatic alterations in the melody, especially use of blue notes; including both major and minor thirds in a chord to create a jazz sound; use of seventh and ninth chords; and employing syncopation and triplet rhythms in the melody. The female impersonator was a common sight at the minstrel shows, although by the 1880s women had started to join the companies, and there were even all-female groups performing (Henderson 2001, p. 738).

Spangled Banner"'. However, the reference was correct in the programme for the tryouts, where it is described as 'an authentic harmonization (1780) of "The Anacreontick Song" which is now better known as "The Star Spangled Banner"'.

[14]   The men who would sit on the ends of the semicircle of performers in the minstrel show; 'simoleon' and 'greenback' are both slang words for 'dollar'.

Thirds, Auxiliary Notes and the *Urmotiv*

There are four main motifs that occur in *1600 Pennsylvania Avenue*, the first of which is the familiar *Urmotiv*. It occurs in eight of the numbers within the show, the majority of the appearances being in the harmonic context of $\hat{4}\hat{3}\hat{1}$ (see Example 7.8).

Example 7.8 Use of the *Urmotiv* within *1600*, showing scale degrees

Interestingly, four of the songs in the first half which feature the *Urmotiv* are sung by the servants. More specifically, these all include Lud, either as a child or adult, and in two of them he is joined by Seena (plus the chorus in another). These songs follow Lud from the point when he first reaches Washington as a child ('If I Was a Dove'), as he falls in love with another servant ('Seena'), marries her ('Lud's Wedding'), and suffers the terror of persecution in the antebellum period

('This Time'). In each song, the *Urmotiv* occurs at a moment of high emotion, a characteristic use of Bernstein's figure throughout his works, and, despite the difference in keys, these motifs all occur on the same pitches: C–B–G. These four songs are also in the half that portrays the time before the Civil War, and as we are told the story of Lud, the motif becomes linked with the Simmons family.

The remaining four songs that use the pattern are sung by the President and his wife in their various incarnations. In the first half, the figure occurs at the beginning of the main verse for 'Take Care of This House' as part of the anacrusis onto the tonic, a figure that will be discussed in detail a little later. Although it is Mrs Adams who is singing here, she is directing her words at Lud, so the $\hat{4}\hat{3}\hat{1}$ configuration should not be that unexpected. However, the remaining uses are not as clear-cut. In the President's 'We Must Have a Ball', the figure is used in an ascending real sequence at the start of the verse, the repetition in different keys lessening the usual emotive effect of the motif. In the final number, 'To Make Us Proud', it appears mid-phrase, and descends from the tonic rather than the fourth degree of the scale. This is a similar harmonic context as its appearance in 'Duet for One' as the opening of the main waltz theme of Lucy Hayes.

The second motif that is employed in *1600* is a lower auxiliary note figure, using a semitone step; this is reminiscent of Strauss's *Radetsky March*, and a similar pattern is used by Bernstein for the opening of 'We Are Women', which he composed for the 1959 London production of *Candide*. This is used in a range of songs, across the different social groups, and also in one of the songs that was cut before the opening. However, it nearly always occurs at the beginning of a song or significant section (the one exception being its position in 'Red, White and Blues') (see Example 7.9).

In six of the nine appearances, it is in the same rhythmic position, on the first beat of the bars, with or without a preceding anacrusis. In two of the remaining examples, the first two notes form the upbeat on to the reiterated note (with a further added note in the case of 'Proud'). The only other version is in the song that was cut, 'Philadelphia', where all three notes are before the downbeat. The harmonic context of the motif is different in the examples, although it is interesting that in the three pieces sung by, or directly related to, the President, the auxiliary note is always a deviation from the tonic.

There is one song that opens with a variation of this figure, both rhythmically and melodically. At the beginning of 'Seena', the semitone step is expanded to a full tone movement from the tonic, most probably to avoid the sharpened seventh that would detract from the blues feel of the song. The motif is also altered so that it is the auxiliary note that falls on the downbeat, shifting the emphasis away from the tonic on either side, and increasing the melancholy sound with an accented discord (see Example 7.3).

The next motif is another previously used by Bernstein, and it has been discussed in connection with *Trouble in Tahiti* and *Mass*. In the context of *1600 Pennsylvania Avenue* the rising minor third and descending major second pattern

Example 7.9 Use of the auxiliary note motif within *1600*, showing scale degrees

($\hat{1}\flat\hat{3}\hat{2}$) is primarily associated with the House itself, as it is first heard when Washington is deciding the location of his capital city (see Example 7.10).

This figure then becomes part of the subsequent march as the two sides confer about the details. It goes on to form an important part of 'Take Care of This House', being used at the beginning of each of the first four phrases of Mrs Adams's song, being a direct reference to the President's thoughts in the earlier song. The three-note motif is used in 'Monroviad' at the opening of the lullaby section, where Eliza Monroe tries to calm her husband, as they talk of the future of

Example 7.10 Use of the 1̂–♭3̂–2̂ 'House' motif within *1600*, showing scale degrees

the staff of the House. In 'This Time' it is Seena's concern for Lud, as a member of that staff, which is portrayed, and the figure appears at a dramatic cadence point. This occurrence of the motif is slightly different, as the rhythm of the phrase is changed into equal-length crotchets, a contrast to the triple-time feel that is found in the previous examples. The rhythmic context of the final appearance of the 1̂♭3̂2̂ pattern is a little less definite, as the metre of the opening solo section of 'Duet for One' is changing from ⁵⁄₄ to ³⁄₂, but there is still a sense of triple time, as the President's wife describes Grant, before taking on the specific persona of Julia Grant.

Perhaps it is coincidental that, following Washington's original ideas about the city and the Presidential Mansion itself, the motif is sung almost exclusively by the women who worry about the building, its employers and employees. The one exception to this is its last use in 'Monroviad', but that is when the President is trying to placate his wife by echoing the lullaby phrase that she has already sung twice to him. Later in the same song, Monroe transforms the motif to an ascending major third and descending major third figure, as he sings of his own strengths and weaknesses. When Eliza replies to this, she transforms the music back to the 1̂♭3̂2̂ configuration.

The final motif that Bernstein uses is another seen in earlier works – the 1̂5̂ or 5̂1̂ pattern (see Example 7.11). This is initially seen in the 'Prelude' before Act I, as a tonic to dominant descent. In retrograde, this figure opens 'Ten Square Miles on the Potomac River', and it is then restored for the beginning of the march later in the same song. It is in the next 'March' that the figure is again used at the opening,

Example 7.11 Use of dominant/tonic figure within *1600*, showing scale degrees

here to emphasize the sound of the brass in the Marine Band. It also appears in two guises in 'Sonatina' and in the previously mentioned 'Monroviad'. Despite the fact that a $\hat{5}\hat{1}$ pattern is perhaps among the most common seen in anacruses, and $\hat{1}\hat{5}$ is seen frequently when basing a melody on the tonic chord, remarkably few of Bernstein's songs in this show have such a figure at their outset. In addition to these songs, all of which are connected to an army, or to the President, the motif is seen only at the beginning of the calypso section of 'Lud's Wedding' in a conventional dominant–tonic anacrusis. Bernstein seems to have saved the figure for its effect in the military environment, which of course could relate to the fact that the tonic and dominant frequently appear in brass music.

Another use of $\hat{1}\hat{5}/\hat{5}\hat{1}$ patterns can be seen in interlocking chains of fourths and fifths, similar to those mentioned in the previous chapter on *Mass*. These only occur in numbers performed by people not connected with the house itself: the British soldiers and the Minstrels. 'Sonatina' begins with a descending chain of interlocking intervals, which reappears periodically throughout the piece, always juxtaposed with curses and exclamations of the British officers: E♭–B♭–C–G–A–D. The performers of the Minstrel section use similar chains in 'Minstrel Parade', where the first descending fifth is diminished, and in 'The Grand Old Party', which uses fourths in the same pattern as seen in 'Sonatina'.

There are just two songs which do not feature any of the four motifs: 'Bright and Black', and 'Pity the Poor'. The absence of motifs in the first of these is most probably related to the fact that, as already mentioned, it was probably first written around 1949, when work on *East Side Story* began.[15] There is no such explanation for 'Pity the Poor', and it may only be missing a motif due to its brevity (it is only 15 bars long). It is more likely, however, that Bernstein did not feel that it merited inclusion in the organic structure that encompassed all the other songs and numbers, as it was parodying Jewish moneylenders.

Musical Scenes

Although *1600 Pennsylvania Avenue* marked a return to conventional musical theatre forms following the 'theatre piece' of *Mass*, one element of Bernstein's earlier works was notably absent: ballet. The narrative dance numbers that could be found in *On the Town*, *Wonderful Town* and *West Side Story* are not used in *1600*, in the same way that they had been omitted from *Candide*. There are dances within songs such as 'Lud's Wedding' and 'We Must Have a Ball', but there are no dream ballets or dance pantomimes to carry the story forward. Perhaps the historical nature of the plot, and the fact that it was based on true events, meant that it was not susceptible to such treatment. In *On the Town* and *West Side Story*, dance had been used to portray emotions and passion, and also to make the violence of the latter palatable to the audience. In *Wonderful Town*, dance was used to show the sisters struggling to make their mark in New York, and to cover the passing of time. As *1600* contains displays neither of love nor violence, and as the timeline is already broken up into episodes, such devices are not needed.

In place of ballet, there are extended musical items that almost fill individual scenes. These are not merely expanded songs, static in the manner of operatic arias, but pieces that combine a variety of styles in clear sections with underscored dialogue or recitative into substantial numbers that advance the action of the story.[16] The three pieces that fit into this category are 'Sonatina', 'The Monroviad' and 'Duet for One'. There are no other connections between these songs apart from their length and function, the first being sung by the British invaders, the second by James and Eliza Monroe, and the last by Julia Grant, Lucy Hayes and the chorus.

The first begins as the British soldiers reach Washington DC during the war of 1812, where they find a state dinner, abandoned by James and Dolly Madison in their rush to leave the capital. After feasting, the troops proceed to smash the furniture and set the White House ablaze, only to see the flames sputter out in a torrential downpour (historically documented) (Harmon 1997b, p. 8). Bernstein's

---

[15]   Before the location of the action in the show moved to the West Side.

[16]   On the recording of *A White House Cantata*, the three items to be discussed are respectively 8'49, 9'01 and 9'48 long.

structural intentions for the piece were made clear in the title of the number, and in the subtitles used on the manuscript, which indicate a three-movement sonata in miniature, as shown in Table 7.1.

Table 7.1   Structure of 'Sonatina'

	Bar Nos.	Details		Key
I	1–4	Introduction		D
Sonata	5–11	1st subject 1st theme	Exposition	D–A
form	12–14	Bridge		D
	15–21	1.1		D–A
	22–26	Bridge		D
	27–34	1.1		c
	35–47	1st subject 2nd theme		E
	48–66	2nd subject		A
	67–72	Codetta		
	73–75	Bridge		E♭
	76–80	1.1	Development	D
	81–85	Bridge		A♭
	86–89	1.1		G
	90–93	1.1		B♭
	94–99	1.1		
	100–110	1.1		C
	110–116	1.2		G
	117–127	Bridge		amb
	128–151	2	Recapitulation	D
	152–159	1.1		D
	160–163	Bridge	Coda	
Bridge	164–173	Fughetta ('Wrecking Music')		d
	174–181	Stretto		D
II	182–207	Minuet		G–F
Minuet	208–233	Trio – 'Anacreon'		B♭
III	234–253	Rondo theme		D
Rondo	254–265	Episode 1		F
	266–277	Rondo theme		C
	278–287	Episode 2		d
	288–310	Rondo theme/coda		D

The first movement of 'Sonatina' (bb. 1–163) concentrates on the plans of the British: they believe that black slaves will join with them to fight against the Americans, and they also intend to burn down Washington's public buildings. The whole of this section is performed in speech, with the rhythm notated without pitch, and the introduction and bridges are based on the fourth motif mentioned previously. The first subject area contains three repetitions of a theme characterized by an Alberti bass and a semiquaver *obbligato*, both features placing the event within the classical era during which it occurred. The second theme within the first subject area contains ascending scale figures and a repeating quaver bass line. The main topic of conversation in this section is the banquet that has been discarded, and their intention to consume it. The following second subject area, which following convention is in the dominant key, is based on the music of 'To Anacreon in Heaven', the tune that also forms the source for a later section (see Example 7.12a).

Bernstein uses the descending and ascending arpeggio from the opening of 'The Star Spangled Banner', the American patriotic anthem derived from the British drinking song, rather than the repeated tonic of the original tune (see Example 7.12b).[17] Above this music, the dialogue has turned to the planned coercion of the slaves to aid the British army. The use of the patriotic music in this scene may have been inspired by a similar utilization by Sherman Edwards in *1776*, where the song 'Cool, Cool, Considerate Men' begins with the same arpeggio, and words also derived from 'The Star-Spangled Banner', 'Oh, say do you see …',

Example 7.12 Comparison of 'Sonatina' and 'To Anacreon in Heaven'

(a) 'Sonatina', bb. 50–53
(b) 'To Anacreon in Heaven', bb. 1–2

_____

[17]   This musical example can be found in Sonneck Society 1976, p. 37.

before moving onto a development of this music, and text which also mentions a minuet at one point. In the development section of Bernstein's sonata form, it is predominantly the first theme of the first subject area that is elaborated upon, with more references to the food and to the slaves. The recapitulation presents two of the themes, back in the tonic key, although the usual order is reversed, as shown in Table 7.1. Following this movement, there is a bridge to the next, based on further development of the 'Anacreon' arpeggio, this time in a fughetta and stretto that provide 'wrecking music' as the British prepare the Presidential Mansion for burning (see Example 7.13).

Example 7.13 'Sonatina', bb. 164–7

This section was a late addition to the number, being absent from some manuscripts of the song. The next part is the dance movement, beginning with a delightful three-part minuet, with alternating four- and two-bar phrases, and a scalic bass line that adds to the classical feel of the piece (see Example 7.14). It is in this section that Admiral Cockburn, leader of the British, sings (rather than speaks) for the first time. The trio of this minuet has slightly less poise, as Cockburn becomes increasingly patriotic, and possibly more intoxicated on the free wine, and calls his men to join him in the drinking song that has been 'stolen' by the Americans. It is here that Bernstein inserts the arrangement of 'To Anacreon in Heaven', in a three-part a cappella version of the song, as mentioned earlier.

The final section of this number begins with a crash of thunder, as the rain begins to fall and extinguish the fire they have just started. The pattern of descending fourths returns, and is followed by a short rondo finale, the theme of which contains the familiar $\hat{1}\sharp\hat{4}\hat{5}$ figure, both in the melody and the bass (see Example 7.15). The two episodes use dotted rhythms that contrast with the quaver and semiquavers of the rondo theme, and the first episode reappears in the coda.

The next scene song is 'The Monroviad', which actually contains two songs (see Table 7.2). The main focus of the scene is a marital argument, and, as was the case with *Trouble in Tahiti*, Bernstein employs sonata form for his husband and wife disagreement. The introduction contains recitative-like phrases over an arpeggiated chord, a longer recitative with accompaniment and punctuating

Example 7.14 'Sonatina', bb. 183–8

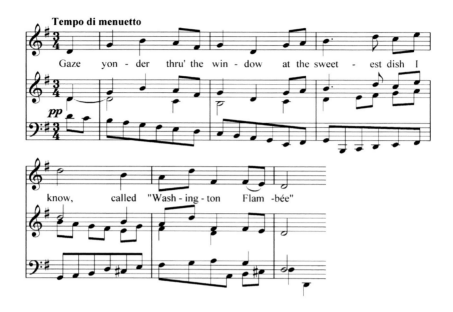

Example 7.15 'Sonatina', bb. 241–4

chords, and an ascending sequence using semiquaver patterns over a dotted rhythm
vamp. The first section is sung completely by the President, James Monroe, as he
asks for guidance in his deliberations over slavery. Following this, there is a shift
to $\frac{9}{8}$, moving away from the simple time of the first section, and in contravention
of tradition, the 'feminine' lyrical theme is presented first (see Example 7.16).

    His wife, Eliza, opens the sonata form proper with this lullaby figure that forms
the first theme, sleepily replying that the staff will stay, a subconscious answer

Table 7.2   Structure of 'The Monroviad'

	Bar Nos.	Detail	Singer	Key	Metre
Introduction	1–4	Recitative	Monroe	amb	$\mathbf{c}$
	5–14	Verse		amb	various
	14–17	Bridge		E	$\frac{2}{4}$
	18–19	Verse		amb	
	20–22	Bridge		E	
	23–24	Verse		amb	$\frac{2}{4}$ $\frac{3}{4}$
Exposition	25–36	Lullaby (1st subject)	Eliza	e	$\frac{9}{8}$
	37–43	2nd subject, 1st theme	Monroe	amb	$\frac{3}{4}$
	44–55	2nd subject, 2nd theme		D	$\mathbf{c}$ $\frac{3}{4}$ $\frac{6}{8}$
	56–62	Codetta			$\frac{2}{4}$
Development	63–74	Lullaby	Eliza	e	$\frac{9}{8}$
	75–77	2.1	Monroe	amb	$\frac{3}{4}$
	78–104	dev of 2.1	Eliza	amb/ e	$\frac{9}{8}$ $\frac{6}{8}$
	105–115	dev of 2.1	Monroe	e	
	116–121	2.2		D	$\mathbf{c}$
	122–146	dev of 2.2	Eliza	e	$\frac{2}{4}$
Recapitulation	147–159	Lullaby		e	$\frac{9}{8}$
Coda	160–185	'Mark of a Man' verse	Monroe	F	$\frac{9}{8}$ $\frac{12}{8}$
	186–209	'Mark of a Man' verse	both	F	
	210–222	Lullaby/coda	both	F	$\frac{9}{8}$

to Monroe's unspoken concern. Monroe then responds with his 'masculine' themes, the second of which is the fanfare figure relating to the Declaration of Independence. His first is connected to the staff and the issue of the deportation of slaves, characterized by short phrases. Eliza counters his protests with a reiteration of the lullaby, beginning the development section. Her husband then reintroduces his two arguments, with the same music referring to the same topics, and both of these are countered by Eliza, developing the musical material. She finally calms him with the recapitulation of her lullaby music. It is noticeable that Eliza's music tends towards E minor, and compound time, while Monroe attempts to stay in simple time signatures and major keys. In the coda, Eliza's influence has clearly won over, as he now sings in the $\frac{9}{8}$ metre which has been associated with his wife, although they compromise and find a new key to sing in. The coda also includes a fragment of the 'Take Care of This House' melody, as the House is what Eliza has been worried about throughout the song, and there is also a clear relationship between the start of the lullaby music, the intervals used in the earlier song, and also in the new music of the 'Mark of a Man' section (see Example 7.17).

The final extended scene is observed in the number in 'Duet for One', where the casting gimmick of having of one woman portray all of the President's wives

Example 7.16 'The Monroviad', bb. 26–9

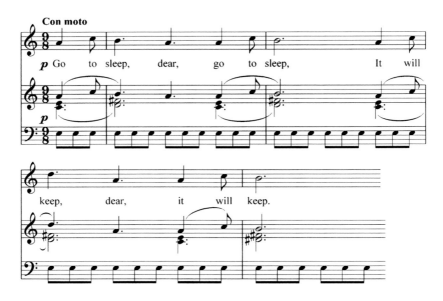

Example 7.17 'The Monroviad', bb. 165–9

creates an interesting situation at the time of a handover of power, as 'at the Inauguration, Julia Grant and Lucy Hayes reflect on their husbands and on one another' (programme notes, *A White House Cantata* 1997) (see Table 7.3).

Table 7.3   Structure of 'Duet for One'

	Bar nos.	Detail	Singers	Key	Metre
1	1–4	Introduction	chorus	D	$\frac{2}{2}$
	5–16	'Hail'		D–B	
	17–21	'Hail' 2		B–D	
	22–38	Verse 1	Grant	D	$\frac{3}{2}\ \frac{5}{4}$
	39–47	'Hail'	chorus		$\frac{2}{2}$
	48–64	Verse 1	Grant		$\frac{3}{2}\ \frac{5}{4}$
	65–68	Bridge	chorus		$\frac{2}{2}$
	69–80	'Hail'		D–B	
	81–85	'Hail' 2		B–D	
	86–99	Fragment of 'Prelude'		Dmin	
2	100–122	Verse 2	Grant/Hayes	F–D	$\frac{7}{8}$
	123–146	Verse 3	Grant/Hayes	D	
	147–158	Verse 4	Grant/Hayes	C	
	159–174	Southern verse	Grant	D	$\frac{6}{8}$
	175–218	Waltz verse	Hayes/chorus	Bmin	$\frac{3}{4}$
	219–235	Southern verse	Grant	D	$\frac{6}{8}$
	236–279	Waltz verse	Hayes/chorus	Bmin	$\frac{3}{4}$
	280	Dialogue	President		
	281–289	Verse 2	Grant	F	$\frac{7}{8}$
	290–296	Verse 3		D	
	297–302	Dialogue	President/Grant/Hayes		
	303–323	Waltz verse	Hayes/chorus	Bmin	$\frac{3}{4}$
	324–349	Coda		D	

This time there are only two sections, divided by a quotation of music from 'Prelude' as the swearing-in group assemble. In the 'gypsy' run-through (script, p. 70) and in the Broadway version the same music was used to underscore Congress voting on the impeachment of Andrew Johnson, but the 'Prelude' was not in its place at the opening of the show at this point.[18] Despite this, the music appears to be connected with moments of constitutional importance, which is possibly why it was later added before the scene that contains the choosing of a

---

[18]   The second section of the 'Prelude', which was previously known as 'Middle C' due to the pedal middle C which continues through the whole number, appears in the 'gypsy' run-through script (p. 90), and was also heard on Broadway towards the end of the show, complete with the humming from the chorus.

location for the capital. Before this point, the music alternates between the crowd's 'Hail's, which appear to be derived from fragments of 'Hail to the Chief', the song traditionally used to welcome the President, and Julia Grant wondering who her husband's successor will be.[19] In reality, there were questions about the triumph of Rutherford B. Hayes in this election in 1876, due to the popularity of the other candidate, Samuel Tilden. The song suggests that Tilden had won the vote, but that they continued to count and recount until the result changed.[20] The uncertainty regarding the identity of the next President is reflected in the alternating $\frac{3}{2}$ and $\frac{5}{4}$ time signatures in Julia Grant's verses in the first section (which may also reflect the instability of her husband, as she remarks about his drinking). At the opening of the second section, the verses that the two First Ladies sing are punctuated by Hayes taking the oath. This is followed by the verses that characterize the differences between the two women, as discussed earlier (see Examples 7.7a and b).

It is also possible to consider '10 Square Miles' as a musical scene song: the action is moved forward by the decisions taken in this song, which is in several sections, but it is just over half the length of the three numbers already studied.

In *1600 Pennsylvania Avenue*, Bernstein uses forms that provide opportunities for development of material, and which resulted in extended pieces of music. This extension of form was perhaps an unconscious preparation for the work that Bernstein would do for his next, and last, musical theatre work, the opera *A Quiet Place*.

---

[19]   Sondheim also utilizes 'Hail to the Chief' in his musical about the presidents, or at least the attempts to remove them forcibly, *Assassins*.

[20]   This foreshadowed the events of the 2000 elections in the US, when there were several recounts before a victor was announced.

Chapter 8
A Quiet Place

'The path of truth is plain and safe'

In June 1978 Bernstein suffered a personal tragedy when his wife Felicia died of lung cancer. Despite his affairs with men, and a brief separation from his wife in 1976, he had returned to Felicia before her final illness started, and her death affected him very badly, coming so soon after her overcoming breast cancer only four years earlier. His grief was magnified by his usual over-emotional and over-dramatic nature, and although it was no doubt an exaggeration when he told a friend in 1985 that 'there's not a minute in my life when I don't think of her' (Burton 1994, p. 451), the statement was based on a sincere emotion. Following Felicia's death, Bernstein concentrated on small-scale compositions, including commissions for Boston Symphony Orchestra (*Divertimento for Orchestra*, 1980), and the Van Cliburn International Piano Competition (*Touches*, 1981), and memorial pieces *A Musical Toast* (to the memory of André Kostelanetz, 1980) and *Halil* (which will be discussed later); he also wrote two songs for Phyllis Newman, the wife of Adolph Green, in 1979, and *Piccola Serenata*, a song for Karl Böhm's 85th birthday. There were other unfinished projects: a musical film with Francis Ford Coppola about the American automotive designer Preston Tucker (1979) and a stage musical called *Alarums and Flourishes* in 1980.

In 1977 Bernstein had completed a larger-scale vocal work, *Songfest*, subtitled 'A Cycle of American Poems for Six Singers and Orchestra'. He had originally begun composing this piece before *1600 Pennsylvania Avenue*, but it had been shelved when work on the show had taken over (Burton 1994, p. 435). After the failure of the musical, Bernstein returned to his song cycle, initially titled *An American Songbook*, and completed it for performance in Washington on 11 October 1977. It formed the second half of an all-Bernstein concert celebrating the inauguration of Mstislav Rostropovich as Music Director of the National Symphony Orchestra. The first half included two other premières: *Slava!* provided the energetic opening under Rostropovich's baton,[1] followed by the first performance of the *Three Meditations from Mass*, with the new music director taking the cello solo and Bernstein conducting. *Songfest* set a variety of poems which 'celebrate America's cultural diversity, executed in as many musical styles as there are songs in the cycle. Blacks, gays, exploited women, contented wives, belly dancers, teenagers and expatriates all have their say' (Burton 1994, p. 443).

---

[1]   Never one to waste good music, Bernstein reused two songs from *1600 Pennsylvania Avenue* in his new concert piece: 'The Grand Old Party' and 'Rehearse!'.

One of the songs, 'To What You Said', recycles music from *1600*, a section originally called 'Middle C'; this would later find its way back into the 'Prelude' of *A White House Cantata*.

The glowing reception which greeted his new song cycle, contrasting so sharply with the failure of *1600*, inspired Bernstein again to operatic writing, and it was shortly after this that he accepted a commission from the Houston Grand Opera for a full-scale work; this would be his last chance to write his 'one real, moving American opera'. He reaffirmed his intentions in a narration for a film about his life called *Reflections* in 1978: 'I have decided at long last to stop experimenting with the Broadway musical and try finally to work in the opera house'.[2]

Felicia's death brought his work on the opera to a temporary halt, but composition resumed in October 1980 when he found a sympathetic librettist with whom to collaborate. Stephen Wadsworth had been at Harvard with Bernstein's daughter Jamie, and initially approached the composer for an interview, adding a special PS to the request letter:

> 'Interested in librettos?' [Bernstein] telephoned me the next day, much more interested in librettos than in yet another magazine story. 'If you bring me a scenario for a sequel to *Trouble in Tahiti* by Tuesday at four o'clock,' he told me (it was Friday), 'I will give you your interview. Fair trade?' So I went to this meeting, and we interviewed each other, and it was a strange afternoon indeed. (Wadsworth 1987, p. 12)

Bernstein's concept of the sequel shared an important element with Wadsworth's libretto: both were centred on a funeral. In common with Bernstein, the young writer had also recently lost a family member, as his sister Nina had been killed in a car crash a year earlier (Wadsworth 1987, p. 12); the dedication line of the opera reflects the mutual grieving: 'To the memory of F.M.B. and N.S.Z.'. From this starting point, the plot of *Trouble in Tahiti II* was mapped out. The title, *A Quiet Place*, came between March and May of 1982, drawn from the final line of the refrain in Dinah's garden aria, the 'quiet place' being the sanctuary she longed for.

In the sequel, as in the first opera, the action takes place over one day, although this time the 24 hours begin in the afternoon. The funeral at the opening is that of Dinah, the wife from *Trouble in Tahiti*. The intervening 30 years had not been kind to her, and she had turned to drink, dying in a car crash that was possibly intentional. The guests gathered at the funeral include her husband Sam, brother Bill, best friend Susie, her Analyst and Doctor, and the Doctor's wife ('Mrs Doc'). Her son Junior, the child who was never seen in *Tahiti*, and his younger sister Dede arrive later, with Dede's husband François, who used to be Junior's lover. The atmosphere at the funeral is tense, and once the other guests leave Sam releases his pent-up rage in a rant against his family and himself. He argues with Junior, who has developed psychological problems, and Scene 1 ends with Sam, Dede

---

2   Script in box 91, folder 3, LBC.

and François storming out of the funeral parlour, leaving Junior with his mother's body in the coffin.

Following an orchestral interlude, Scene 2 picks up the story later that day, when the family are back at their house, and father and daughter begin a reconciliation as they go through Dinah's belongings. François tries to comfort Junior, who appears to remember an incident in his childhood when he believes he committed incest with his sister, although the truth of this memory is never quite clear, and François gives the impression that it is part of Junior's fantasy. This scene is played out in a double duet, one pair of characters in each adjacent room. The setting of this is very similar to the scene that was cut from *On the Town*, when the two couples (Chip and Hildy; Ozzie and Claire) performed the two songs that were then juxtaposed, 'Say When' and 'I'm Afraid It's Love', in two apartments on stage.

That night, Bill and Mrs Doc consider their respective relationships with Dinah in an Interlude. Early the next day, the family members face each other in the garden, which was Dinah's sanctuary during her troubled marriage, bonding with each other by playing childhood games. The friends from the funeral earlier arrive, and in the middle of a game of tag Sam finally welcomes François to the family: the tension is dissipated in laughter. Following another Interlude, where time moves on to late afternoon, the family begin to unite, until a minor disagreement escalates into another heated argument. It is François that calms the situation, using a letter left by Dinah, addressed 'To Whom It May Concern', and finally they begin to reach out towards each other, leading to a resolution of some of their problems and conflicts.

A Quiet Place portrays the development of several of the relationships from *Trouble in Tahiti*, most notably that of Dinah and Sam. The score for the earlier opera indicates that Junior is nine years old, and a line in the sequel states that Dede is 30, compared to Junior's age of 40. This suggests that Dede was probably conceived very soon after the events of the first opera. Could there have been a last-ditch effort to save the marriage by having another child? Whether this was the case or not, the couple had indeed stayed together, although not in a state of happiness; an interesting touch in the 1986 Vienna staging of *A Quiet Place*, directed by Wadsworth himself, is that the sleeping arrangements in the master bedroom change from a scene in *Trouble in Tahiti*, where the couple shared a double bed, to twin beds in a scene from the later opera.[3] Another relationship that appears to have faltered since the 1950s is between Sam and his brother-in-law, Bill. Although Dinah's brother did not appear in *Trouble in Tahiti*, following his introduction in the sequel we can assume that he is the Bill to whom Sam is lending money in his Scene 2 aria in the earlier work.

When Bill becomes transformed into the brother in the sequel, the lending of money in *Trouble in Tahiti* takes on a new angle, as Sam is probably enjoying the

---

[3]   The first photograph can be found together with the review by Fanning (www.spingal.plus.com/aquietplace.html), and the second is in Gottlieb 1988, p. 66.

fact that he is being benevolent to Dinah's brother, without her knowing. Certainly the relationship between the two men has not improved by the funeral, as it is made known that it is Bill and not Sam who is paying for the service.

Although the story does lead on from the ideas planted in the first opera, there are undoubtedly aspects of autobiographical writing, as least from Bernstein. In her biography, Peyser suggests that the characters had their basis in members of the Bernstein family, not altogether surprising after the autobiographical nature of some of the incidents in the earlier *Tahiti*. In addition to Sam embodying Bernstein's father, and Junior representing Bernstein himself, Dede seems to be based on his sister Shirley (Peyser 1987, p. 408), although in reality the age gap between them was only five years, rather than ten. The parallel between the Bernstein siblings and the operatic brother and sister is underlined by Junior's confused memory of a sexual encounter with his sister when they were children. Shirley Bernstein remembered a more innocent event from her own life, when she was four and her brother was about nine:

> He wanted to see how you do things, genitally. So who better to try it out than me? And evidently I went screaming to my mother that 'Lenny tried to put his jibbick in my wo-wo' and my mother went after him with a broom and he scuttled under a bed way into a corner where she couldn't get at him with the broom. (Quoted in Burton 1994, p. 10)

Bernstein himself had also related this tale to a friend (Peyser 1987, p. 409), but it does seem strange for him to play out this memory in an opera, treating it almost as therapy on the public stage. As Peyser goes on to say: 'Bernstein indulges in a rite of purification without ever quite confessing to the sin itself. He behaves like the penitent in a confessional booth who, after asking for forgiveness, then says, "But, in all truth, father, I may just have imagined this"' (Peyser 1987, p. 410).

Peyser suggests a further point of reference from Bernstein's life: that the character of Mrs Doc is based on Lillian Hellman, who 'had become attached to Felicia' when Hellman and the Bernsteins had stayed on Martha's Vineyard (1987, p. 408). The nocturnal interlude that showed Mrs Doc's affection for the deceased Dinah, who represents Felicia, was cut following the première, as 'Wadsworth felt the public did not want to know about grumpy old Mrs Doc's lesbian feelings for Dinah' (Burton 1994, p. 469).

The story seems very angst-ridden and self-indulgent with its 'soap opera' style ending, but the overwrought nature of the piece is perhaps one of its strengths: 'the breakdown in communication is a ready-made metaphor for Bernstein's music, undercutting most of the reasons that might be advanced for resisting it' (Fanning 1988). So why did Bernstein consider a story of such domestic anguish for the subject of his opera? Even taking personal factors into account, Bernstein must still have wanted this work to succeed, so was there an audience for this kind of tale?

Although American operas of the years between the two Bernstein pieces did not look to domestic situations for their inspiration, there was a precedent in English opera: Tippett's *The Knot Garden* (1970). There are several parallels between the two works, particularly in the characters; both have a wife who finds sanctuary in the garden, and a domineering husband, as well as a gay character, and a man who appears to be bi-sexual. There are further parallels in the plots: both include an act that consists of duets and ensembles between the various characters, and in both there is some resolution through the playing of games, a psychological concept. The conflicts and tensions found in *A Quiet Place* have a definite precursor in Tippett's piece: 'The main subject matter is the inner as opposed to the public lives of the characters, and from this emerges the main dramatic ideal, which is a question: can people yet learn to live with each other when their personalities and personal relationships have reached crippling deadness or bitterness?' (Kemp 1984, p. 404).

An American operatic influence can be found, although from over 30 years earlier, featuring an equally dysfunctional family, in Marc Blitzstein's *Regina*. Based on Lillian Hellman's *The Little Foxes*, the story focuses on the Hubbard family, living in the American South in 1900, and the efforts of brothers Oscar and Benjamin to swindle money out the dying husband of their sister Regina. The power-hungry trio resort to lying, cheating, stealing bonds, and in a final act of depravity Regina leaves her husband Horace to die while grasping for his heart medication. As described by Morse: 'Hellman paints a damning portrait of those who live only in order to exploit others ... Their brutality and unscrupulousness does not leave their personal relationships unaffected' (1993, p. 73). Regina's cold-heartedness alienates her daughter, and at the end of the opera Regina is left alone. Bernstein was intimately acquainted with Blitztein's operatic version of the tale; it appears that he was present at an early run-through of the work on 26 April 1949.[4] Bernstein also attended the première on 31 October 1949, according to his date book, but perhaps more significant is the article that he write for *The New York Times*, and which was published the day before the opening in support of Bliztstein's new work, and its place in the field of opera. Bernstein spoke of the truth behind Hellman's story; '"The Little Foxes", on which the work is based, is about ugliness: ugly people engaged in ugly dealings with one another' (1949, p. X1). The ugliness of the human condition, and the harshness with which people can treat each other, is surely at the heart of Bernstein's later opera, although with a brighter ending than Blitzstein's work.

In addition to Hellman's play, American drama had been exploiting unhappy families and troubled marriages for several decades. Tennessee Williams's *A Streetcar Named Desire* (1947) and *Cat on a Hot Tin Roof* (1955), and Eugene

---

[4]   In his date book, an entry for that date: '8.30 Run thru Little Foxes' (box 321, LBC). It should be noted that the final title of *Regina* was only decided on in the August of that year (Gordon 1989, p. 324).

O'Neill's *Long Day's Journey into Night* (1941, first American production in 1956) focussed on the disturbed members of dysfunctional families; *Who's Afraid of Virginia Woolf* by Edward Albee (1962) had at its centre a particularly volatile marriage. Miller's *The Death of a Salesman* (1949) featured an ordinary man who was wrapped up remembering happier times, and who also died in a car crash.[5] These works mirrored society in general during these years: 'what they managed to capture was a turning point in national consciousness: a move from confidence to doubt. In the land of success, they wrote, obsessively, about the unsuccessful' (Wardle 1993, p. 209).

One important aspect of *A Quiet Place* was the approach that the two collaborators took when beginning to write the work. They had specific aims, and also methods and ideals that they wanted to avoid. In their intention to write an American opera, about American people coping with American problems, using the American language, they shunned some more 'traditional' techniques: 'We worked hard to avoid writing in schemes, to avoid the disease we coined "schematoma". Rhyme schemes, meter schemes, closed forms, "well-made play" schemes were viewed suspiciously and only grudgingly allowed' (Wadsworth 1987, p. 13).

Wadsworth wrote in a vernacular style, in 'the American language as is it spoken by Americans to express their American selves' (Wadsworth 1987, p. 13); a lot of the anxiety of the situations is reflected in the text, and subsequently in the music. In the first act, especially, there are unexpected breaks in the lines, with 'half-finished sentences and social gaffes' (Miles 1988). The disturbed states of Junior and Sam often lead to swearing and bad language, which must be considered part of the vernacular. On several occasions, *Sprechstimme* is used, suggesting that the emotions of the character prevent them from finding the correct pitches convincingly, and their voices waver. In addition, atonal music prevents the attaching of emotional truisms to the vocal line and any feeling of melodic cliché. The words, perhaps obviously, play an important part with the opera, and they are never obscured by the music; 'at times the conversations suggest speech which has been only heightened, not transformed, by music, with the orchestra providing the depth for which the characters cannot find words' (Conrad 1992b, p. 1202).

In contrast to *Trouble in Tahiti*, the sequel does not utilize the musical vernacular, except in one or two specific moments. The artificial sweetness and optimism presented by the Radio Trio and the influence of popular music in the 1952 opera are gone, replaced with some quite stark musical textures and sounds. This was intentional on Bernstein's part, as he wanted to show the difference between the family then, and the illusion that surrounded them, and the disjointed group now, as he stated in a memo to Harry Kraut in September 1981:

---

[5]   Again, Bernstein had visited the theatre to watch most of these: the O'Neill in April 1957, Albee's play in October 1962, and the Miller in April 1949, as listed in his date books in boxes 335, 336 and 337, LBC.

[The new opera] will be in totally other style, *TinT I* having been a deeply serious (even tragic) theme clothed in the lightest of disguises; jazzy, tuneful (in a pop sense), etc. for reasons of caricature, irony, satire, etc. The characters *were* cardboard. *TinT II*, au contraire, goes deeply into each character, plus a good number of new ones. The music no longer avails itself of strophic or stanzaic song-forms (as did *TinT I*); it is anything but 'pop'; musical styles range from dodecaphonic, strictly serial, to diatonic chorales ... Except for special purposes, it avoids obvious rhyme and sequential forms, as in pop music, but plays subtly with vernacular elements in a way that LB believes takes that famous 'next step' toward whatever LB once hoped 'American Opera' could one day be.[6]

This musical style could be viewed as a culmination of the development of Bernstein's compositional technique throughout his theatre works. From the popular song forms and jaunty jazz-influenced melodies of *On the Town*, the musical theatre works show an evolution of writing style. This reached a climax in *West Side Story*, with the integration of symphonic and song writing. Following this, Bernstein introduced many new ideas and styles in *Mass*, and then reverted to more traditional ideas in *1600*. *A Quiet Place* then moves to a new arena of composition, leaving the popular song structures behind and embracing the concept of through-composed music. This could also be seen as a direct result of the influence of Wagner, as in 1981 Bernstein had finally recorded *Tristan und Isolde*, the work he considered 'the central work of all music history, the hub of the wheel' (quoted in Burton 1994, p. 462).

Unfortunately, this huge distinction between the music styles of the two operas created problems in the original production at Houston in 1983, when *Tahiti* was performed before the interval, and the four scenes of *Quiet Place* were played after without a break. These scenes appeared to have a familiar structure, as noted by Andrew Porter in *The New Yorker*: 'the underlying form is that of the four-movement symphony, with the linked nocturnal duets as the slow movement and games in the garden as a scherzo' (1983, p. 88). However, the sudden shift from the style of one opera to the other was not successful, as the light music of the first gave way to the dark and complex mood of the second, which was also much longer. To solve this problem, the two pieces were rearranged into a more conventional three-act opera before the performances at La Scala in June 1984, as shown in Table 8.1.

Tahiti was placed in the new second act, becoming two flashbacks between the action of the old Scene 2. Scenes 3 and 4 became the final act, losing the interlude containing the other characters from the funeral, and a letter from Dinah that prompted the reconciliation was replaced by the device of her old diaries. This new version received a positive reaction from the Italian critics, and the opera has remained in this form for subsequent productions; as the original version has been withdrawn and is unavailable, it is the music of the revised version that I have

---

[6]   Box 93, folder 29, LBC.

Table 8.1   Structure of *A Quiet Place*

Premiere: Houston, 17 June 1983 (from programme)	Revised version: La Scala, 19 June 1984

Trouble in Tahiti
Prelude
Scene 1
Scene 2
Scene 3
Scene 4
Interlude
Scene 5
Scene 6
Scene 7

Act I
Prologue
A Quiet Place Scene 1
Postlude

Act II
A Quiet Place Scene 2 – Sam
Trouble in Tahiti (Prelude to Scene 4)
A Quiet Place Scene 2 – Double Duet
Trouble in Tahiti (Interlude to end)

A Quiet Place
Scene 1 – The Funeral
Orchestral Interlude
Scene 2 – Sam & Double Duet
Interlude – Bill and Mrs Doc
Scene 3 – Garden Games
Orchestral Interlude
Scene 4 – Argument and Reconciliation

Act III
Prelude
A Quiet Place Scene 3 (without secondary characters)
A Quiet Place Scene 4

used for analysis. Despite this, an adjustment of the structure does not address the criticisms that were levelled at the music of the opera, and the story that was being told through it. Some of the reviews of the première were quite harsh in their assessments of Bernstein's new work:

> The eclectic *A Quiet Place* is fundamentally tonal, but its melodies only infrequently blossom, as if Bernstein were inhibited by 30 years of modernism from writing the kind of straightforward, expressive music that obviously agrees with him. Instead, he has compromised with a bloated, percussive score that, stripped of its bluster and its 'commitment', is too often little more than a plaintive bleat. (Walsh 1983, p. 69)

If Bernstein has lost most of the easy, slangy arrogance of his early music – above all the grand Broadway scores for *On the Town* and the much-underrated *Wonderful Town* – he can still command the grand gestures needed to sock a point home. But the gestures themselves have paled ... the spectacle of a prodigious talent in decline, or at least in eclipse, is never a heartening one. (Rich 1983, p. 97)

It seems that, despite all of Bernstein's hopes and aspirations for his opera, and for its place in the history of American music, it was not to be. *A Quiet Place* has not passed into the opera repertory, and, in spite of all his efforts, his most popular score has remained *West Side Story*.

Serialism

As mentioned previously, many of Bernstein's musical theatre works contain chromatic melodies, beginning with the melody of 'Presentation of Miss Turnstiles' in *On the Town*, and the opening clarinet phrase in *Trouble in Tahiti*. From *Candide* onwards, the chromaticism becomes more obviously 12-tone in nature, being utilized primarily for dramatically tense situations, and, as in his orchestral works, not usually being subjected to strict serialist techniques.[7]

Both his second and third symphonies contain serial writing, although it is in *Kaddish* that use of the technique is more advanced. Whereas *The Age of Anxiety* 'employs, in a harmonic way, a 12-tone row out of which the main theme evolves' (Bernstein, programme note), in *Kaddish* we are presented with inversions and transpositions of the row, in addition to the prime row. The construction of the series used in *Kaddish*, based on fourths and semitones, results in certain retrogrades being identical to inversions, meaning that there are only 24 permutations, rather than the full 48: P1 = RI8, P2 = RI9, and so on. Despite the use of different versions of the row, Bernstein is still not overly strict on his employment of serialist methods: the accompanying chords are not precisely derived from the row, and incomplete rows are also used.

It is possible that Bernstein felt some pressure to embrace 12-tone techniques as his friend and mentor Aaron Copland had utilized the methods in his Piano Quartet (1950), *Piano Fantasy* (1957) and *Connotation for Orchestra* (1962). Copland described how he found the approach 'liberating' in 1968: 'it forces the tonal composer to unconventionalize his thinking with respect to chordal structure, and it tends to freshen his melodic and figurational imagination' (1968, p. 168); other America composers who had integrated serial aspects into their work included

---

[7] In a letter to Jack Gottlieb, Bernstein also points out his use of a 12-tone row in the 'Galop' variation in *Fancy Free* (Gottlieb 2010, p. 146). The two phrases of the main melody contain 16 quavers, and so four of the 12 tones are necessarily repeated: D–D♯–E–C–C♯–F♯–G–B♭, F–F♯–G–E–G♯–A–B♭–B♮.

Roger Sessions and Milton Babbitt. Bernstein could see the attraction that the methods held for composers who were searching for fresh sounds: 'They must feel it as something new and vital. Perhaps it attracts them because it offers a way out. It guarantees a system whereby music can be written that sounds new, or at least different from the great body of world music';[8] he also accepted, if grudgingly, that he had not escaped the temptation himself:

> It was a such a welcome gift to the crisis-ridden twentieth-century composer that it took instant strong hold, capturing the imagination of such composers as Alban Berg and Anton Webern … and persisting to this very day (with evolutionary modifications, of course) in the music of composers such as Stockhausen, Boulez, Wuorinen, Kirchner, Babbitt, Foss, Berio – and sometimes, though very rarely, even in mine. (1976, p. 281)

However, Bernstein felt that the real challenge was creating new music within the bounds of tonal music; 'The real hard thing is to make something fresh in C major'.[9] In fact, Bernstein appeared genuinely disappointed that Copland had succumbed to the draw of the intellectual, suggesting that it had stifled his creativity. In a birthday tribute to his old friend in 1970, Bernstein wrote that

> When he [Copland] started writing twelve-tone, I figured that it was inevitable – everybody has to fool with serialism … But still I asked him, "Of all people, why you – you who are so instinctive, so spontaneous? Why are you bothering with tone rows and with the rules of retrograde and inversion, and all that?" And he answered me, "Because I need more chords. I've run out of chords". And that lasted for four more pieces and then he didn't write any more. How sad for him. How awful for us. (reprinted in 1982, p. 290)

This may be one reason he diluted the dodecaphonic techniques with tonal aspects, and saw them as disparate elements that competed with each other, often until one style 'overcame' the other, as in his composition *Halil*. In this piece, written between *Mass* and *A Quiet Place* in 1981 as a memorial to an Israeli flute player who was killed in the conflict in the Middle East, Bernstein uses a 12-tone row in the solo flute line at the beginning, and creates a struggle with the more tonal music that follows, in: 'It is a kind of night-music which, from its opening 12-tone row to its ambiguously diatonic final cadence, is an ongoing conflict of nocturnal images: wish-dreams, nightmares, repose, sleeplessness, night-terrors and sleep itself, *Death's twin brother*' (programme note, 1981).

However, as with his previous serial compositions, the row is not used as the sole basis for the musical development, and there is repetition within the initial presentation of the series. Bernstein's strictest use of dodecaphonic methods prior

---

8   From 'Notes on Atonality', an undated sheet of paper, box 104, folder 18, LBC.
9   Ibid.

to *A Quiet Place* can be seen in the baritone solo in *Songfest*, 'The Pennycandystore Beyond the El'. In this setting of the poem by Lawrence Ferlinghetti, all the material used, except for one six-note descending phrase, is derived from the row presented in the introduction. A number of different transformations are utilized – P0, P9, R9, I9, I10, RI3, P2 and RI3 – in addition to fragments of the same rows. Bernstein makes use of imitation of short sections of the rows, occasionally omits notes from the patterns, and adds harmonies beneath appearances of P2; at one point he also splits a row, moving the first four notes to the end, so as to create better counterpoint with a different presentation of the row. This slightly contradicts the programme note for the piece, which describes the song as 'a hushed, jazzy scherzo employing strict 12-tone technique' (Gottlieb 1976, in score). An unpublished work from this time also contains dodecaphonic ideas: a number from *Alarums and Flourishes*, an unfinished project from 1980, labelled '12-tone Serenade'.[10]

In both the row from *The Age of Anxiety*, and the ascending phrase of *Trouble in Tahiti* we begin to see a use of semitones within the row, a characteristic that develops through the subsequent examples of serial 'melodies' (see Example 8.1).

Example 8.1   Rows used within Bernstein's musical theatre works, semitones shown bracketed

As can be seen in the other four rows, three of the initial intervals, and all of the final intervals are semitones;[11] there are also a large number of semitones within these four rows. Each of the rows has other characteristics, in part shaped

---

[10]   It is also called 'My Twelve Tone Melody', and is not the same as another number with the same title, written for Irving Berlin's 100th birthday celebrations in 1988.

[11]   If the octave displacement in 'Quiet' is discounted.

by the nature of the show and other motifs used, and by the context of each song. As the tension in the palace in *Candide* becomes unbearable, it is represented in the song 'Quiet', which combines ascending and descending chromatic lines, both starting on B, with the intervals between the lines widening as tempers rise. The 'Cool' row is divided into three patterns of four notes, with specific intervals in each group, as discussed in the chapter on *West Side Story*, in the particularly edgy atmosphere leading up to the Rumble. The 'theme' of 'Credo' includes a reiterated note (the bracketed A), and has certain notes repeated in each presentation; the tension perhaps stems from the statement of belief at a time when faith was waning among the American public. In *A Quiet Place* there is certainly a tense emotional context, as the row is introduced at the opening of the funeral scene, but in this work there is a more disciplined employment of 12-tone methods, although still not as strictly applied as by some composers. The row used in the opera is derived from a song that Bernstein wrote called 'Play Some More', the manuscript for which is undated (see Example 8.2).

Example 8.2 'Play Some More', verse bb. 1–4, from manuscript

In these previous works, use of transformations of rows has been limited, with 'Credo' using the inverted row, and 'Quiet' employing both transpositions and inversions: P0, P2, I11, P11 and I10. In Dialogue 1 of *A Quiet Place* we are presented with all four variants of the row at the outset, in the order P0, R0, I0 and RI0. Bernstein designed the row in such a way that elision was possible from one version to another, by placing the first and last notes a tritone apart. This means that each version of the untransposed row starts and ends on either an E♭ or an A, and that each one can lead not only on to its own retrograde, but also on to another variation of the row.

In Dialogue 1 Bernstein employs only the original versions of each transformation, and the second transposition of the prime, P2. To create interest in the movement, he employs canonic techniques, and later presents three versions of the row contrapuntally, a texture he used in the serial song of *Songfest* seven years previously (see Examples 8.3a and b). In the canon, there is elision in the first line where RI0 moves to P0, but in the echo the E♭ is repeated, as P0 begins an octave higher, displacing the harmony by a quaver. In the homophonic passage, four notes are altered within the rows, presumably for tonal reasons (those notes marked by x), but the combination still results in several octaves between the

Example 8.3   Use of the row in Dialogue 1

(a) Dialogue 1, bb. 117–22
(b) Dialogue 1, bb. 124–6 (an x indicates an altered note)

rows, and also several tritones. This alteration is typical of Bernstein's embrace of the 12-tone techniques, which is always quite superficial.

Within the structure of Dialogue 1, it can be seen that there are only occasional deviations from the serialist technique. The introduction contains the first four notes of the prime row, but with the B and the C reversed, creating a motif that recurs in the opera, and that will be mentioned later (see Example 8.4). The four-note pattern leads onto a pedal B that underpins the first 16 bars of this section, combining with A and E♭ pedals that linger at the end of rows. This arrangement of notes suggests a tonality of B major, with a seventh, which goes against strict 12-tone technique by implying a tonal centre. There are only three other bars that do not conform with serialist methods: b. 123, which contains arpeggio figures based on A, E♭ and D♭, and bb. 128–9, which contain tremolos. After the initial

Example 8.4   Dialogue 1, b.1

presentation of the rows in Dialogue 1, they reappear in later sections of the opera, either in full[12] or in part:

Dialogue 2	end of R0 begun in accompaniment in Dialogue 1
	fragment of P0 (P0f) in accompaniment
Dialogue 3	P0f in accompaniment
Dialogue 4	P0 sung by Funeral Director
	P0, I0, R0 and RI2 in accompaniment
	P0f in accompaniment
Dialogue 5	P0 sung by Doctor
	R0 and P0f sung by Funeral Director
Dialogue 11	P0 and R0 sung by Funeral Director
Dialogue 13	P0, R0, P0f, P9 and R6 sung by Funeral Director
	R0 and I0 in accompaniment

It is significant that the rows are first heard in the conversation between the Funeral Director and Bill, and it is the former that initiates the majority of the statements of the row. The Funeral Director is obviously, by virtue of his vocation, connected to the stressful situation that the characters find themselves in, and they are constantly reminded of this by his presence; he is present in all the Dialogues where the complete rows are found; in Dialogue 5 one row is sung by the Doctor, but this follows directly after one sung by the Funeral Director: the Doctor responds to the prime row of the Funeral Director with the retrograde, beginning on the same E♭. All of the fragments heard in the Dialogues are derived from the prime row, although the length of these varied from four to ten notes, forming a link between various conversations.

In Act II, Scene 3, following Sam's solo section, Dede's entrance marks the beginning of a passage that utilizes portions of rows (bb. 708–742), either notes 1 to 5, or 1 to 6, of the 12. The rows used here are I11, P7, and later I0. The

---

[12]   This definition includes rows with only one note omitted.

connection between the first two can be seen in the first and last notes of each hexachord:

I11	D	E♭	F♯	F	E	B♭
P7	B♭	A	F♯	G	G♯	D

This again allows elision between the two fragments used. However, the serial material is set against a more tonally based background, and the melodies soon move away from their 12-tone origins. This section is mirrored in the passage from b. 743 to b. 766, as the duet between Sam and Dede gives way to a parallel duet between François and Junior. This begins with a transposition of the melodies of bb. 708–711, up a fourth, in bb. 743–6, but with a slightly altered accompaniment. This means that new row fragments are being used, but with the same properties as the earlier pair:

I4	G	A♭	B	B♭	A	E♭
P0	E♭	D	B	C	D♭	G

In this section there are two further row segments used: first P6, which begins on an A, a tritone away from the opening note of P0; and also I9, which is utilized only once, and which appears to have been chosen for tonal rather than serial reasons, as it forms a sequence a fourth above I4, used two bars before.

It is interesting, and perhaps significant, that Tippett's *The Knot Garden* also features a 12-tone row, which is utilized at the beginning of the first and second acts. The latter's function is to 'create the nightmarish atmosphere of Act II and with it the impression of an ineludable, malevolent force against which resistance is useless' (Kemp 1984, p. 429).

Some of the techniques and characteristics employed by Bernstein reflect elements that can be found in the 12-tone works of Webern: the use of the semitone, elision, canonic writing and overlapping. Bernstein had encountered Webern's work through conducting pieces during his time at the NYPO in 1957 and 1967. It is interesting that Bernstein used dodecaphonic techniques at all, as he made his opinion of the Second Viennese School clear during his lectures at Harvard in 1973. In the fifth of the lectures he gave whilst holding the Norton Professorship, 'The Twentieth Century Crisis', he describes the evolution from atonal to 12-tone music, and discussed Schoenberg's methods:

> The trouble is that the new musical 'rules' of Schoenberg are not apparently based on innate awareness, on the intuition of tonal relationships. They are like rules of an artificial language, and therefore must be learned. This would seem to lead to what used to be called 'form without content', or form at the expense of content – structuralism for its own sake. (Bernstein 1976, p. 283)

This perhaps explains why Bernstein never completely embraced the dodecaphonic approach, and why he always maintained some sense of tonality within his 12-tone writing. The struggle between an intellectualized approach and a more spontaneous and creative approach was, in Bernstein's mind, always going to be won by the latter. He summed up his thoughts on the subject in a simple sentence: 'I feel atonality is the end of something, not the beginning.'[13]

'Resolution' and Other Motifs

As *A Quiet Place* was designed to be a sequel to *Trouble in Tahiti*, and as the two shows share characters, it is not surprising that motifs from the earlier work reappear in the second. One example, the Resolution motif, from *Trouble in Tahiti*, plays an important part in the second opera, appearing in all three acts, both in its original version and also in variations and retrogrades (see Example 8.5). There are ten variants on the three intervals in the motif, as shown in Table 8.2. Wadsworth described the motif as 'an old certainty "churned up again," to quote Old Sam, like all the others things that "never worked"' (1987, p. 14). Many of the appearances are related to Dinah, or to a reflection on the past, in particular in the Readings, where the motif is heard in canon in its full version as the lid is closed on Dinah's coffin.

Table 8.2   Variations on the Resolution motif

Variation	Intervals		
Original	perfect 5	maj 3	min 7
1	TT	maj 2	min 6
2	maj 3	maj 2	min 6
3	min 6	min 3	min 6
4	TT	min 3	maj 6
5	min 6	maj 2	min 6
6	min 6	maj 2	maj 7
7	TT	min 3	min 6
8	perfect 5	maj 3	perfect 5
9	perfect 5	min 3	maj 6
10	perfect 5	maj 3	maj 6

In the original arrangement, when *A Quiet Place* was placed after *Tahiti* in a double bill, all quotations of motifs in the second half were reminiscences, with a definite point of reference in music already heard: the initial emotional context had previously been experienced. However, the nature and function of the motifs

---

[13]   From 'Notes on Atonality', box 104, folder 18, LBC.

more closely resembles the *Tahiti* pattern. Following its appearance at the opening of Dialogue 1, it is heard twice more, at the start of Sam's Act I solo, where it begins a ritornello that recurs throughout the aria, and at the outset of Act II, where the ritornello is repeated, and where Sam has a further solo. These last two examples imply that the motif is linked to Sam, although this is contradicted by its use in Dialogue 1. Although Sam does not participate in this conversation, he is present at that time, as he 'stands motionless, his back to the audience' (Bernstein and Wadsworth 1984, p. 10). Perhaps it is his turmoil that we are hearing in the music, as he is the only character to remain from *Tahiti*, and is thus the one we would connect with.

Wadsworth states that a further important 'cell' within *A Quiet Place* is the chorale that is sung by the chorus (see Example 8.7):

> This was music newly composed by Lenny. It takes over from the *Tahiti* cluster at the beginning of the Prologue ... The chorale seems to presage a revelation every time it comes around – the trauma of the accident, the discovery of a cure in Act II, the healing of the final Scene. (Wadsworth 1987, p. 15)

The first phrase of this chorale bears a strong resemblance to a figure from *Dybbuk*, sung by the tenor and baritone soloists. In this context, it is accompanying a line from the Song of Songs in the Old Testament, 'Ēnayich yonim' ('Thine eyes are as doves'), relating more to romance and adoration than revelation.

The chorale is heard twice in the Prologue, first before the accident and under the comments of the chorus at the scene of the car crash, and second in phrases between sarcastic and mocking remarks from those about to attend the funeral. In Act II, it is Dede who is humming the chorale melody (supported by the sopranos

Example 8.7 Prologue, bb. 19–22 and bb. 27–30

of the chorus) as she and her father sort through Dinah's things. The 'cure' is a reconciliation between father and daughter triggered by Dede trying on one of Dinah's dresses, one that her mother wore in *Tahiti*, reminding Sam of happier times and of the fact that he really does love his daughter. There is a further iteration of the chorale in Act II, as Sam almost kisses his sleeping son, attempting to bridge the gap between them, but can't bring himself to do it. In Junior's room he finds the handball trophy that he won in *Tahiti* and this starts him reminiscing, leading into the second flashback, which is the second half of *Tahiti* itself. The final appearance of the chorale is near the end of Act III, when the family has so very nearly come back together, only to be driven apart again by an argument. Junior knocks Dinah's diary into the air, and the chorale is heard twice: 'first cold, in a skittish, syncopated "wrong" setting for orchestra with yawning gaps between phrases, then warm, in a perfectly simple, smooth statement hummed by the ubiquitous offstage voices' (Wadsworth 1987, p. 15).

It seems that at this point in his compositional career that Bernstein's motivic writing was now second nature, a fact that is hardly surprising as he had been using these techniques for 40 years:

> Whereas [Bernstein] was deeply aware and appreciative of my constant recycling of fragments of his old *Trouble in Tahiti* libretto, he seemed rarely to plant musical references – references to either *Tahiti* or to completed sections of *A Quiet Place*. There were countless times when Lenny realized *after* composing something that it was indeed related to X or Y moment. (Wadsworth 1987, p. 15)

Act I

The first act of *A Quiet Place* is the longest single movement ever written by Bernstein: as a whole it lasts over 45 minutes,[14] and substantial passages of this are uninterrupted music. From the Prologue to the end of Dialogue 13 is one such section, a single musical section that, although subdivided into various segments, is continuous and only breaks after more than 22 minutes of music. Bernstein had only written one longer piece without interruptions or halts: the 'Symphonic Dances from *West Side Story*' (22'57); in all three of his symphonies, and in the majority of his other orchestral works, the music was divided into separate movements with clear boundaries. To sustain the musical momentum in Act I he uses three main techniques, particularly in linking together the Dialogues that form the main part of this act. The Dialogues are just that, conversations between guests at the funeral, and they are divided into two groups by Dede's Arietta (see Table 8.3). The significance of the Arietta is that it is the first time a direct member

---

[14]   All timings are taken from Bernstein's own Deutsche Grammophon recording of the pieces mentioned; in Act I there are several optional cuts, in Dialogues 1, 3, 5 and 13, which are made on the recording, and which remove a total of 36 bars.

Table 8.3   Structure of Act I of *A Quiet Place*

	Prologue	1	2	3	4	5	6	Arietta	7	8	9	10
Bill	B	B		B		B				B	B	
Funeral Director		FD			FD	FD						
Susie			Sus			Sus	Sus		Sus	Sus		
Analyst			A			A						
Doctor				Doc		Doc				Doc		
MrsDoc					MD	MD						MD
Dede							Dede	Dede	Dede	Dede		
François										F	F	F
Junior												
Sam												
Chorus	Ch			Ch		Ch			Ch	Ch	Ch	Ch
Characters		2	2	2	2	6	2	1	2	5	2	2
Bars	98	35	31	57	32	92	3	56	53	21	33	23

	11	12	13
Bill			B
Funeral Director	FD		FD
Susie			Sus
Analyst	A		A
Doctor			
MrsDoc		MD	MD
Dede		Dede	Dede
François		F	F
Junior			
Sam			
Chorus	Ch	Ch	Ch
Characters	2	2	7
Bars	28	24	45

	Readings	Chorale	Aria	Trio	Finale	Postlude
Bill	B					
Funeral Director	FD					
Susie	Sus					
Analyst	A					
Doctor	Doc					
MrsDoc	MD					
Dede	Dede			Dede	Dede	
François	F			F	F	
Junior	J			J	J	
Sam			Sam		S	
Chorus	Ch	Ch				
Characters	9		1	3	4	
Bars	115	7	181	38	63	33

of Dinah's nuclear family has 'spoken';[15] although Sam is present at the funeral from the beginning, he has been silent until now, and will remain so until the guests have departed.

Bernstein uses three techniques to create connections between the Dialogues, the first the same as a method he employed in his second symphony, *The Age of Anxiety*, in 1949. In the 'Seven Ages' movement of the piece, Bernstein created a set of seven variations, which were linked by the fact that the main theme in each variation was based on melodic material from the previous section: 'Each variation seizes upon some feature of the preceding one and develops it, introducing, in the course of the development, some counter-feature upon which the next variation seizes. It is a kind of musical fission' (prefatory note in score). This is used clearly on at least three occasions in *A Quiet Place*, linking Dialogues 2 to 3, 3 to 4, and 9 to 10. In two of these it is the very last phrase of one dialogue that becomes the first phase of the next, and in the other example (Dialogues 3 to 4), it is a section of the vocal line in the first conversation that plays an important part in the accompaniment of the following dialogue (see Example 8.8). Dialogue 3 contains a further interesting phrase: a new 12-tone row heard in canon between the voices of the chorus and the orchestra. This row, in a version a semitone lower, was written on the top of the manuscript page that contains the aforementioned 'Play Some More'.[16]

Example 8.8 Showing transitions between dialogues

Dialogue 2, b. 164

Dialogue 3, b. 165

Dialogue 3, bb. 176-77

Dialogue 4, b. 230

Dialogue 9, b. 511

Dialogue 10, b. 512

There are three other examples of this kind of development, although the phrases are not reproduced as exactly as in the previous cases. Dialogue 6, which at only three bars is by far the shortest and serves as an introduction to Dede's Arietta, begins with a descending minor third interval, as Susie greets Dede; this is the same interval Bill used to welcome his niece near the end of Dialogue 5. A rising linear minor third that is frequently used in Dede's Arietta is then utilized

---

15   Dede has one bar in Dialogue 6 that leads directly into the Arietta proper.

16   On a manuscript in LBC.

at the opening of the succeeding Dialogue 7; sections of the accompaniment from the Arietta also appear in this Dialogue. Finally, François's first words echo Susie's welcome to him in Dialogue 8, and a number of his subsequent phrases, in both Dialogue 8 and then also in 9, follow the same intervallic outline, sometimes in inversion.

The second technique is only used twice, and is perhaps the simplest of the methods used. In moving from Dialogue 1 to 2, and 12 to 13, Bernstein continues some aspect of the accompaniment to link the two sections. In the first of these it is the retrograde version of the row that forms the connection; in the second it is the semiquaver pedal A♭.

The final method first appears in Dialogue 5. By this point six of the characters have been introduced, and all of these are involved, at some point, in this conversation. To reflect this, elements from the previous four dialogues are brought in: the Funeral Director's retrograde row from Dialogue 1; Susie's phrase from Dialogue 2, and her repetition of a phrase of the Doctor from Dialogue 3; the Doctor himself is accompanied by a variation on the figure that was used to connect Dialogues 2 and 3, and his 'passage of time' phrase from Dialogue 3; and Mrs Doc's characteristic cadence figure, originally heard in Dialogue 4, is taken up by the Analyst as he talks to her. The same technique is employed in Dialogue 8, the next conversation involving more than two characters: Susie welcomes François with a variant of her greeting to Dede in Dialogue 6; Dede's opening phrase resembles a passage she sang in the preceding Dialogue; Doc reiterates his rising seventh motif; and Bill has an ascending minor third, possibly derived from Dede's previous music. Similar reuse of musical ideas occurs in the last four Dialogues. In Dialogue 10 Mrs Doc makes fun of Susie and the Funeral Director by imitating them and repeating snatches of their music. Dialogue 11 includes the prime and retrograde versions of the row as part of the Funeral Director's speech. Dialogue 12 recycles the figure from bb. 176–7 of Dialogue 3 in a more extended form, and in Dialogue 13 we get rows from the Funeral Director, and the repetition of an accompaniment from Dialogue 5 when Mrs Doc approached the Analyst, now heard as he approaches François.

The Prologue begins with the Resolution motif and associated chord, and provides the immediate background to *A Quiet Place*. In this it serves the same function as the Prologue of *West Side Story*, which shows the gang tension rising prior to the main story of the musical; the two pieces use motifs based on the same four notes, as mentioned in Chapter 5. In *A Quiet Place*, the time span is unspecified, but the aftermath of the car crash is revealed by the comments of the onlookers in *Sprechstimme*, interspersed with the sung chorale. This introduction also underlines the basic role of the chorus in the opera: from their offstage position, they remark on the onstage action and emphasize particular emotional moments, reflecting the function of the radio singers in *Tahiti*: 'the jazz trio of the earlier work finds a counterpart in the offstage chorus which echoes and comments throughout the later opera' (Conrad 1992b, p. 1202). It seems that the Prologue of the opera was added following the première, as neither it nor the chorus is mentioned on the Houston programme, meaning that the audience at the opening may not have been immediately aware of the reason for the funeral.

The readings are separated from the dialogues by a moment of silence, and for the most part they are unaccompanied. The different vocal lines occasionally converge where the passages they are reading have the same words, for example, 'children', 'Dinah' and 'apart' (see Example 8.9). There is also some imitation in the melodies of Bill and Susie, who are both talking of personal memories rather than reading poems or speeches. Bernstein may have intended more formal counterpoint to be used at this point, as he wrote a late-night poem to Stephen Wadsworth when they were in the process of writing *A Quiet Place*: 'And then, O Wonder, *Readings* could ensue, / And reminiscences of Bill and Sue. / In Contrapünktisch Cancrizanserei' (in Wadsworth 1987, p. 16).

Example 8.9 Readings, bb. 643–4

The readings are rudely interrupted by Junior's entrance, the last member of the family to arrive, but, following his outburst, the poems and homilies are resumed, ending with a full appearance of the Resolution motif by the orchestra as the guests move to leave. There is a short chorale, sung by all except the four family members, as the guests file out, but this is different from the opening chorale.

The remainder of Act I features Sam, Dede, François and Junior, and begins with Sam's first words in the opera, an angry outburst aimed at his children, his dead wife and himself. This aria, which includes material recycled from a number rejected from *1600 Pennsylvania Avenue*,[17] is in ritornello form, one of the few occasions where Bernstein employs a formal structure in *A Quiet Place*; it is somewhat ironic that his angry and confused eruption should be contained within such a traditional and organized form. Sam alternates between talking to himself and berating those around him, mainly in a time signature of $\frac{6}{8}$, continuing the characterization begun in *Tahiti*, where Sam's two solo scenes are both in compound time. The ritornello theme is developed from the descending pattern already mentioned (see Example 8.10).

Following Sam's emotional outburst, the other three are drawn into their own memories of their fathers: Dede and Junior remember letters they sent to Sam

---

[17]   The second episode of the ritornello was originally part of a number in *1600* called 'The Switch', which never made it into the show (manuscript in LBC).

Example 8.10 Act I aria 'You're Late...', bb. 1–3

from school and camp, and François recalls questions he asked his dead father. There is an underlying rondo form here, with elements of the accompaniment being repeated: A–B–A–C–A–C¹–B–A–C². In addition to the Resolution motif, there is a semitone figure that appears in all three of the contrapuntal vocal lines: an E–E♭, or E♭–E pattern, which always occurs in the first or second bars of the A section, creating a connection between the emotions of the three singers (see Example 8.11).

Example 8.11 Act I Trio, bb. 943–4

The reverie is broken by Junior's sharp return to reality, and all his tension and fear are unleashed in a mock striptease, directed towards his father; this tune was originally destined for Bernstein's version of *Lolita*, which Bernstein had sent to Harry Kraut in October 1977, and is the source for most of Junior's musical material (see Example 8.12).

The Finale begins with two accompaniments drawn from Sam's earlier solo aria, and, following the ensuing arguments and recriminations, Sam, Dede and François leave. There is an orchestral postlude as Junior 'runs his hand tenderly across the coffin lid, wondering' (Bernstein and Wadsworth 1984, p. 92), and the music accompanying this is based on Junior's music from his entrance and strip song, combined with a bass riff from the latter; he is left alone on the stage.

Example 8.12 Act I Finale, bb. 1011–14

Acts II and III

The revised second act of *A Quiet* Place is predominantly taken up with the two flashbacks to *Trouble in Tahiti*, although these are framed by two other scenes. The first of these presents Sam alone in the master bedroom, later that day after the funeral, as he begins to go through his wife's belongings. He has found her diary, and is reading portions of it aloud. The music of this scene begins with a repetition of the ritornello theme from Sam's Act I aria, although now the vocal line is changed to reflect his change in mood (see Example 8.13).

Example 8.13 Act II, Scene 1, bb. 1–10

The second half of this short scene introduces a new melody, which is marked 'like a lullaby, gently rocking', as Sam apologizes to the absent Dinah for their problems. This lullaby music had originally been intended for the abandoned show *Alarums and Flourishes* around 1980, when it was called 'Saquina's Lullaby'. The same music also appears as part of the number 'Play Some More', which as already mentioned provided the basis for the 12-tone row in this opera, and is connected to a chorus phrase in Dialogue 3. The scene ends as Sam slips into his memory, and the first half of *Trouble in Tahiti* unfolds.

Scene 3, which follows the first flashback, returns to Sam and his reading of the diary, but gradually the other members of the family also appear. The music begins once more in $\frac{6}{8}$, one of Sam's musical characteristics, but changes to ¢ when Dede enters the room to talk to her father. As discussed earlier, this section of the scene uses fragments of the row, as both Dede and Sam, and Junior and François begin to work out their problems, and it is also in this section that the Resolution motif appears several times. There is a significant change in the music when Junior begins to tell the fantasy tale of his incest with Dede, and her voice is heard in counterpoint in some phrases, as she looks through her mother's dresses in the next room. Junior's supposedly revelatory tale is strophic, and he repeats his music four times, with some variation and development as the story continues, before François brings Junior's ranting to a halt. When Dede appears wearing one of Dinah's dresses, there is a further shift, and the music is dominated by references to *Trouble in Tahiti*, mainly in the use of the Garden music beneath their conversations. One of the more poignant moments, although not employing a direct quotation, is when Dede refers to her mother's garden, using Dinah's words, as she suggests that she will clear the weeds away the following day (see Example 8.14).

The family members gradually end their conversations, and retire for the night, and Junior goes to sleep in his old room. As Sam approaches his son, the lullaby music is heard again, suggesting that Sam is sorry for what Junior has been through, and perhaps feels responsible for his problems, although he still cannot manage to give his son a goodnight kiss. As he spies the handball trophy on the shelf, the memories of 30 years ago stir once more, and, following a repeat of the chorale by the chorus, the second half of *Trouble in Tahiti* is presented.

The final act of the opera is also a continuous piece of music, after the opening Prelude, this time lasting nearly 30 minutes.[18] Originally some of the other characters from Act I were present in the garden scene, and also in an interlude during which 'deep in the same night, Bill and Mrs Doc – in other parts of the town – try to come to terms with conflicted feelings about Dinah' (Houston programme notes); the revision altered this so that only the four major family members remain in this section of the opera. The act begins with only Dede on the stage, and she is joined gradually by Junior, François and Sam. As would be expected in a final

---

[18]   29'13 on the Bernstein recording.

Example 8.14 Act II, Scene 3, bb. 1030–32

act, there are musical reminiscences of earlier events and themes, but not all of the music is borrowed from within the opera itself.

The Prelude contains music that was sung in Dialogue 3 by the chorus, and also uses Junior's music. Dede begins the following scene with a solo aria, the final example of a piece with a formal structure in this opera, in the form A–B–C–B^1 followed by C^1 in the orchestra. Two interesting points are that the B section of this aria is based on 'This Time' from Bernstein's previous stage work, and that a further phrase that appears three times here bears a striking resemblance to a figure from 'Thank You' in *Mass*; in both of these earlier examples, there are references to happier times which are now in the past. When Junior enters, Bernstein quotes from another composer for the only time in *A Quiet Place* with a passage from the finale of Mendelssohn's Violin Concerto; Junior appears to be remembering a cereal advertisement, which Dede also recalls and joins in with. This does not appear to be a real advertisement, but is probably a joke from Bernstein's days with the Boston Symphony Orchestra, when they used to make up words to go with famous melodies.[19] This leads into another musical borrowing, but this time of Bernstein's own material, as the rituals of breakfast stir up memories, and there is a four-bar quotation from the opening scene of *Tahiti*, with Dede and Junior taking the parts of their parents. The next thing they remember is a childhood clapping game, although neither of them can recall it perfectly: Dede claps in the wrong place, and Junior repeatedly gets the kiss wrong. Another fragment of the *Tahiti*

---

[19]   Suggestion from Wayne Shirley, conversation with author in the Library of Congress, August 2002.

breakfast is replayed, and the A section of Dede's aria is repeated. The siblings recall another game, and they begin to play tag, the rules of which are: 'Stoop and say a slogan to avoid being tagged. When tagged, turn around and count to ten (to allow the other player to get away) before going after him or her. Counting to ten not necessary when more than two play' (Bernstein and Wadsworth 1984, p. 267). Junior is first to say a slogan, and his phrase is a variation on his music from Act I. It is during this game that François enters, avoiding being tagged by singing a snippet from *Candide*. (Is Bernstein saying that the line had become well known by then, or was it just self-quotation?) As Dede and François embrace, a further memory surfaces, and the trio re-enact Dede's birthday, when she was first introduced to François, who was still with Junior at the time. This scene parallels the trio in Act I, when the three of them called to mind the relationships each had with their father, but there is no musical connection between the two trios. Sam joins in the game as the tag resumes, and when he 'stalks' Junior, it is with his son's own music (see Example 8.15).

Example 8.15 Act III, Tag 2, bb. 282–3

The game gradually slows and stops as Sam brings out Dinah's diary. As he begins to read from it, the music and the mood change dramatically, and the voice of Dinah can be heard, as her written words bring her memory to the forefront of her family's consciousness. Her vocal line contains snatches of melodies from *Tahiti*, and some scat phrases (see Example 8.16). The comments in her diary cause some amusement, and her husband and children (and the chorus) begin to laugh until they are rolling in hysterics, releasing the tension and anxiety between them. It seems that things are resolved, and the music from the Prelude of *Trouble in Tahiti* is reused as an accompaniment, implying that the perfection that the Radio Trio sang of in the earlier opera is close at hand. However, the peace is soon broken by an argument over the mundane matter of the sleeping arrangements, and the situation deteriorates once more until Junior throws his mother's diary in the air. The chorale is reiterated here as the family finally realize how foolish they are being, and begin to be brought closer together. Junior begins by reaching out to his father, first with his own music from Act I, but then accompanied by the lullaby music, again implying some real remorse on the part of both father and son (see Example 8.17).

As the others join in, another section of Sam's music, this time from his Act I aria, is reused, before Junior makes his final gesture towards his father, singing his own music as he has finally gained enough confidence in himself. When Sam at last

Example 8.16 Act III, bb. 345–64

Example 8.17 Act III Finale, bb. 566–7

accepts his son, we hear the music from the Prelude of this act, and it is this music that ends the opera, with the closing 'Amen' from the chorus (see Example 8.18).

Example 8.18 Act III Finale, bb. 617–20

As with all of his previous works for the musical theatre, *A Quiet Place* ends with a sense of hope that things will get better: the sailors and girls hope they will meet again, Sam and Dinah attempt to reconcile their differences, Ruth and Eileen look forward to their new lives, Candide and friends try for a new way of life, the two gangs are brought together in grief, love overcomes religious failings, and America looks to the new century. Perhaps this is the essence of his works: that, no matter what the problems and difficulties, love and optimism win through.

Conclusion

The Final Years

After *A Quiet Place*, Bernstein would never find another collaborator to help him in his quest for his American opera. In 1984, he gave a fresh slant to one of his older works in the Deutsche Grammophon recording of *West Side Story*. A starry cast of opera singers was drawn together under Bernstein's baton, and a documentary was made of the recording process: the meeting of Broadway music and operatic voices was not always successful, and the programme revealed the problems as well as the triumphs. In a touching moment, Bernstein's children Alexander and Nina took on the speaking parts of Tony and Maria during the balcony scene.

In December 1984, Bernstein's oldest daughter, Jamie, married David Thomas, and three years later Bernstein's first grandchild was born: Francesca Anna Maria Thomas. These two events provided moments of happiness in what was becoming an increasingly hard time for Bernstein. Although he was kept busy with conducting engagements all over the world, his creative juices were not flowing freely; he was searching for a theme for his next opera, but couldn't find the right subject. In 1988 sections of his incidental music from *The Lark* were given a new breath of life as the *Missa Brevis*; in the same year he produced his last song cycle in *Arias and Barcarolles* – soprano and tenor soloists are accompanied by piano duet, and the overwhelming themes are love and relationships. As his final composition with text, the work provides an interesting epilogue to his compositional output. Burton described it as 'Bernstein's last contribution to his musical autobiography; it is intimate, at times wryly self-mocking and bewilderingly eclectic, always unpretentious and blessedly free of guilt, breast-beating and all aspects of faith lost or retrieved' (1984, p. 493). An orchestral piece called *Jubilee Games*, originally written for the Israel Philharmonic Orchestra in 1985, was expanded from two movements to three, and then developed further in to four, changing title along the way to *Concerto for Orchestra* in 1989 (in the process Bernstein had inserted two other pieces, *Opening Prayer* and *Seven Variations on an Octatonic Theme*). In the same year he completed his final work, a *Dance Suite* for brass quintet. There were two more attempts to return to opera and musical theatre, the first being a project originally started in 1968 as an adaptation of Brecht's *The Caucasian Chalk Circle*. This was revived in 1987 as *The Race to Urga*, but still did not reach the stage. A similar fate befell Bernstein's Holocaust opera, which he had begun in 1985 with Stephen Wadsworth; work on this continued up to February 1990. By this time, Bernstein's health was declining, and the breathing problems that had dogged him through out his life were becoming increasingly challenging; a scan had also revealed a tumour in his lungs, and, although this was removed, he was weakened by the treatment. A visit to Japan in early summer 1990 placed his body under more stress, and he had to withdraw from several conducting engagements. On returning to America, Bernstein took his place at Tanglewood once more, and conducted a concert on Sunday 19 August, but the effort was almost too much for the ailing maestro, as he visibly suffered on the podium; this would be his last concert. Realizing that he could not continue, Bernstein announced his retirement from conducting on 9 October; he died less than a week later on 14 October, suffering a cardiac arrest in his home in New York.

Closing Thoughts

Following this survey of Bernstein's musical theatre works, what conclusions can be drawn regarding his compositional techniques? First, Bernstein was indeed eclectic, a label that he himself accepted and used about his work, but that he also applied to other composers. With his usual outspokenness he claimed that 'the greater the composer, the better case you can make for his eclecticism. This combination of Haydn, Mozart and Bach, and everything else that goes into making up Beethoven, plus the magic factor which is the individuated thing we call Beethoven, that voice, that personal sound' (quoted in Laird 1999, p. 1).

It was from his influences that he drew the motivic methods that he utilized so much in his works, the organicism that creates relationships within the shows and operas, and gives them an underlying unity of sound. This is one element common to all his works, and the development of Bernstein's approach can be seen through his theatre works. The manipulation of motifs in *On the Town*, both to underline the integration of the musical numbers and as a basis for generating music from a small amount of basic material, evolves through the succeeding works, as the number of motifs decreases and the organicism throughout the show increases. The unity provided by the manipulation of motifs reached a climax in *West Side Story*, with the principal motif being treated as a leitmotif, changing depending on the context and the character. After this show, it seems that Bernstein's approach to composing changed, and his priority shifted from the need to connect everything motivically to the idea of longer structures that were linked by other means, evident in the extended sections of *1600 Pennsylvania Avenue* and *A Quiet Place*; perhaps he thought that he had taken the motivic ideas as far as they could go within the genre, although they are still present in the remaining pieces but with a less prominent function. I think that both of the approaches derived from his highbrow writing: the first from a need to include symphonic ideas in the shows, almost to remind people that he was a serious composer before coming to Broadway, and the second from a desire to create his serious American opera. A further significant element that was imported from the serious compositions was the use of academic and traditional structures, transplanted into the form of the Broadway musical. Although it is perhaps less unexpected for the structures and techniques of Western art music to appear in his operas (although, conversely, they contain vernacular sounds and ideas), to find fugues, sonata forms, 12-tone rows and symphonically based ballets in a popular genre is a little unusual. I think it was his eclecticism that led him to combine the aspects of the differing styles in the piece he was writing at the time, as it also should be remembered that his non-musical theatre compositions often included popular elements.

Unfortunately, this eclecticism did not always lead to critical acclaim. In his ambition to remain within current compositional trends, his attempts sometimes resulted in an unsuccessful juxtaposition of styles and genres, which confused rather than delighted the listener. *Mass* was criticized for its clumsy mixture of musical influences, and *A Quiet Place* was too brash for many opera-goers. In embracing the surrounding styles and blending them with his own compositional ideas, Bernstein almost 'diluted' the American sounds and concepts he had so much success with in the 1940s and 1950s. Indeed, some of his later works are quite difficult to appreciate on first hearing, as they are so distant from his early compositions; the serialism and dissonance in *A Quiet Place* does not appeal to people in the same way as the jazzy popular music of *On the Town*. In his attempt to expand his musical vocabulary, Bernstein alienated the public he had entertained with his earlier works; the cleverness of his later music does not necessarily make it easy to listen to.

This eclecticism also leads to a further point about Bernstein's compositions: although he was a great musician (considered by some to be the greatest American musician), and a strong musical ambassador, I do not believe that he was a *great* American composer. Although he introduced highbrow musical techniques into popular genres, these techniques had existed in serious music for many years; it was merely the application of them that was original. His music was frequently derivative, and reflected trends and sounds of the time; Bernstein was never really innovative, but absorbed and manipulated the music around him. Despite his protestations and all the serious works he created, it will be for the popular works – *West Side Story*, the Overture to *Candide* and *Chichester Psalms* – that he will be remembered, and quite rightly too, I think, as these pieces demonstrate what Bernstein did best: that mix of Carnegie Hall and Tin Pan Alley that appealed to the American audiences.

But Bernstein's eclecticism was not limited merely to musical experiences, which raises the second conclusion that has emerged from this study. Bernstein was aware of the fact that music does not just reflect the influence of other music, but of a variety of external stimuli: 'Who are you if you are not the sum of everything that's happened before? Everything that you've experienced at least, not everything that has happened, but everything that has been significant in your experience, unconscious mainly' (quoted in Laird 1999, p. 5). With this thought, Bernstein was echoing one of his ideas from his 1939 bachelor's thesis, where he pointed out that 'a composer's music is the sum of all his experience (including musical experience)' (Bernstein 1982, p. 55). These beliefs underpin the second issue, that the theatre works of Bernstein provide a musical autobiography. The main themes of each show reflect aspects of Bernstein's own life at the time that they were composed.

On the Town focuses on the search for romance and fun. Bernstein was 26 years old, and had been in New York for two years. He was enjoying life with his friends and with his new-found success. *Trouble in Tahiti* demonstrates the quest for marital happiness. Following the conflicts and tensions in the marriage of his parents, Bernstein was exorcising these memories before embarking on his own married life with Felicia. It is the hunt for a job and happiness in the city that is shown in *Wonderful Town*, reflecting the fact that, at the beginning of the 1950s, Bernstein was torn between conducting and composing, and had still not gained the job that he really wanted with the New York Philharmonic. In *Candide*, the search is for love, a happier and simpler existence, and the perfect world. Bernstein was away from home frequently during 1955 and 1956, at a time when his children were growing up. The US was also recovering from the supposed threat of Communism and the HUAC trials, which had touched Bernstein through his friends.

His next theatre work is based on the struggle for freedom and tolerance. The theme of *West Side Story* was possibly the one closest to Bernstein's heart, as he strived to reach as many people as he could with music, through his TV programmes as well as his compositions. In his own words: 'I believe in people. I feel, love, need, and respect people above all else ... One person fighting for truth can disqualify for me the platitudes of centuries. And one human being who meets with injustice can render invalid the whole system which has dispensed it' (Bernstein 1982, p. 137).

Within his own life, Bernstein's role and recognition as a conductor was increasing, while he remained frustrated at the lack of acceptance for his compositions. In *Mass*, the search is for God. Not only was the country reeling following the wars in Korea and Vietnam, and the Kennedy assassinations, but Bernstein had been hit by the deaths of his friend and mentor Marc Blitzstein in 1964 and his father in 1969. These events were followed by the start of his relationship with Tom Cothran, as he struggled to come to terms with changes in his life. Some of these issues had appeared in *Kaddish*, and Bernstein's struggle with God continues in *Mass*, until the conclusion is reached that love can bring people together. The odd-one-out is *1600 Pennsylvania Avenue*, portraying the search for a national identity through the tensions between black and white, a less personal or specific aim than in the previous works.[1] Although there seems to be no immediate parallel in his life, at this time Bernstein was struggling with his homosexual side, and 1976 saw a trial separation between him and Felicia (Burton 1994, p. 437). Perhaps the dualism in the country, shown in *1600*, is in some way representative of the two sides of Bernstein's life at that time? In *A Quiet Place*, the hope is for family security and inner peace. This opera is the most autobiographical of the works. Having lost Felicia to cancer in 1978,

---

[1]   It was in 1970 that Bernstein controversially showed his public support of the Black Panthers (Burton 1994, p. 390).

Bernstein uses the opera as a means of therapy, in order to work out the issues he had with his own father.

The idea of the composer's life having a direct bearing on his musical output is by no means a new concept, but musicologists are beginning to see musical biography as a new direction and discipline, and it is a natural progression from the sociomusciology that developed in the late 1990s. There is, however, a further connection between the themes of Bernstein's musical theatre works: the idea of searching for something, predominantly love, or God. This suggests that, beneath Bernstein's extrovert exterior, there was ultimately insecurity, a need for people to love him, and a search for approval and acceptance. The striving for God may be in part derived from his Jewish heritage, and the scholarly traditions of his family. However, investigations of these concepts would require a move into the realms of psychology and theology, and are beyond the scope of a musicological study.

Despite the reaching and searching, and struggling and fighting, each of the works considered has an optimistic conclusion, if not an outright happy ending, underlining a further important ideal of Bernstein's: the hope for something better to come. Even in the tragedy that ended his version of *Romeo and Juliet*, there is a sense of hope in the truce between the gangs, as they join together to carry Tony's body away. At this point, and in Bernstein's other shows, there is a link between hope and the perfect fifth, as the interval recurs in several of his works, and the transparency of the interval relating to the purity of the emotion. This is balanced by the concept of striving and searching, which Bernstein portrays musically in the interval of the seventh, as in *Candide*. The concept of hope was very important to Bernstein, and it was a value that he longed to spread to others, particularly to the younger generations. In two speeches to students, one at Tanglewood in 1970, and the other at Johns Hopkins University in 1980, he stressed the importance of having hope, especially in the face of tragedy and conflict: 'You've got to recognize the hope that exists in you, but not let impatience turn it into despair' (Bernstein 1982, p. 283); 'you are the generation of hope. We are counting on you ... to find new truths: true answers, not merely stopgaps, to the abounding stalemates that surround us' (Bernstein 1982, p. 357).

Bernstein's hope for the future was also reflected in his passion for education, beginning with the Young People's Concerts, and continuing throughout his life. He viewed learning as an essential part of life, and credited his own love of knowledge to his father: 'I think that probably the greatest gift my father bestowed on us children was to teach us to love learning' (1982, p. 174). Through his television lectures and live concerts, his conducting seminars and his connections with Tanglewood, Bernstein attempted to engender in all a love of not just music but also of all the arts, and saw education as the conduit through which a society could better itself. When called to testify to the House Subcommittee of Select Education in 1977, regarding a bill calling for a White House Conference on the Arts, he restated these views:

> Only a society prepared by education can ever be a truly cultured society ... We
> *can* become a cultured nation, we have only to learn how to first to apply our
> energies and public dollars in the right places. Let us be proud of America, and
> of our limitless resources and potential. And our children will be proud of us.
> (Reproduced in Bernstein 1982, pp. 332 and 335)

Bernstein's educational ideals continue after his death, with the Leonard
Bernstein Centre for Learning, established in 1992, through the 'Artful
Learning' methodology: an arts-based teaching and learning model that has been
implemented in a number of schools through the US, educating both pupils and
teachers through Bernstein's philosophy that 'the best way to "know" a thing is
in the context of another discipline' (1976, p. 3). Another aspect of his legacy
comes in the 'Bernstein Beat' concerts, a series of events in the spirit of the Young
People's Concerts, formulated by his daughter Jamie and the conductor Michael
Barrett in 1999, but with a focus on Bernstein's own music, and performed all over
the world.

In conclusion, I believe that Bernstein's experiences formed the basis for
his works, and so it is not unexpected that his profoundest beliefs should be
encapsulated in them. I think the piece that was closest to achieving his aims, both
musical and personal, is *Mass*: the juxtaposition of musical styles, the religious
argument at its heart, and the final image of the touch of peace being passed from
performers to audience embody Bernstein's dreams and expectations. As described
by Seckerson: '*Mass* is Bernstein's personal credo, perhaps even his epitaph ... An
act of faith, if you like, its music a universal symbol of that faith with the power to
move and heal, to break down and transcend the cultural and religious barriers that
divide us' (1988, p. 259). The title of this book reflects my belief that Bernstein
was searching for his own place in the world, for that place where he would find
true happiness and contentment. His longing for a brighter future is summed up in
more of Sondheim's words for *West Side Story*, which perhaps provide a motto for
the composer's hopes and attitude:

Somehow, someday, somewhere!

Bibliography

Unpublished Primary Sources

The Leonard Bernstein Collection, which houses many of the composer's personal papers, manuscripts and photographs, is maintained at the Library of Congress in Washington; in the citations in this book, the abbreviation LBC is used for the Collection. It is an invaluable resource in the research of Bernstein's music and life. At this time, the majority of the Collection, including correspondence, photographs and other personal papers, has been sorted, and can be called according to box numbers (which are listed in the Collection Finding Aid). However, music is the last area to be classified and, as yet, has not been allocated boxes. There are also scripts and materials pertaining to *On the Town*, *Wonderful Town* and *West Side Story* in the Comden and Green Collection at the New York Public Library, Performing Arts Section.

General Books and Articles

Anon. (1957), 'Wunderkind', *Time*, 69 (5), 4 February, 68–70, 72, 75
— (1968), 'The Symphonic Form is Dead', *Time*, 92 (9), 30 August, 53
Atkinson, Brooks (1940), '"My Sister Eileen", a Comedy of the Village', *The New York Times*, 27 December, 23
— (1941), '"My Sister Eileen", In Praise of the Season's First Gay Antic – the Case of G. S. Kaufman', *The New York Times*, 5 January, X1
Auden, W. H. (1968), *Collected Longer Poems*, London: Faber and Faber
Bailey, Kathryn (1991), *The Twelve-Note Music of Anton Webern*, Cambridge: Cambridge University Press
Balanchine, George and Francis Mason (1978), *Balanchine's Festival of Ballet*, London: W. H. Allen
Banfield, Stephen (1993), *Sondheim's Broadway Musicals*, Michigan: University of Michigan Press
— (1998), 'Popular Song and Popular Music on Stage and Screen', in Nicholls 1998
Banks, R. A. (1991), *Drama and Theatre Arts*, London: Hodder and Stoughton
Bauch, Marc (2003), *The American Musical*, Marburg: Tectum Verlag
Beebe, Lucius (1936), 'An Adult's Hour is Miss Hellman's Next Effort', *New York Herald Tribune*, 13 December, reproduced in Bryer 1986
Bindas, Kenneth, ed. (1992), *America's Musical Pulse: Popular Music in Twentieth Century Society*, Connecticut: Praeger
Biner, Pierre (1972), *The Living Theatre*, New York: Horizon Press

Block, Geoffrey (1997), *Enchanted Evenings: The Broadway Musical from* Show Boat *to Sondheim*, New York: Oxford University Press

Bordman, Gerald (1980), *Jerome Kern: His Life and Music*, New York: Oxford University Press

— (1992), *American Musical Theatre: A Chronicle*, 2nd edn, New York: Oxford University Press

Bryer, Jackson, ed. (1986), *Conversations with Lillian Hellman*, Mississippi: University Press of Mississippi

Budd, John (1946), 'Introduction to *Candide*', in Voltaire 1947.

Burlingame, Jon (2003), 'Leonard Bernstein and *On the Waterfront*: Tragic Nobility, a Lyrical Song, and Music of Violence', in Rapf 2003

Burn, Carol Lucha (1986), *Musical Notes*, Connecticut: Greenwood Press

Burton, Humphrey (1994), *Leonard Bernstein*, London: Faber and Faber

Burton, William Westbrook (1995), *Conversations About Bernstein*, New York: Oxford University Press

Butterworth, Neil (1985), *The Music of Aaron Copland*, London: Toccata Press

Carpenter, Humphrey (1992), *Benjamin Britten: A Biography*, London: Faber and Faber

Chase, Gilbert (1966), *America's Music from the Pilgrims to the Present*, New York: McGraw-Hill Book Co.

Chujoy, A. and P. W. Manchester (1967), *The Dance Encyclopedia*, 2nd edn, New York: Simon and Schuster

Cipolla, F. and R. Camus (2001), 'Bands', in Koskoff, Ellen, ed., *The Garland Encyclopedia of World Music: The United States and Canada*, New York: Garland

Citron, Stephen (1991), *The Musical from the Inside Out*, London: Hodder and Stoughton

— (1995), *The Wordsmiths: Oscar Hammerstein 2nd and Alan Jay Lerner*, New York: Oxford University Press

Cohen, Selma, ed. (1998), *International Encyclopedia of Dance*, 6 vols, New York: Oxford University Press

Cole, Hugo (1966), 'Aaron Copland', *Tempo*, 76, 2–6, and 77, 9–15

— (1971), 'Popular Elements in Copland's Music', *Tempo*, 95, 4–10

Collier, James (1986), 'Jazz', in Hitchcock and Sadie 1986, 2

Cooke, Melvin (1996), *Britten: War Requiem*, Cambridge Music Handbooks, Cambridge: Cambridge University Press

Copland, Aaron (1968), *The New Music 1900/60*, London: MacDonald

Cunliffe, Marcus, ed. (1993), *American Literature Since 1900*, London: Penguin

Dickinson, Peter (1975), 'Copland at 75', *The Musical Times*, 116, November

— (1979), 'The Achievement of Ragtime: An Introductory Study with Some Implications for British Research in Popular Music', *Proceedings of the Royal Musical Association*, 105, 63–76

Dramatists Guild (1970), 'Lillian Hellman Reflects upon the Changing Theater', *Dramatists Guild Quarterly*, Winter 1970, 17–22, reproduced in Bryer 1986

Drew, David (1990), 'Motifs, Tags and Related Matters', in Hinton 1990

Dusella, Reinhold and Helmut Loos (1989), *Leonard Bernstein: Der Komponist*, Bonn: Boosey and Hawkes

Earhart, Will and Edward Brige (1953), *Songs of Stephen Foster*, Philadelphia: University of Pittsburgh Press

Engel, Lehman (1972), *Words With Music*, New York: Macmillan

Ericson, Raymond (1963), 'Records: Britten's *War Requiem*', *The New York Times*, 16 June, 13

Esslin, Martin (1987), *The Field of Drama*, London: Methuen

Ewen, David (1957), *Richard Rodgers*, New York: Henry Holt and Co.

— (1968), *The World of Twentieth Century Music*, New Jersey: Prentice Hall

Fleischmann, Aloys, ed. (1998), *Sources of Irish Traditional Music c.1600–1855*, 2 vols, New York: Garland.

Forte, Allen (1973), *The Structure of Atonal Music*, Connecticut: Yale University Press

— (1995), *The American Ballad of the Golden Era 1924–1950*, New Jersey: Princeton University Press

Fuld, James J. (1966), *The Book of World-Famous Music*, New York: Crown

Gänzl, Kurt (1994), *The Encyclopedia of the Musical Theatre*, 2 vols, New York: Schirmer

Gershwin, Ira (1978), *Lyrics on Several Occasions*, London: Omnibus

Gilbert, Martin (1999), *Challenge to Civilization: A History of the Twentieth Century 1952–1999*, London: Harper Collins

Gordon, Eric (1989), *Mark the Music: The Life and Work of Marc Blitzstein*, New York: St Martin's Press

Gottlieb, Jack (1964), 'The Music of Leonard Bernstein: A Study of Melodic Manipulations', DMA, University of Illinois

— (1968), 'The Choral Music of Leonard Bernstein, Reflections of Theatre and Liturgy', *American Choral Review*, 10 (2), Summer, 156–75

— (1980), 'Symbols of Faith in the Music of Leonard Bernstein', *The Musical Quarterly*, 66 (2), 287–95

— (1988), *Leonard Bernstein: A Complete Catalogue of His Works*, 2nd edn, New York: Jalni

— (1998), *Leonard Bernstein: A Complete Catalogue of His Works*, 3rd edn, New York: Leonard Bernstein Music Publishing Company

— (2003), Programme notes for CD recording *Leonard Bernstein: A Jewish Legacy*, Naxos 8.559407

— (2004), *Funny, It Doesn't Sound Jewish: How Yiddish Songs and Synagogue Melodies Influenced Tin Pan Alley*, New York: SUNY

— (2010), *Working With Bernstein: A Memoir*, New York: Amadeus Press

Gow, David (1960), 'Leonard Bernstein: Musician of Many Talents', *The Musical Times*, 101, July, 427–9

Gradenwitz, Peter (1949), 'Leonard Bernstein', *Music Review*, 10 (1), February, 191–202

— (1987), *Leonard Bernstein: The Infinite Variety of a Musician*, Leamington Spa: Berg Publishers

Gräwe, Karl Dietrich (1989), '"Optimismus mit Trauerflor, kämpfend" Leonard Bernstein und seine Opern', in Dusella and Loos 1989

Green, Stanley (1974), *The World of Musical Comedy*, New York: A. S. Barnes and Co.

— (1980), *Encyclopedia of the Musical Theatre*, New York: Da Capo

Greenfield, Edward (1988), 'Leonard Bernstein at 70: Leonard Bernstein talks to Edward Greenfield', *Gramophone*, 66 (783), August, 257

Gruen, John (1968), *The Private World of Leonard Bernstein*, New York: Ridge Press

Guernsey, Otis (1985), *Broadway Song & Story: Playwrights/Lyricists/Composers Discuss their Hits*, New York: Dodd, Mead and Co.

Hamm, Charles (1979), *Yesterdays*, New York: W. W. Norton and Co.

Hasse, John, ed. (1985), *Ragtime: Its History, Composers and Music*, London: Macmillan

Henderson, Clayton (2001), 'Minstrelsy', in Sadie and Tyrell 2001, 16

Henehan, Donald (1990), 'A Prophet Ultimately Honoured', *The New York Times*, 21 October, 2: 1, 9

Hindemith, Paul, (1937), *Craft I*, trans. A. Mendel, London: Schott and Co.

Hinton, Stephen, ed. (1990), *Kurt Weill: Threepenny Opera*, Cambridge Opera Handbooks, Cambridge: Cambridge University Press

Hitchcock, H. Wiley (1969), *Music in the United States: A Historical Introduction*, 2nd edn, New Jersey: Prentice Hall

— and Stanley Sadie, eds (1986), *The New Grove Dictionary of American Music*, 4 vols, London: Macmillan

Holde, Artur (1961), *Leonard Bernstein*, Berlin: Rembrandt Verlag

Hoppin, Richard (1978), *Medieval Music*, New York: Norton

Idelsohn, Abraham (1992), *Jewish Music*, New York: Dover

Ilson, Carol (1989), *Harold Prince, from* Pajama Game *to* Phantom of the Opera, Michigan: UMI Press

Jaensch, Andreas (2003), *Leonard Bernsteins Musiktheater: auf dem Weg zu einer amerikanischen Oper*, Kassel: Bärenreiter

Jenkins, Philip (1997), *A History of the United States*, London: Macmillan

John, Nicholas, ed. (1991), *Oedipus Rex/The Rake's Progress*, English National Opera Guide, London: John Calder

Joseph, Charles M. (1983), *Stravinsky and the Piano*, Michigan: UMI Press

Jowitt, Deborah (2004), *Jerome Robbins: His Life, his Theater, his Dance*, New York: Simon and Schuster

Joyner, David (1998), 'Jazz from 1930 to 1960', in Nicholls 1998

Kemp, Ian (1984), *Tippett: The Composer and his Music*, London: Eulenberg Books

Kendall, Alan (1976), *The Tender Tyrant: Nadia Boulanger, A Life Devoted to Music*, London: MacDonald and Janes

Kennedy, Michael (1981), *Britten*, Master Musicians, London: Dent

Kenny, Anthony (1998), *A Brief History of Western Philosophy*, Oxford: Blackwell

Kernfeld, Barry (2002), *The New Grove Dictionary of Jazz*, 2nd edn, 3 vols, London: Macmillan

Kingman, Daniel (1979), *American Music*, New York: Schirmer

Kirk, Elise (1986), *Music at the White House*, Illinois: University of Illinois Press

— (2001), *American Opera*, Illinois: University of Illinois Press

Kislan, Richard (1995), *The Musical*, New York: Applause

Klain, Jane (1994/5), 'Cris Alexander: In Tune, In Focus', *Show Music*, Winter, 10 (4), 35–9

Kolodin, Irving, et al. (1986), 'New York', in Hitchcock and Sadie 1986, 3

Kowalke, Kim (1990), '*The Threepenny Opera* in America', in Hinton 1990

Laird, Paul (1999), 'Leonard Bernstein: Eclecticism and Vernacular Elements in *Chichester Psalms*', *The Sonneck Society for American Music Bulletin*, 25 (1), Spring, 1, 5–8

— (2002), *Leonard Bernstein: A Guide to Research*, New York: Routledge. Includes essay: 'Leonard Bernstein's Musical Style'

Lamb, Andrew (2000), *150 Years of Popular Musical Theatre*, London: Routledge

Larkin, Colin (1992), *The Guinness Encyclopedia of Popular Music*, London: Guinness

Laufe, Abe (1978), *Broadway's Greatest Musicals*, London: David and Charles

Laurents, Arthur (2000), *Original Story By*, New York: Applause

Lawson, Steven (2000), 'Bernstein and the MacDowell Colony', *Prelude, Fugue and Riffs*, Winter, 4

Lawson-Peebles, Robert, ed. (1996), *Approaches to the American Musical*, Exeter: University of Exeter Press

Ledbetter, Steven, ed. (1988), *Sennets and Tuckets: A Bernstein Celebration*, Massachusetts: Boston Symphony Orchestra

Lees, Gene (1991), *The Musical Worlds of Lerner and Loewe*, London: Robson Books

Leibniz, Gottfried Wilhelm (1973), *Philosophical Writings*, ed. G. H. R. Parkinson, trans. M. Morris and G. H. R. Parkinson, London: Dent

Lerner, Alan J. (1987), *A Hymn to Him: The Lyrics of Alan Jay Lerner*, London: Pavilion

Lorenz, Megaera and Brenna (1999), 'Betty Boop in *Minnie the Moocher*', on www.heptune.com/minnbett.html

Mandelbaum, Ken (1991), *Not Since Carrie: Forty Years of Musical Flops*, New York: St Martin's Press

Manuel, Peter (1988), *Popular Musics of the Non-Western World: An Introductory Survey*, New York: Oxford University Press

Meckna, Michael (1986), *Virgil Thomson, A Bio-Bibliography*, Connecticut: Greenwood Press

Mellers, Wilfrid (1964), *Music in a New Found Land*, London: Rockcliffe and Barrie

Moody, Richard (1972), *Lillian Hellman*, New York: Pegasus

Mordden, Ethan (1983), *Broadway Babies*, New York: Oxford University Press

— (1998), *Coming Up Roses: The Broadway Musical in the 1950s*, New York: Oxford University Press

Morse, David (1993), 'American Theatre: The Age of O'Neill', in Cunliffe 1993

Myers, Paul (1998), *Leonard Bernstein*, London: Phaidon Press

Nanry, Charles (1992), 'Swing and Segregation', in Bindas 1992

Neumeyer, David (1986), *The Music of Paul Hindemith*, Connecticut: Yale University Press

Nicholls, David, ed. (1998), *The Cambridge History of American Music*, Cambridge: Cambridge University Press

Oja, Carol J. (1989), 'Marc Blitzstein's *The Cradle will Rock* and Mass-song style of the 1930s', *Musical Quarterly*, 73, 445–75

Oliver, Paul (1986), 'Spirituals, §II. Black', in Hitchcock and Sadie 1986

Peyser, Joan (1987), *Leonard Bernstein*, London: Bantam Press

Phillips, John and Anne Hollander (1965), 'The Art of the Theater I: Lillian Hellman – An Interview', *Paris Review*, 33, Winter–Spring, reproduced in Bryer 1986.

Pollack, Harold (1999) *Aaron Copland: The Life and Work of an Uncommon Man*, London: Faber and Faber.

Prince, Harold (1974), *Contradictions: Notes on Twenty-six Years in the Theatre*, New York: Dodd

Ramey, Phillip (n.d.), 'A Talk With Leonard Bernstein', a photocopy of an article, with no indication of original publication, dating from between 1971 and 1974, in Box 90, folder 15, LBC

Rapf, Joanna, ed. (2003), *On the Waterfront*, Cambridge Film Handboooks, Cambridge: Cambridge University Press

Rice, Robert (1958), 'The Pervasive Musician I, II', *The New Yorker*, 33 (47), 11 January, 37–63; 33 (48), 18 January, 35–65

Riddle, Ronald (1985), 'Novelty Piano Music', in Hasse 1985

Robertson, Alec (1968), *Requiem: Music of Mourning and Consolation*, Connecticut: Greenwood Press

Rodgers, Richard (1975), *Musical Stages*, New York: Random House Press

Routh, Francis (1975), *Stravinsky*, London: J. M. Dent and Sons

Rye, Howard and Barry Kernfeld (2002), 'Jump', in Kernfeld 2002, 2

Sadie, Stanley, ed. (1992), *The New Grove Dictionary of Opera*, 4 vols, London: Macmillan

— and John Tyrell, eds (2001), *The New Grove Dictionary of Music and Musicians*, 2nd edn, 29 vols, London: Macmillan

Salzman, Eric (1988), *Twentieth Century Music*, New Jersey: Prentice Hall

Schiff, David (1997), *Gershwin: Rhapsody in Blue*, Cambridge Music Handbooks, Cambridge: Cambridge University Press

— (2001), 'Bernstein, Leonard' in Sadie and Tyrell 2001, 3

Schneider, Otto (1985), *Tanz-Lexicon*, Vienna: Verlag Brüder Hollinder

Schoenberg, Arnold (1975), *Style and Idea*, ed. Leonard Stein, trans. Leo Black, London: Faber and Faber.

Schulberg, Budd (2003), 'Introduction: "The Mysterious Way of Art"', Making a Difference in *On the Waterfront*', in Rapf 2003.

Schuller, Gunther (1968), *Early Jazz*, New York: Oxford University Press

— (1989), *The Swing Era*, New York: Oxford University Press

Seckerson, Edward (1988), 'Leonard Bernstein at 70: The New York Years', *Gramophone*, 66 (783), August, 258–9

— (1990), 'Review: Bernstein *Songs and Duets*', *Gramophone*, 68 (805), June, 93

— (1991), 'Music I Heard With You', *Gramophone*, 69 (819), August, 38–9

Secrest, Meryle (1995), *Leonard Bernstein: A Life*, New York: Vintage Books

— (1998), *Stephen Sondheim: A Life*, London: Bloomsbury

Seldes, Barry (2009), *Leonard Bernstein: The Political Life of an American Musician*, California: University of California Press

Shiloah, Amnon (1992), *Jewish Musical Traditions*, Michigan: Wayne State University Press

Sklan, Robert (1994), *Movie-Made America*, New York: Vintage Books

Smith, Helen (1998), 'The Art of Glorification: A History of Pastiche, and its Use within Sondheim's *Follies*', *British Postgraduate Musicology*, 2, 24–31.

— (2003), 'The Musical Development of Leonard Bernstein, as Demonstrated Through His Works for the Musical Theatre', PhD, University of Birmingham

— (2006), '*Peter Grimes* and Leonard Bernstein: An English Fisherman and his Influence on an American Eclectic', *Tempo*, 60 (35), January, 22–30

Sonneck Society and Queensborough Community College (1976), *Two Centuries of Music in America*, A Bicentennial Conference, New York: Queensborough Community College

Southern, Eileen (1997), *The Music of Black Americans: A History*, 3rd edn, New York: Norton

Stravinsky, Igor (1942), *Poetics of Music, in the Form of Six Lessons*, trans. A. Knodel and I. Dahl, Massachusetts: Harvard University Press

Suskin, Stephen (1992), *Show Tunes 1905–1991*, New York: Limelight Editions

Swain, Joseph (1990), *The Broadway Musical: A Critical and Musical Survey*, New York: Oxford University Press

Swan, Claudia, ed. (1999), *Leonard Bernstein: The Harvard Years, 1935–1939*, New York: The Eos Orchestra

Thomson, Virgil (1970), *American Music Since 1910*, London: Weidenfeld and Nicolson

Visser, Joop (1997), Programme notes for CD, *52nd Street: The Street of Jazz*, Germany: Charly, CDGR 1812

Vlad, Roman (1967), *Stravinsky*, trans. Frederick and Ann Fuller, 2nd edn, London: Oxford University Press

Walsh, Stephen (1993), *Stravinsky: Oedipus Rex*, Cambridge Music Handbooks, Cambridge: Cambridge University Press

Wardle, Irving (1993), 'American Theatre Since 1945', in Cunliffe 1993

Waters, Arthur (1927), '*Show Boat* Review', *Philadelphia Public Ledger*, 16 December, quoted in Kreuger, Miles (1977), *Show Boat: The Story of a Classic American Musical*, New York: Oxford University Press, 55

Webster, James (2001), 'Sonata Form', in Sadie and Tyrell 2001, 23

Weiss, Peter (1965), *The Persecution and Assassination of Marat as Performed by the Inmates of Charenton under the Direction of the Marquis de Sade*, English version by Geoffrey Skelton, London: Caldere and Boyars

Werner-Jenson, Arnold (1979), 'Beethoven: Missa Solemnis', trans. J. Coombs, notes with the Bernstein/Deutsche Grammophon recording, DG 469 546-2

Whitney, David and Robin Vaughn (1993), *The American Presidents*, 8th edn, New York: Reader's Digest

Whittall, Arnold (1977), *Music Since the First World War*, London: Dent

Wilder, Thornton (1958), *Three Plays by Thornton Wilder*, New York: Bantam Books

Williams, William H. C. (1996), *'Twas Only an Irishman's Dream: The Image of Ireland and the Irish in American Popular Song Lyrics, 1800–1920*, Illinois: University of Illinois Press

Williams, Tennessee (1976), *Cat on a Hot Tin Roof and Other Plays*, London: Penguin

Wollen, Peter (1992), *Singin' in the Rain*, London: BFI

Work, John W. (1940), *American Negro Songs and Spirituals*, New York: Bonanza Books

Wright, David (1999), 'Bernstein at Harvard: The Artist and the Escape Artist', in Swan 1999

Writings by Bernstein

(1949), 'Prelude to a Musical', *The New York Times*, 30 October, 2: 1, 3

(1956), 'Colloquy in Boston', *The New York Times*, 18 November, 2: 1, 3. Bernstein's draft for this reproduced as 'Candide or Omnibus', on www.leonardbernstein.com/candide_notes.htm

(1966), *The Infinite Variety of Music*, New York: Simon and Schuster

(1969), *The Joy of Music*, London: Panther Books [first published in New York in 1959]

(1976), *The Unanswered Question, Six Talks at Harvard*, Massachusetts: Harvard University Press

(1982), *Findings*, London: MacDonald and Co.

(2004), *The Joy of Music*, New Jersey: Amadeus Press [as earlier edition above]

(2005), *Leonard Bernstein's Young People's Concerts*, New Jersey: Amadeus Press [first published in 1962 in New York]

Libretti and Sources

Chodorov, Jerome and Joseph Fields (1941), *My Sister Eileen*, New York: Dramatists Play Service

Comden, Betty and Adolph Green (1997), *The New York Musicals of Comden and Green*, New York: Applause [contains libretto for *On the Town* by Comden and Green, and for *Wonderful Town* by Chodorov and Fields]

Hellman, Lillian (1957), *Candide*, New York: Random House

— (1972), *The Collected Plays*, Massachusetts: Little, Brown and Company

Laurents, Arthur and Stephen Sondheim (1958), *West Side Story*, Oxford: Heinemann

Lehman, Ernest (2003), *West Side Story*, screenplay for 1961 MGM film, reproduced in book included with special edition DVD, 15930BCDVD

McKenney, Ruth (1938), *My Sister Eileen*, New York: Harcourt, Brace and Co.

Shakespeare, William (1993), *Romeo and Juliet*, New York: Dover

Voltaire (1947), *Candide, or Optimism*, trans. John Butt, London: Penguin

— (1992), *Candide et autres contes*, Paris: Gallimard

Wheeler, Richard (1988), *Candide*, Scottish Opera Version, unpublished, hired from Boosey and Hawkes

The Libretto for *1600 Pennsylvania Avenue* is unavailable, although Amberson kindly allowed me to see a copy of the version recreated by Eric Haagenson for his 1992 Indiana University Opera Theatre production of the 'gypsy run-through' version of the show.

Reviews and Show-Specific Writings

Fancy Free

Martin, John (1944), 'Ballet by Robbins called smash hit', *The New York Times*, 19 April, 27

On the Town

Barnes, Howard (1944), 'Fresh New Musical', *New York Herald Tribune*, 29 December, 2: 1

Burton, Humphrey (2005), 'On the Town', programme note for English National Opera production of *On the Town*, March 2005

Haagenson, Erik (1994/5), 'Still a Helluva "Town!"', *Show Music*, Winter, 10 (4), 27–34

Kreuger, Miles (1972), 'The Broadway Composer', *High Fidelity Magazine*, February, 78–9

Mordden, Ethan (1999), 'The Dance Musical', in *Beautiful Mornin': The Broadway Musical in the 1940s*, New York: Oxford University Press

Morrison, Richard (2005), 'An Accolade for One Helluva Show', *Prelude, Fugue and Riffs*, Summer/Spring, 1–3

Nichols, Lewis (1944), 'The Play', *The New York Times*, 29 December, 11

Smith, Helen (2005), '"A Helluva Town": A New York Soundscape', programme note for English National Opera production of *On the Town*, March 2005

Snelson, John (2005), 'Town and Country', programme note for English National Opera production of *On the Town*, March 2005

Trouble in Tahiti

Atkinson, Brooks (1955), '"Trouble in Tahiti", Draper, "27 Wagons"', *The New York Times*, 20 April, 40 [review of Broadway production in 1955]

Burkat, Leonard (1953), 'Current Chronicle – Boston', *Musical Quarterly*, 39 (1), January

Burton, Humphrey (1993), 'Trouble in Tahiti', *Prelude, Fugue and Riffs*, Winter, 1 and 7

Keathley, Elizabeth L. (2005), 'Postwar Modernity and the Wife's Subjectivity: Bernstein's *Trouble in Tahiti*', *American Music*, 23 (2), Summer, 220–56

Oja, Carol J. (2005), 'Review – Leonard Bernstein: *Trouble in Tahiti*', *American Music*, 23 (4), Winter, 526–7 [review of BBC/Opus Arte DVD of the opera]

Sargeant, Winthrop (1958), 'Musical Events: Whither?', *The New Yorker*, 34 (9), 19 April, 138–9 [Review of 1958 Broadway performance]

Wonderful Town

Anon. (1994), '*Wonderful Town*: A Conversation with Comden and Green', *Prelude, Fugue and Riffs*, Fall, 1, 5

Atkinson, Brooks (1953a), 'At the Theater', *The New York Times*, 26 February, 22

— (1953b), 'Wonderful Town: Rosalind Russell as the Head Clown in a Big Broadway Musical Show', *The New York Times*, 8 March, 2: 1

Downes, Olin (1953), 'Wonderful Time: Bernstein's Musical is Brilliant Achievement', *The New York Times*, 10 May, 2: 7

Drew, David (1955), '*Wonderful Town* (A Musical Comedy)', *The Score*, 12, June, 77–80

Oja, Carol J. (2007), '*Wonderful Town* and McCarthy-Era Politics', *Prelude, Fugue and Riffs*, Spring/Summer, 6

Taubman, Howard (1953), 'Tunesmith of "Wonderful Town"', *The New York Times*, 5 April, 2: 1

Candide

Atkinson, Brooks (1956a), 'Candide', *The New York Times*, 3 December, 40

— (1956b), 'Candide: Lillian Hellman and Leonard Bernstein Turn Voltaire Satire into Fine Play', *The New York Times*, 9 December, 2: 5

Bernstein, Nina (1997), 'Candide's Travels', *Prelude, Fugue and Riffs*, Spring/Summer, 1, 4

Chapin, Theodore S. (1985), Article included in CD liner notes in recording of 1982 Opera House version of *Candide*, NW 340/341-2

Conrad, Jon Alan (1992a), 'Candide', in Sadie 1992, 1

Crist, Elizabeth B. (2006), 'Mutual Responses in the Midst of an Era: Aaron Copland's *The Tender Land*, and Leonard Bernstein's *Candide*', *The Journal of Musicology*, 23 (4), Fall, 485–527

Gibbs, Wolcott (1956), 'The Theatre: Voltaire Today', *The New Yorker*, 32 (43), 15 December, 52–3

Gottlieb, Jack (1997), '*Candide* Goes to College', *Prelude, Fugue and Riffs*', Spring/Summer, 5

Kerr, Walter (1956), 'Candide', *New York Herald Tribune*, 3 December, reproduced at www.leonardbernstein.com/candide_publications.htm

Mauceri, John (1988), '*Candide* or No Exit', programme for 1988 Scottish Opera production, reproduced at www.spingal.plus.com/candide.html

Porter, Andrew (1982), 'Musical Events: How to Live in Grace', *The New Yorker*, 58 (37), 1 November, 152–3 [review of City Opera production]

— (1991), '*Candide*: An Introduction', article included in CD liner notes in recording of 1989 London Symphony Orchestra performance, DG 429 734-2

Prince, Harold (1976), 'Foreword', in vocal score for 1976 version of *Candide*, NW 340/341-2

— (1985), Article included in CD liner notes in recording of 1982 Opera House version of *Candide*.

Ross, Don (1956), 'Voltaire's "Candide" Is Set to Music', *New York Herald Tribune*, 25 November, reproduced at www.leonardbernstein.com/candide_publications.htm

Ryan, George (1956), 'Eggheads Ahoy!', *The Pilot*, October, reproduced at www.leonardbernstein.com/candide_publications.htm

Schwarte, Michael (1995), 'Parodie und Entlehnung in Leonard Bernsteins *Candide*: Bermerkung zu einem musikgeschichtlichen Gattungs-Chamäleon', in Beer, Axel and Lütteken, Laurenz, eds, *Festschrift Klaus Hortschansky zum 60. Geburtstag*, Tutzing: Verlagt bei Hans Schneider

Sutton, Martin (1995), *The Musicals Collection: Candide*, 31, Peterborough: Orbis Publishing

Wells, John (1991), 'Bernstein and Voltaire', article included with video liner notes of 1989 London Symphony Orchestra performance, VMP 072 423-2

West Side Story

Anon. (1957), 'New Musical in Manhattan', *Time*, 70 (15), 7 October, 48–9

Atkinson, Brooks (1957a), 'Theatre: The Jungles of the City', *The New York Times*, 27 September, 14

— (1957b), 'West Side Story: Moving Music Drama on Callous Theme', *The New York Times*, 6 October, 2: 1

Bauch, Marc (2003), *The American Musical* [includes chapter on *West Side Story*], Marburg: Tectum Verlag

Block, Geoffrey (1993), 'The Broadway Canon from *Show Boat* to *West Side Story* and the European Operatic Ideal', *The Journal of Musicology*, 11 (4), Fall, 525–44

Burton, Humphrey (1985), 'Bernstein's *West Side Story*: A Session Report', *Gramophone*, 62 (743), April, 1195–6

Conrad, Jon Alan (1992c), 'West Side Story', in Sadie 1992, 3

Garebian, Keith (1995), *The Making of West Side Story*, Ontario: Mosaic Press

Gräwe, Karl Dietrich (1987), 'Ein Mozart für Amerika "West Side Story" von Leonard Bernstein', in Danusen, H., Kämper, D. and Terse, P., eds, *Amerikainsche Musik seit Charles Ives*, Laaber: Laaber Verlag

Gussow, Mel (1990), '"West Side Story": The Beginnings of Something Great', *The New York Times*, 21 October, 2: 5

Kerr, Walter (1957), 'West Side Story', *New York Herald Tribune*, 27 September, reproduced at www.westsidestory.com/archives_herald2.php

Laurents, Arthur (1957), 'The Growth of an Idea', *New York Herald Tribune*, 4 August, reproduced at www.westsidestory.com/archives_herald1.php

Mellers, Wilfrid (1996), 'West Side Story Revisited', in Lawson-Peebles 1996

Simeone, Nigel (2009), *Leonard Bernstein: West Side Story*, Aldershot: Ashgate

Stearns, David P. (1985), '*West Side Story*: Between Broadway and the Opera House', essay with Deutsche Grammophon recording, DG 072 106-3

Stempel, Larry (1988), 'Broadway's Mozartean Moment, or An Amadeus in Amber', in Ledbetter 1988

—— (1992), 'The Musical Play Expands', *American Music*, 10 (2), Summer, 136–69

Taubman, Howard (1957), 'A Foot in Each Camp', *The New York Times*, 13 October, 2: 9

Wells, Elizabeth A. (2000), '*West Side Story* and the Hispanic', *Echo*, 2 (1), Spring, at www.echo.ucla.edu/volume2-Issue1/wells/wells-article.html

Mass

Barnes, Clive (1971), 'Animated Ailey Troupe Infuses Piece with a Ritualistic Power', *The New York Times*, 9 September, 51

Bell, Christopher and Michael Richardson (1989), '*Mass* – The Man, the Music', programme for 1989 Edinburgh production, reproduced at www.spingal.plus.com/mass.html

Bender, William (1971), 'A Mass for Everyone, Maybe', *Time*, 98 (12), 20 September, 41–3

Berlinski, Herman (1972), 'Bernstein's "Mass"', *Sacred Music*, 99 (1), 3–8

Goemanne, Noel (1973), 'Open Forum: The Controversial Bernstein Mass: Another Point of View', *Sacred Music*, 100 (1), 33–6

Gottlieb, Jack (2005), 'The Little Motive That Could', *Prelude, Fugue and Riffs*, Fall/Winter, 6–7

Henahan, Donal (1972a), 'Bernstein's *Mass* Opens Engagement at Met', *The New York Times*, 29 June, 34

— (1972b), 'Is it Bernstein's "Parsifal"? Or...', *The New York Times*, 9 July, D9

Hilferty, Robert (2008), 'Mass', article included in CD liner notes in 2009 Naxos recording, 8.559622-23

Hume, Paul (1975), 'A Reaffirmation of Faith', *Atlanta Arts* (monthly magazine of the Atlanta Memorial Arts Centre), May/June, 6–12

— (1988), 'Liturgy on Stage: Bernstein's *Mass*', in Ledbetter 1988

Minear, Paul (1987), 'Leonard Bernstein: *Mass*: A Cry for Peace', in *Death Set to Music*, Georgia: John Knox Press

Sargeant, Winthrop (1972), 'Musical Events: Missa cum Laude', *The New Yorker*, 48 (20), 8 July, 58

Sheppard, W. Anthony (1996), 'Bitter Rituals for a Lost Nation: Partch's *Revelation in the Courthouse Park* and Bernstein's *Mass*', *The Musical Quarterly*, 80 (3), 461–99

Zadikov, Rosemarie Tauris (1971), 'Leonard Bernstein Talks About His Music', *Time*, 98 (12), 20 September, 44

1600 Pennsylvania Avenue (and *A White House Cantata*)

Anon. (1976), '*1600*: Anatomy of a Turkey', *Time*, 107 (23), reproduced at www.time.com/magazine/article/0,9171,947691,00.html

Barnes, Clive (1976), '"1600 Pennsylvania Avenue" Arrives', *The New York Times*, 5 May, 48

Haagensen, Erik (1992), '1600 Pennsylvania Avenue: The Show That Got Away', *Show Music*, 8 (3), Fall, 25–32

Harmon, Charlie (1997a), Programme notes for *A White House Cantata*, 8 July 1997

— (1997b), '*A White House Cantata*: Scenes from *1600 Pennsylvania Avenue*', article included in CD liner notes in Deutsche Grammophon recording, released in 1998, DG 463 448-2

Higgins, John (1997), 'Warmed-over Turkey', *The Times*, 10 July, 2: 37

Hoge, Warren (1997), 'Saving Bernstein Pearls Lost with a '76 Show', *Prelude, Fugue and Riffs*, Fall, 1 and 4

Norris, Geoffrey (1997), 'Making a Shambles out of the White House', *The Telegraph*, 10 July, 29

Oberdorfer, Don (1974), 'A Bernstein–Lerner Musical', *The Washington Post*, 6 September, Style: 1–2

A Quiet Place

Conrad, Jon Alan (1992b), 'A Quiet Place', in Sadie 1992, 3

Fanning, David (1988), Review of *A Quiet Place*, Deutsch Grammophon recording, reproduced at www.spingal.plus.com/aquietplace.html

Hayes, Malcolm (1986), 'First Performances: *A Quiet Place*', *Tempo*, 168, March, 45–6

Heumann, Scott (1983a), 'And the Natives Sing: Leonard Bernstein in Search of an American Opera', *Opera Cues* (Houston Grand Opera Guild Magazine), 23 (3), March/April/June, 19–21

— (1983b), Interview with Stephen Wadsworth, *Houston Stage*, June, 12–14

— (1983c), 'The New Bernstein', *Opera*, 34, 1117–20

Miles, Rodney (1988), 'Towards the Great American Opera', *Opera*, 39, 1167–73

Porter, Andrew (1983), 'Music Events: Harmony and Grace', *The New Yorker*, 59 (21), 11 July, 88–9

— (1984), 'Musical Events: Love in a Garden', *The New Yorker*, 60 (28), 27 August, 60–62

Rich, Alan (1983), 'Lenny's Soap Opera', *Newsweek*, 27 June, 97

Wadsworth, Stephen (1987), '*A Quiet Place* Librettist's Notes', essay with Deutsche Grammophon recording, DG 447 962-2

Walsh, Michael (1983), 'Trouble in Houston for Lenny', *Time*, 121 (26), 27 June, 69

Scores, Programme Notes and Score Forewords

Bernstein's compositions (up to *A Quiet Place*), published by Boosey and Hawkes unless otherwise marked. Any score forewords and programme notes by Bernstein (unless denoted JG, by Jack Gottlieb).

1600 Pennsylvania Avenue, see *A White House Cantata*
Afterthought, 1945
The Age of Anxiety, Symphony 2, revised 1965
Bernstein on Broadway, Amberson/G. Schirmer, 1981
The Birds, unpublished, manuscript in the LBC, 1938
'La Bonne Cuisine', in *Song Album*
Brass Music, 1950
Candide, original version, 1956 (vocal score)
    'Chelsea' version, 1973, Schirmer (vocal score, includes libretto)
    Opera House version, 1982, unpublished, hired from Boosey and Hawkes (vocal score, includes libretto)
    Scottish Opera version, 1994 (full score)
Chichester Psalms, 1965, JG
Clarinet Sonata, Warner Bros., 1943
Divertimento for Orchestra, 1980, in *Orchestral Anthology Vol. 2*
Dream With Me, 1992
Dybbuk, unavailable, on hire from Boosey and Hawkes
Facsimile, 1950
Fancy Free, 1950, JG (LB programme note 1946)
Fanfares, 1995

Five Anniversaries, 1964
Four Anniversaries, 1948
Halil, 1981
Haskiveinu, 1946
'I Hate Music', in *Song Album*
Jeremiah, Symphony 1, 1943, JG
Kaddish, Symphony 3 (revised version), 1985
The Lark, 1964, JG
Mass, 1971 (vocal score)
A Musical Toast, 1980, JG
'My New Friends', in *Bernstein on Broadway*
On the Town, 1997 (vocal score)
On the Town – Three Dance Episodes, 1946
On the Waterfront Symphonic Suite, in *Orchestral Anthology Vol. 2*
Orchestral Anthology, Vols 1 and 2, 1998
The Peace, unpublished, manuscript in LBC, 1940
Peter Pan, some songs in *Song Album*
Prelude, Fugue and Riffs, 1950
A Quiet Place, revised edition 1984 (vocal score)
Salome, unpublished, manuscript in LBC, 1955
Serenade, 1956
Seven Anniversaries, M. Witmark and Sons, 1944
Shivaree, 1970
'Silhouette', in *Song Album*
Slava!, 1977, JG
Song Album, 1988, JG
Songfest, 1976, JG
'So Pretty', in *Song Album*
Thirteen Anniversaries, 1990
Touches, 1981
Trouble in Tahiti, 1953
Two Love Songs, in *Song Album*
Warm Up, 1970
West Side Story, 1957 (vocal score); 1994 (full score)
A White House Cantata, unpublished, full score on hire from Boosey and Hawkes, 1998
Wonderful Town, Leonard Bernstein Music Publishing Co., Boosey and Hawkes and Hal Leonard, 2004 (vocal score)
Yigdal, manuscript in LBC, 1950

Other Sources: Radio Programmes, TV Programmes and TV Scripts

Burton, Humphrey (Dir.) (1991), *Candide*, performance of 1989 London Symphony Orchestra performance, VMP 072 423-3

— (1996/7), *Composer of the Week; Leonard Bernstein*, BBC Radio 3, 30 December–3 January

Cairns, Tom (2003), *Trouble in Tahiti*, BBC/Opus Arte, DVD 0A 0838 D

Rosen, Peter (1978), *Reflections*, Peter Rosen Productions, 1 July, script in LBC

Swann, Christopher (1985), *West Side Story*, recording of 1985 recording, conducted by Bernstein, Deutsche Grammophon 072 106-3

Unknown director (1986), *My Musical Childhood*, BBC, script in LBC

Unknown director (1996), *Musicals Great Musicals: The Arthur Freed Unit at MGM*, Alternate Current, NHK and Turner Entertainment Co.

Leonard Bernstein Pieces Index

General Index

Federal Theatre Project, 44
Fields, Joseph, 3, 74, 75, 77, 78 n.3, 79, 88
Fiorello, 207 n.1
Fisk Jubilee Singers, 215
Flagstad, Kirsten, 73
Foss, Lukas, 248
Foster, Stephen, 222
Four Cohans, 88
Friml, Rudolph, 7
    Rose Marie, 124
Fryer, Robert, 75

Gagnon, Roland, 3
Gelber, Jack
    Connection, The, 174
Gershwin, George, 7, 11, 42, 78,
    American in Paris, An (film), 36
    Piano Concerto, 37
    Porgy and Bess, 67, 145, 173, 217,
        218, 223
    Rhapsody in Blue, 81
Gershwin, Ira, 90
Gilbert, Henry, 10
Gilbert, W.S., 125
Goberman, Max, 3
Goodman, Benny, 74, 91
Gottlieb, George, 89
Gottlieb, Jack, 1 n.1, 19, 20, 21 n.13, 35
    n.22, 41 n.27, 77, 91, 93, 94, 97,
    113, 114, 117 n.12, 126, 134, 147,
    162, 193, 199, 200 n.23, 247 n.7
Gottschalk, Louis Moreau, 215
Gounod, Charles
    Faust, 123, 124
Gräwe, Karl, 114, 150
Green, Adolph, 3, 12, 13, 21, 71, 74, 77,
    78, 79, 82, 84, 87, 89, 90, 92 n.20,
    93, 94, 99, 172, 177, 201, 239
Grieg, Edvard, 19
Guthrie, Tyrone, 3

H.M.S. Pinafore (Gilbert and Sullivan), 125
Hair (Rado, Ragni, MacDermot), 191 n.14
Hammerstein, Oscar II, 7, 145, 214
Hammett, Dashiell, 99
Harrigan and Hart, 88
Harris, Charles K., 213
Harris, Roy, 9

Hart, Lorenz, 7,
Harvard University, 1, 4, 5, 9, 14 n.6, 15,
    18, 28, 33, 44, 45, 79, 109, 165,
    208, 240, 253
Haydn, Joseph, 272
    Mass in the Time of War, 207
    String Quartet op. 50 no. 5, 132
Hellman, Lillian, 3, 99, 101, 103, 105, 110,
    111, 122, 126, 127, 130, 131, 140,
    242
    Children's Hour, The, 100,
    Lark, The, 100, 101, 198
    Little Foxes, The, 100, 243
Henderson, Fletcher, 73, 74
Herman, Woody, 91
Herriman, George
    Krazy Kat, 7
Hindemith, Paul, 9, 34, 35
    Sonata no. 2 for Piano, 33
Horwitt, Arnold, 74, 75
House Subcommittee of Select Education,
    275
House Un-American Activities Committee
    (HUAC), 99, 100, 101, 128, 132,
    274
Houseman, John, 44
Howard, Ken, 207 n.2
Huber, Harold, 93
Hussey, Walter, 201, 202

Indiana University Group, 210
Israel Philharmonic Orchestra, 271

Jackson Five, 190
Jaensch, Andreas, 21 n.12, 30 n.16, 51 n.8,
    62, 87 n.12, 112, 150, 158
Järvi, Kristjan, 1
Johns Hopkins University, 275
Joplin, Janis, 191
Joplin, Scott
    Treemonisha, 215
Jumbo (Rodgers and Hart), 73

Kay, Hershy, 191
Kazan, Elia, 99, 100, 101
Kelly, Gene, 36 n.25
Kennedy Centre, 3, 171, 207, 210
Kennedy, Jackie, 171